The Economics of Public Issues

THIRTEENTH EDITION

Roger LeRoy Miller
Institute for University Studies
Arlington, Texas

Daniel K. Benjamin
Clemson University
and PERC, Bozeman, Montana

Douglass C. North
Washington University, St. Louis

Addison
Wesley

Boston San Francisco New York
London Toronto Sydney Tokyo Singapore Madrid
Mexico City Munich Paris Cape Town Hong Kong Montreal

Editor-in-Chief: Denise Clinton
Acquisitions Editor: Victoria Warneck
Associate Editor: Roxanne Hoch
Managing Editor: James Rigney
Production Supervisor: Katherine Watson
Marketing Manager: Adrienne D'Ambrosio
Design Manager: Regina Kolenda
Cover Designer: Patti McKinnon
Senior Manufacturing Buyer: Hugh Crawford
Composition and Prepress Services: Pre-Press Co., Inc.
Printer and Binder: R.R. Donnelley & Sons
Cover Photo: © 2002 PhotoDisc

Library of Congress Cataloging-in Publication Data

Miller, Roger LeRoy.
   The economics of public issues / Roger LeRoy Miller, Daniel K.
Benjamin, Douglass C. North.—13th ed.
      p. cm.
   Includes bibliographical references and index.
   ISBN 0-321-11873-1 (alk. paper)
   1. Economics. 2. Industrial policy. 3. Economic policy. I. Benjamin,
Daniel K. II. North, Douglass Cecil. III. Title.

HB171 .M544 2002
330.973'0931—dc21   2002025585
5 6 7 8 9 10—DOC—06 05 04

To Renaud and Martine,
Knowing and working with
you has been, and will continue to be,
a great honor and pleasure for me.

R.L.M

To Jack McGuire Benjamin:
navigator of the future

D.K.B.

Contents

Preface

This book is about some issues of our times. Several of these issues are usually thought of as being inherently non-economic. Others provide classic illustrations of the core of economic science. Many are controversial and thus are likely to evoke non-economic reactions to what we have to say. In our view, however, the one feature that ties all of the issues together is that they illustrate the power of economics in explaining the world around us. And, we might add, we hope all of them illustrate that economics can be entertaining as well as informative.

Over the years, we have sought to select issues for this book that—in addition to the attributes noted above—possess a sense of immediacy. We hope you will find the issues we have added for this edition meet this criterion. The new issues include the following:

- *The Costs of Terrorism*
- *Lights Out in California*
- *The Internet Economy*
- *The Perils of Product Differentiation*
- *The Euro*
- *Money and Interest Rates*
- *The Disappearing Surplus*

In addition, numerous readers have requested that we bring back two chapters from prior editions, and so we have complied. The returning chapters (updated, of course) are:

- *Contracts, Combinations, and Conspiracies*
- *Coffee, Tea, or Tuition-Free?*

Longtime users will recognize that Part Seven has both a new title—*Global and Macroeconomic Affairs*—and new material that reflects a recurrent theme in the requests we have received from users. In addition to chapters on international trade, we now have three chapters on macroeconomic issues: the euro, the federal deficit, and monetary policy. We think they enhance the value of the book for use in one-semester survey courses—and include enough microeconomics to be useful in purely micro classes too.

All of the other chapters in this edition have been partially or completely rewritten, and every chapter is, of course, as up-to-date as we can make it. What you will consistently find is a straightforward application of economic principles as they are taught in virtually all courses in economics, public policy, and the social sciences. This book can be understood by those who have taken a course in economics, are taking a course in economics, or have never taken a course in economics. In other words, we have made it self-contained, as well as accessible to a wide range of students.

The chapters are organized into seven parts. Part One examines the foundations of all economic analysis, including the concepts of scarcity, tradeoffs, opportunity cost, marginal analysis, and the like. In a sense, the four chapters in this introductory part set the stage for the remaining twenty-eight chapters. The second through sixth parts of the book cover the topics—such as demand and supply, market structures, environmental issues, and the impact of government policies—that are integral to virtually every course in which economics plays a role. At the end of the book, Part Seven examines global and macroeconomic affairs, because these matters are an essential part of the public issues of today.

Every part has a short introduction that prepares the reader for the material that is included in the following chapters. These part openers summarize and tie together the relevant issues, thus serving as launch pads for the analyses that follow. We hope you will have your students read these part openers before they embark on any of the subsequent chapters.

Every instructor will want to order a copy of the *Instructor's Manual* that accompanies *The Economics of Public Issues*. In writing this manual we have tried to incorporate the very best of the teaching aids that we use when we teach from *The Economics of Public Issues*. For each chapter, the features of this manual are:

- A synopsis that cuts to the core of the economic issues involved in the chapter.
- A concise exposition of the "behind the scenes" economic analysis upon which the discussion in the text is based. In almost all cases, this exposition is supplemented with one or more

diagrams that we have found to be particularly useful as teaching tools.
- Answers to the Discussion Questions posed at the end of the chapter—answers that further develop the basis economic analysis of the chapter, and almost always suggest new avenues of discussion.

The world of public issues continues to evolve. By the time you read this preface, we will be working on the next edition. If you have any particular subjects you would like included in the future, let us know by writing us in care of Addison Wesley.

Several chapters in this edition draw on the "Tangents" column that Benjamin writes for *PERC Reports*. We are grateful to the Political Economy Research Center (PERC) for permission to use that material. In addition, literally dozens of kind users of the last edition of this book, as well as several extremely diligent and thoughtful reviewers, offered suggestions for the current edition. Although scarcity precluded us from adopting all of their recommendations, we believe the reviewers—Harjit Arora (Le Moyne College), David Moewes (Concordia College), Thomas Dee (Swarthmore College), Janet Gerson (University of Michigan), Andrew Herr (Saint Vincent College), John McAdams (Marquette University), Bruce Petersen (Washington University), Ken Peterson (Furman University), Randal Rucker (Montana State University), Richard Vogel (SUNY, Farmingdale)—will be able to identify the impact they each had on this edition. To them and to our users who wrote to us—especially our perpetual critic Roger Meiners—we offer our sincere thanks and hope that the end result was worthy of their time and concern. We also thank Roxanne Hoch for shepherding the project, and Robbie Benjamin, whose editorial skills once again have improved the final product. All errors remain, of course, solely our own.

R.L.M.
D.K.B.
D.C.N.

Part One

The Foundations of Economic Analysis

INTRODUCTION

Our world is one of **scarcity;** we want more than we have. The reason is simple. Although we live in a world of limited **resources,** we have unlimited wants. This does not mean we all live and breathe solely to drive the fastest cars or wear the latest clothes. It means that we all want the right to make decisions about how resources are used—even if what we want to do with those resources is to feed starving children in Third World nations.

Given the existence of scarcity, we must make choices; we cannot have more of everything, so to get more of some things, we must give up other things. Economists express this simple idea by saying that we face **trade-offs.** For example, a student who wants higher grades generally must devote more time to studying and less time to, say, going to the movies; the trade-off in this instance is between grades and entertainment.

The concept of a trade-off is one of the (surprisingly few) basic principles you must grasp to understand the economics of public issues. We illustrate the simplicity of these principles with Chapter 1, "Killer Airbags." It is possible you thought that the government mandated the use of automobile airbags to save people's lives. Indeed, that may well have been the motivation. But it turns out that airbags also kill some automobile occupants and induce drivers of airbag-equipped cars to drive in ways that endanger themselves and other persons. So, like many of the issues explored in this book, there is more to automobile safety—and government policy making—than meets the eye, but with the use of some simple economic principles, you can greatly expand both your vision and your understanding of them.

Chapter 2, "Terrible Trade-off," examines a behind-the-scenes trade-off made every day on our behalf by the U.S. Food and Drug Administration (FDA). This federal government agency is charged with ensuring that the new prescription medicines that reach the market are both safe and effective. In carrying out its duties, the FDA requires pharmaceutical companies to subject proposed new drugs to extensive testing before the drugs may be introduced to the market. When the FDA requires more exhaustive testing of a drug, this improves the chances that the drug will be both safe and effective. But additional testing slows the approval of new drugs, thus depriving some individuals of the ability to use the drugs to treat their illnesses. The drug approval process undoubtedly reduces pain and suffering for some people, and even saves the lives of others, because it reduces the chances that an unsafe or ineffective drug will reach the market. Yet because the process also reduces the rate at which drugs reach the market (and may even prevent some safe, effective drugs from ever being introduced), the pain and suffering of other individuals is increased. Indeed, some individuals die as a result. This, then, is the terrible trade-off we face in Chapter 2: Who shall live and who shall die?

If trade-offs, or choices, are present in all our activities, we must face the question of how we may make the best choices. Economists argue that doing so requires the use of what we call **marginal analysis:** The term *marginal* in this context means incremental, or additional. All choices involve costs and benefits—we give up something for anything that we get. As we engage in more of any activity (eating, studying, or sleeping, for example) the **marginal benefits** of that activity eventually decline: The *additional* benefits associated with an *additional* unit of the activity get lower. In contrast, the **marginal costs** of an activity eventually rise as we engage in more and more of it. The best choices are made when we equate the marginal benefits and marginal costs of activity; that is, we try to determine when engaging in any more of a given activity would produce additional costs in excess of the additional benefits.

In Chapter 3, "Flying the Friendly Skies?", we apply the principles of marginal analysis to the issue of airline safety. How safe is it to travel at 600 miles per hour 7 miles above the ground? How safe *should* it be? The answers to these and other questions can be explored using marginal analysis. One of the conclusions we reach is that *perfect* safety is simply not in the cards: Every time you step into an airplane (or even across the street) there is some risk that your journey will end unhappily. As disconcerting as this might sound at first, we think you will find after reading this chapter that once the costs and benefits are taken into account you would have it no other way.

Every choice we make entails a **cost:** in a world of scarcity something must be given up to obtain anything of value. Although economics makes no pretense of being able to address all of the emotional and other human impacts of our lives, we can fairly readily estimate the economic losses implied by almost any choice. We see this clearly in Chapter 4, "The Costs of Terrorism," where we assess the economic effects of the September 11, 2001 terrorist attack on America. Not only can we determine the costs implied by the property destroyed that day, we can estimate the likely costs of the added security and other behavioral adjustments required to reduce the chance of another attack of this sort. By examining the decisions individuals make when they choose among factors affecting their own risks of death, we can even estimate the economic costs that resulted from the 3,000 fatalities that occurred in the attacks.

Once we compile these costs, we find that although the human toll of that day was horrific, the economic losses America suffered were small relative to the size of our economy, and ones from which we will likely soon recover. The point is not that the September 11 attacks were unimportant, nor that the human tragedy of that day should be forgotten. The point is rather that the U.S. economy has both the size and the strength to recover: The very capitalist machine that apparently helped incite the attacks is what will make it possible for us to survive and quickly repair the economic damage. The events of September 11 have made us poorer, but they have not made us poor.

1

Killer Airbags

Federal law requires that new cars be equipped with devices that kill drivers and passengers. If this sounds odd, the story gets stranger when you realize these devices are supposed to—and sometimes do—*save* lives. The devices in question are airbags, and their saga illustrates almost all of the important principles you should know to understand the economics of public issues.

The airbag story begins in 1969, when the Nixon Administration first proposed requiring "passive" restraints that would protect motorists during collisions even if they took no actions to protect themselves. The ideal system was thought to be airbags that would automatically inflate in the event of a collision. But a special government study commission found the airbags then available were not only extremely costly and unreliable but were in fact dangerous to the occupants of cars, especially to young children.[1] So, instead of airbags, the government tried requiring seat belts that prevented cars from being started unless the belts were fastened. Inconvenienced consumers who disliked seat belts quickly rejected these, and the idea of airbags was revived and eventually mandated by the federal government. In anticipation of the requirements that 1998 cars have them on both the driver and

---

[1] *Cumulative Regulatory Effects on the Cost of Automobile Transportation (RECAT): Final Report of the Ad Hoc Committee,* Office of Science and Technology, Washington, D.C., 1972.

passenger sides, carmakers began installing airbags on selected models in 1989. By 1997, more than 65 million cars had driver-side bags, and about 35 million had them on the passenger side, too.

At first it seemed as though the earlier problems with airbags had been solved. The installed cost of about $400 apiece was far less than it would have been when the bags were initially proposed, and their reliability was dramatically increased. News reports soon began appearing with stories of seemingly miraculous survival by occupants of airbag-equipped cars in collisions. By the end of 1995, it was estimated that airbags had saved more than 1500 lives since 1989.

As the population of cars with airbags grew, however, another set of stories began to appear: Airbags deploy at speeds up to 200 mph and are designed to be most effective when used in conjunction with seat belts. It soon became apparent that people who failed to use belts, people who sat closer than the normal distance from the steering wheel or dashboard, and—most ominously— children anywhere in the front seat were at increased risk of serious injury or death due to airbag deployment. By late 1997 it was estimated by the federal government that although a total (since 1989) of perhaps 2600 people owed their lives to airbags, there were more than 80 people, most of them children, who had been killed by the force of normally deploying airbags.

The outcry over the deaths of children killed in low-speed crashes by the very devices that were supposed to protect them generated action by both the private sector and the federal government. Auto manufacturers and their suppliers began developing "smart" airbags that sense the severity of a collision, the size of the person in the front seat, and whether the person is properly belted. Then, depending on the results of those measurements, the bag decides whether to deploy and at what speed it will do so. As an interim solution, in November 1997 (four and a half years after the first documented airbag fatality) the Department of Transportation announced that consumers would be allowed to apply for permission to have airbag cutoff switches installed in their vehicles. The estimated cost to consumers who have the switches installed is $150 to $200 per car. State governments also got in the act, with many of them mandating that children under a certain age or size be prohibited from occupying the front seat of an automobile.

Beginning with the 1998 model year, manufacturers also began installing less powerful airbags that inflate 22 percent less quickly on the driver side and 14 percent less quickly on the passenger side. The result has been a sharp reduction in (although not an elimination of) airbag-induced fatalities. By 2002, 120 million driver-side airbags were on the road, along with 94 million passenger-side bags. The federal government had credited the devices with saving 7600 lives in serious, high-speed crashes since 1989, at a cost of about 200 people—half of them children—killed by airbag deployments in low-speed crashes.

What can we learn from the airbag episode that will guide us in thinking about other public issues of our times? There are several general principles:

1. *There is no free lunch.* Every choice, and thus every policy, entails a **cost**—something must be given up. In a world of scarcity, we cannot have more of everything, so to get more of some things, we must give up other things. Simply put, we face trade-offs. In this case, although airbags increase the safety of most adults, there is both a monetary cost of $800 per car and a reduced level of safety for children riding in the front seat.

2. *The cost of an action is the alternative that is sacrificed.* Economists often express costs (and benefits) in terms of dollars, because this is a simple means of accounting for and measuring them. But that doesn't mean costs have to be monetary, nor does it mean economics is incapable of analyzing costs and benefits that are very human. In the case of airbags, the cost that induced action by consumers, manufacturers, and government officials was the lost lives of scores of children.

3. *The relevant costs and benefits are the marginal (or incremental) ones.* The relevant question is not whether safety is good or bad; it is instead how much safety we want—which can only be answered by looking at the added (or marginal) benefits of more safety compared to the added (marginal) costs. One possible response to the child fatalities would have been to outlaw airbags on new cars and mandate that all installed airbags be deactivated. That would have guaranteed that no more children would have been killed by airbags. But for many people (such as those without young children), this solution to airbag fatalities would not be sensible, because the marginal cost would exceed the marginal benefit.

4. *People respond to incentives.* A rise in the apparent costs of using airbags (due to airbag fatalities among children) reduced consumers' desire to utilize airbags and induced them to put pressure on the federal government—pressure that convinced the Department of Transportation to change the regulations. Moreover, the simultaneous rise in the rewards of developing alternatives to today's airbags sent suppliers scurrying to find those alternatives, including "smart" airbags.

5. *Things aren't always as they seem.* Many analyses of the effects of government policies take an approach that doesn't fully recognize the behavior people otherwise *would* have undertaken. Thus, official pronouncements about the consequences of policies routinely misrepresent their impact—not because there is necessarily any attempt to deceive, but because it is often so difficult to know what would have happened otherwise. For example, the claim that 7600 lives have been "saved" by airbags is portrayed as the benefit of the government mandate that all new cars have airbags. In fact, absent the airbag regulations, it is highly likely that automobile manufacturers would have devised other systems—better seat belts, vehicles with additional "crush space" in the passenger compartment, or perhaps even some form of optional passive restraint system—that would have saved many of the lives supposedly saved by government-mandated airbags. Moreover, as we discuss more fully in Principle 6 (below), individuals themselves would have behaved much differently absent the airbag regulations. Given the speculative nature of such hypothetical behavior, the people reporting the numbers are (justifiably) reluctant to estimate the effects; we are thus served up the far safer statistic of "7600 lives saved."

6. *Policies always have unintended consequences, and as a result, their net benefits are almost always less than anticipated.* Information, like all goods, is costly to obtain, and sometimes the cheapest way to learn more about something is simply to try it. When it is tried, new things will be learned, not all of them pleasant. More importantly, in the case of government regulations, Principle 3 (above) fails to make good headlines. Instead, what gets politicians reelected and regulators promoted are fundamental, *absolute* notions, such as "safety" (and motherhood and apple pie). Thus, if a little safety is good, more must be better, so why not simply mandate that all front-seat passengers in all cars be protected

by airbags that are all the same? Eventually, the reality of Principle 3 sinks in, but in this case not before scores of children had lost their lives.

Although these basic principles of public issues are readily apparent when looking at the children who have been killed by airbags, they are just as present in two other features of airbags—neither of which has received much attention. First, most airbag deployments occur in relatively low-speed accidents (under 30 miles per hour), when the added safety benefits to properly belted occupants is low. But once the bags are deployed, they must be replaced, and often so must the windshield (blown out by the passenger-side bag) and sometimes even the dashboard (damaged as the airbag deploys). The added repair cost per car is currently estimated to be between $2000 and $2500. Thus, not only are automobile repair costs soaring due to airbags, many cars that routinely would have been repaired are now being written off completely because it is too costly to fix them.

Second, and more significantly, cars that are airbag-equipped tend to be driven more aggressively, apparently because their occupants feel more secure. The result is more accidents by such cars, more serious accidents (such as rollovers) that kill occupants despite the airbags, and a higher risk of pedestrian fatalities—none of which are accounted for in the lives-saved figures that we quoted earlier.[2] In addition, when seat belts are worn, they are almost as good as airbags in preventing fatalities among automobile occupants. Belts reduce the fatality rate by 45 percent; adding an airbag increases this only to 50 percent. The net effect is that even though airbags are both better and less costly than they were when first proposed, it is still not clear they yield benefits that exceed their costs.

DISCUSSION QUESTIONS

1. Under what circumstances is it appropriate to trade off human lives against dollars when making decisions about safety?

---

[2] Steven Peterson, George Hoffer, and Edward Millner, "Are Drivers of Air-Bag-Equipped Cars More Aggressive? A Test of the Offsetting Behavior Hypothesis," *The Journal of Law & Economics,* October, 1995, pp. 251–264.

2. Do you think government action allowing airbag deactivation and depowered airbags would have been as swift or as likely if all the fatalities had been among adults rather than chiefly among small children?

3. Do you think government regulators do (or should) distinguish between the *voluntary* choices adults make for themselves (such as not wearing motorcycle helmets or seat belts), versus the decisions to which young children are *involuntarily* exposed by adults (such as being placed unbelted in an automobile or subjected to second-hand cigarette smoke)?

4. Most people—and without any government regulation requiring it—have locks on their doors to protect them from intruders. If airbags are so good at protecting people from injuries and death, why were government regulations required to get them installed on automobiles?

2

Terrible Trade-off

How would you rather die? Due to a lethal reaction to a drug prescribed by your doctor? Or because your doctor failed to prescribe a drug that would have saved your life? If this choice is one you would rather not make, consider this: Employees of the United States Food and Drug Administration (FDA) make that decision on behalf of millions of Americans many times each year. More precisely, the FDA decides whether new medicines (prescription drugs) should be allowed to go on sale in the United States. If the FDA decides to allow a drug to be sold, doctors may prescribe it, in the expectation that the beneficial effects of the drug will outweigh whatever adverse side effects the drug may have. But if the FDA prohibits the drug from being sold in the United States, doctors here may not legally prescribe it, even if thousands of lives are saved by the drug each year in other countries.

The FDA's authority to make such decisions dates back to the passage of the Food and Drugs Act of 1906. That law required, among other things, that medicines be correctly labeled as to their contents and that they not contain any substances poisonous or harmful to the health of consumers. Because of this legislation, Dr. Hostetter's celebrated Stomach Bitters and Kickapoo Indian Sagwa, along with numerous rum-laden concoctions, cocaine-based potions, and supposed anticancer remedies, disappeared from druggists' shelves. The law was expanded in 1938 with the passage of the federal Food, Drug, and Cosmetic Act, which forced manufacturers to demonstrate the safety of new drugs before being allowed to offer them for sale. (This legislation was driven by the deaths of 107 individuals who had taken an elixir of sulfanilamide, which happened to contain diethylene glycol, a poisonous substance usually contained in antifreeze.)

The next step in U.S. drug regulation came after the birth of 12,000 deformed infants whose mothers during pregnancy had taken a sleeping pill called thalidomide. When these deformities first became apparent, the drug already was widely used in Europe, and the FDA was moving toward approving it in the United States. In fact, about 2.5 million thalidomide tablets were in the hands of U.S. physicians as samples. The FDA ordered all the samples removed and prohibited the sale of thalidomide in the United States. Using this incident as ammunition, Senator Estes Kefauver secured passage of a bill known as the 1962 Kefauver–Harris Amendments to the 1938 Food, Drug, and Cosmetic Act. This legislation radically altered the drug approval process in the United States.

Prior to the 1962 amendments, the FDA usually approved a new drug application within a 180-day time limit, unless the application failed to demonstrate that the drug was safe for use in the proposed manner. The 1962 amendments added a "proof of efficacy" requirement and also removed the time constraint on the FDA. Thus, since 1962, manufacturers wishing to introduce a new drug must demonstrate to the FDA's satisfaction that the drug is safe to use in the proposed manner, and also that it will accomplish the intended therapeutic outcome. Moreover, the FDA is free to determine how much and what evidence it will demand before approving a drug for sale, and it may take as long as it wants before either giving or refusing approval.

The most noticeable impact of the 1962 amendments was a reduction in the number of new drugs coming onto the market. Researchers have estimated that the 1962 amendments cut new drug introductions by as much as two-thirds. This occurred because the amendments sharply increased the costs of introducing a new drug and markedly slowed the approval process. Prior to the 1962 amendments, for example, the average time between filing and approval of a new drug application was seven months; by 1967, it was 30 months; and by the late 1970s, it had risen to eight to ten *years*. Although the average approval time has since dropped, it still takes ten times as long for a new drug to be approved as it did before the 1962 amendments. The protracted approval process involves costly testing by the drug companies and delays the receipt of any potential revenue from new drugs. Moreover, once all of the test data is in, the FDA may decide against the company's application. Overall, the expected profitability of new drugs has been sharply reduced by the 1962 amendments, so fewer of them have been brought onto the market.

The rationale behind the FDA regulations is presumably protection of consumers, because generally consumers do not have the ability to obtain or analyze the information necessary to make accurate choices about the safety or efficacy of particular drugs. Consumers are at the mercy of the physicians who prescribe the drugs. But the physicians are also, in a sense, at the mercy of the drug companies, for it is almost impossible for each individual doctor to keep up with all of the technical literature about drugs and be aware of the advantages and disadvantages of each of them. Doctors must rely on the so-called detail people sent out by the drug companies to inform physicians about new drugs and give them samples to dispense to their patients, so that doctors can see for themselves how effective the new drugs really are. Without FDA regulations, it is argued, the drug companies might introduce drugs that are not completely safe or simply do not work as well as they might.

Countering this argument is that doctors, hospitals, and drug companies have strong incentives to prescribe, market, and produce drugs that are both safe and effective. After all, if it can be proven that side effects from a drug cause harm to an individual, or that an individual was harmed because a drug did not perform as promised, the ensuing lawsuit can cost the doctor, hospital, or manufacturer millions of dollars. Moreover, doctors, hospitals, and drug companies rely heavily on their reputations, and serious errors in prescribing, marketing, or producing drugs can damage those reputations beyond repair.

Although debate remains over exactly how much regulation is appropriate to ensure that drugs are both safe and efficacious, there is little doubt that the 1962 amendments have resulted in a U.S. "drug lag." The number of drugs marketed in the United Kingdom that are not available in the United States, for example, is very much larger than the number marketed in the United States that are not available in the United Kingdom. Although the FDA and its supporters note that it takes time to ensure that patients benefit from rather than are harmed by new drugs, regulation-induced drug lag can *itself* be life-threatening. Dr. George Hitchings, a winner of the Nobel Prize in Medicine, estimated that the five-year lag in introducing Septra (an antibacterial agent) to the United States "killed 100,000, maybe a million people" in this country. Similarly, the introduction of a class of drugs called beta blockers (used to treat heart attack victims and people with high blood pressure) was delayed nearly a decade in this country relative to its introduction in Europe. According to several researchers, the lag in the FDA approval of these drugs cost the lives of at least 250,000 Americans.

Now we can see the terrible trade-off in the market for prescription drugs: Although lives are saved because unsafe or ineffective drugs are kept off the market, the FDA regulatory process delays (or even prevents) the introduction of some safe and efficacious drugs, thereby costing lives. If the only cost of FDA-mandated testing were the millions of dollars that drug companies must spend on those procedures, there probably would not be many critics of the FDA. But the fact is that many persons could have benefited greatly—perhaps to the extent of being alive today—had the 1962 Kefauver–Harris Amendments not delayed the introduction of so many drugs.

With this thought in mind, let us take a more systematic look at the trade-off we face. Every time a new drug is introduced, there is a chance that it should not have been—either because it has adverse side effects that outweigh the therapeutic benefits (it is not safe), or because it really does nothing significant to help the individuals who take it (it is not effective). When such a drug is introduced, we shall say that a **Type I error** has been committed. Since 1962, incidence of Type I error—the thalidomide possibility—has been reduced by increasing the amount of prior testing for new drugs. People have surely benefited from this reduction in Type I error by incurring fewer adverse side effects and by being spared the costs of taking ineffective drugs. But other people have been the victims of what is called **Type II error.** Their cost is the pain, suffering, and death that occur because the 1962 amendments have prevented or delayed the introduction of safe, efficacious drugs. Type II error occurs when a drug *should* be introduced but is not, because of FDA regulation.

Does the apparently high incidence of Type II errors by the FDA over the past 40 years imply that the regulatory process should be overhauled radically? Possibly, but even doing so would not eliminate the fundamental trade-off. The FDA's long, intensive review of new drug applications does produce benefits: The drugs that eventually reach the market are safer and more effective. As we have seen, the costs are that some safe, effective drugs never make it to the market, and many others are substantially delayed. Expediting the review process would enable more drugs to reach the market sooner, but it would also increase the chances that a harmful or ineffective drug might slip through the screening process.

It seems that for every benefit there is a cost. Indeed, this simple fact is so pervasive in our lives that economists have even coined a phrase summarizing it—*There is no such thing as a free lunch*—which simply means that in a world of scarcity, every choice we make entails a cost. By choosing to reduce the risk of introducing another thalidomide, we also choose to increase the risk of delaying another Septra or beta blocker. Trade-offs such as this are an inescapable fact.

The principles involved in making the best choices among trade-offs are discussed in Chapter 3. On the drug front, outcries over the high incidence of Type II errors by the FDA have in some cases induced the agency to shorten the testing period for drugs when the costs of Type I error are insignificant compared to the possible damage due to Type II error—as is the case with terminally ill patients. Thus, since the 1980s, the FDA has accelerated the approval process for several drugs used in treating patients with terminal diseases. One of the most famous of these drugs is azidothymidine (AZT), which emerged in 1986 as a possible treatment for AIDS. AZT received FDA approval after a testing period of only 18 months when it was found that the drug increased the life expectancy of AIDS patients. In effect, the FDA decided that the costs associated with Type I error—such as headaches and nausea—were outweighed by the many deaths that would result if the drug were not approved quickly.

In light of the expedited review that some drugs receive, it is worth asking two questions. First, how is it possible that the costs of delays for other drugs might greatly outweigh the benefits? The answer appears to be a principle called "rational ignorance." The fact is that for most people most of the time, it doesn't pay to learn all there is to know even about important issues such as medical care. Thus, voters simply don't know enough to enable them to put sufficient pressure on their elected representatives or the FDA to improve the approval process: It is rational for most voters to remain ignorant and ineffective, because the costs of learning and doing more outweigh the likely benefits. But what, then, explains the outbreak of consumer interest and pressure leading to relatively quick approval on drugs such as AZT for AIDS and Taxol, used to treat breast cancer? The answer seems to reside in the existence of narrow, clearly identifiable groups of individuals who have enormous personal costs or benefits at stake. In the case of AZT, gay men took the lead in putting pressure on the FDA, while in the case of Taxol, it was women, particularly those coming from families with a history of breast cancer. In each case, the potential benefits of learning about the advantages of the drug and acting on that knowledge were large relative to the costs—it was rational for consumers to be knowledgeable rather than ignorant in these cases. The result was pressure on the FDA, and expedited approval.

Ultimately, despite the expedited review of AZT and a number of other drugs used to treat AIDS or cancer, most of the agency's critics remain convinced that the FDA has too often weighed the terrible trade-off of drug regulation in a way that has produced tragedy for patients. As the battle against AIDS continues, there is little doubt that pressure on the FDA to expedite the drug review process will increase. Only time and careful scrutiny will enable us to determine whether future choices by the FDA help us or harm us.

DISCUSSION QUESTIONS

1. Does the structure of the drug industry have any bearing on the types of errors that drug firms are likely to make? That is, would a drug industry comprised of numerous highly competitive firms be more or less likely to introduce unsafe drugs than would an industry comprised of a few large firms?

2. How could the incentives facing officials at the FDA be changed to reduce the incidence of Type II errors?

3. What would be the advantages and disadvantages of a system in which, rather than having the FDA permit or prohibit new drugs, the FDA merely published its opinions about the safety and efficacy of drugs, and then allowed physicians to make their own decisions about whether to prescribe them for their patients?

4. Suppose, for simplicity, that Type I and Type II errors resulted in deaths only. Keeping in mind that too little caution produces Type I errors and too much caution produces Type II errors, what would be the best mix of Type I and Type II errors?

3

Flying the Friendly Skies?

Most of us hop into our car with little thought for our personal safety, beyond perhaps the act of putting on seat belts. Yet even though travel on scheduled, commercial airlines is safer than driving to work or to the grocery store, many people approach air travel with a sense of foreboding, if not downright fear.

If we were to think carefully about the wisdom of traveling 600 miles per hour in an aluminum tube seven miles above the earth, several questions might come to mind: How safe is this? How safe should it be? Because the people who operate airlines are not in it for fun, does their interest in making a buck ignore our interest in making it home in one piece? Is some form of government regulation the only way to ensure safety in the skies?

The science of economics begins with one simple principle: We live in a world of **scarcity,** which implies that to get more of any good, we must sacrifice some of other goods. This is just as true of safety as it is of pizzas or haircuts or works of art. Safety confers benefits (we live longer and more enjoyably), but achieving it also entails costs (we must give up something to obtain that safety).

As the degree of safety rises, the total benefits of safety rise but the marginal (or incremental) benefits of additional safety decline. Consider a simple example: Adding exit doors to an airplane increases the number of people who can escape in the event of an emergency evacuation. Nevertheless, each *additional* door adds less in safety benefits than does the previous one; if the fourth door enables, say, an extra ten people to escape, the fifth may enable only an extra six to escape. (If this sounds implausible, imagine having a door for each person; the last door added will enable at most one more person to escape.) So we say that the marginal (or incremental) benefit of safety declines as the amount of safety increases.

Let's look now at the other side of the equation: As the amount of safety increases, both the total and the marginal (incremental) costs of providing safety rise. Having a fuel gauge on the plane's instrument panel clearly enhances safety, because it reduces the chance that the plane will run out of fuel while in flight.[1] It is always possible that a fuel gauge will malfunction, so having a backup fuel gauge also adds to safety. Because having two gauges is more costly than having just one, the total costs of safety rise as safety increases. It is also clear, however, that while the cost of the second gauge is (at least) as great as the cost of the first, the second gauge has a smaller positive impact on safety. Thus, the cost per unit of additional (incremental) safety is higher for the second fuel gauge than for the first.

How much safety should we have? For an economist, the answer to such a question is generally expressed in terms of marginal benefits and marginal costs. The economically *efficient* level of safety occurs when the marginal cost of increasing safety just equals the marginal benefit of that increased safety. Put somewhat differently, if the marginal benefits of adding (or keeping) a safety feature exceed the marginal costs of doing so, then the feature is worth it. But if the added benefits of a safety device do *not* exceed the added costs, we should refrain from installing the device. Note there are two related issues here: How safe should we be, and how should we achieve that level of safety?

Both of these issues took on added urgency on the morning of September 11, 2001, when terrorists hijacked four U.S. commercial jetliners. The hijackers deliberately crashed two of the planes into New York's World Trade Center and flew another into the side of the Pentagon. The fourth plane crashed in a Pennsylvania field, probably in the midst of a struggle for control between the passengers and hijackers. Most people were stunned with the ease with which the hijackers were able to carry out their mission, for it suggested that air travel, particularly in the U.S., was far less safe than

---

[1] Notice that we say "reduces" rather than "eliminates." In 1978 a United Airlines pilot preoccupied with a malfunctioning landing gear evidently failed to pay sufficient attention to his cockpit gauges. Eight people were killed when the plane was forced to crash land after running out of fuel.

previously believed. Immediately, it was clear that we should devote additional resources to airline safety; what was not clear was how *much* additional resources should be thus devoted, nor precisely *what* changes should be made. For example, some airline pilots wanted the right to carry firearms on flights, to help them prevent future hijackings. Other people objected, noting the high potential costs of such an action: an errant shot from a pistol could puncture a plane's skin, resulting in catastrophic cabin depressurization. Similarly, almost everyone agreed that more careful screening of passengers (and baggage) at airports would produce important safety benefits. But again, the question arose: how should we achieve this? Should carry-on bags be prohibited, or just examined more carefully? How thoroughly should checked luggage be screened for bombs? The precise answers to these questions will be decided upon only as we learn more about the extent of the threat and the costs of alternative responses to it. Nevertheless, throughout the process, economic principles can help us make the most sensible decisions.

In general, the efficient level of safety will not be perfect safety, because perfection is simply too costly to achieve. For example, to be absolutely *certain* that no one is ever killed or injured in an airplane crash, we would have to prevent all travel in airplanes. This does not mean it is efficient to have air disasters become a daily feature on the evening news. It does mean that it is efficient for there to be *some* risk associated with air travel. The unavoidable conclusion is that if we wish to enjoy the advantages of flying, we must be willing to accept some risk—a conclusion that each of us implicitly accepts every time we step aboard an airplane.

Changes in circumstances can alter the efficient level of safety. For example, if a technological change reduces the costs of bomb scanning equipment, the marginal costs of preventing terrorist bomb attacks will be lower. It will be efficient to have more airports install the machines, and to have extra machines at large airports to speed the screening process. Air travel will become safer because of the technological change. Similarly, if the marginal benefits of safety rise for some reason—perhaps because the president of the United States is on board—it could be efficient to take more precautions, resulting in safer air travel. Given the factors that determine the benefits and costs of safety, the result of a change in circumstances will be some determinate level of safety that generally will be associated with some risk of death or injury.

Airplanes are complex systems, and an amazing number of things can go wrong with them. Over the century that humans have been flying, airplane manufacturers and airlines have studied every one of the things that has gone wrong thus far, and put into place design changes and operating procedures aimed at preventing recurring error. Of course consumers have the greatest incentive to ensure that air travel is safe, and if information were free, we could assert with some confidence that the actual level of safety supplied by firms was the efficient level of safety. Consumers would simply observe the safety offered by different airlines, the prices they charge, and select the degrees of safety that best suited their preferences and budgets—just as with other goods. But, of course, information is not free; it is a **scarce good,** costly to obtain. As a result, it is possible that passengers are unaware of the safety records of various airlines, or the competency of the pilots and the maintenance procedures of an airline's mechanics. Indeed, it is possible that even the *airlines* are uncertain about the efficient level of safety, perhaps because they have no way of correctly estimating the true threat of terrorist attacks, for example. Both of these possibilities have been used to argue that it is appropriate for the federal government to mandate certain minimum levels of safety, as it does today through the operation of the Federal Aviation Administration (FAA). Let's look at this issue in some detail.

One argument in favor of government safety standards rests on the presumption that, left to their own devices, airlines would provide less safety than passengers actually want to have. This might happen, for example, if customers could not tell (at a reasonable cost) whether or not the equipment, training, procedures, and so on employed by an airline are safe. If passengers cannot cheaply gauge the level of safety, they will not be willing to reward airlines for being safe or punish them for being unsafe. If safety is costly to provide and consumers are unwilling to pay for it because they cannot accurately measure it, airlines will provide too little of it. The conclusion, at least as reached by some, is that government experts—such as the FAA—should set safety standards for the industry.

This conclusion seems plausible, but it ignores two simple points. First, how is the government to know what the efficient level of safety is? Even if the FAA is fully knowledgeable regarding the efficacy and costs of all possible safety measures, it still does not have enough information to set efficient safety standards, because it does not know the value that people place on safety. Without such information, the FAA has no way of assessing the benefits of additional safety, and thus no means of knowing whether those benefits are greater or less than the added costs.

The second point is that it is likely that people are really interested in reaching their destinations safely, and not in whether they got there because of a good plane, a good pilot, or a good mechanic. Even if they cannot observe whether an airline hires good pilots or bad pilots, they can observe whether that airline's planes land safely or crash. If it is *safety* that is important to consumers—and not the obscure, costly-to-measure set of reasons for that safety—the fact that consumers cannot easily measure metal fatigue in jet engines may be totally irrelevant to the process of achieving the efficient level of safety.

Interestingly, evidence shows that consumers *are* cognizant of the safety performance of airlines, and that they "punish" airlines that perform in an unsafe manner. Researchers Mark Mitchell and Michael Maloney have found that when an airline is "at fault" in a fatal plane crash, consumers appear to downgrade their safety rating of the airline (i.e., revise upward their estimates of the likelihood of future fatal crashes). As a result, the offending airline suffers substantial, adverse financial consequences, over and above the costs of losing the plane and being sued on behalf of the victims. These research findings suggest a striking degree of safety awareness on the part of supposedly ignorant consumers.

Of course this discussion leaves open the issue of how to handle safety threats posed by terrorists and the like. For example, much of the information that goes into assessing terrorist threats is classified as secret, and its revelation to airlines or consumers might well compromise key sources of the data. Hence there could be an advantage to having the government try to approximate the efficient safety outcome by mandating certain screening provisions, without revealing exactly why they are being chosen. Similarly, because airlines are connected in networks (so that people and baggage move from one airline to another in the course of a trip) one might argue that achieving the efficient level of safety necessitates a common set of screening rules for all airlines. Even so, this does not inform us whether the government should impose those rules, or the airlines should come to a voluntary joint agreement on them.

We began this chapter by repeating the commonplace observation that airlines are safer than cars. Yet many people *still* worry for their safety every time they get on an airplane. Are they being irrational? Well, the answer, it seems, is in the eye of the beholder. Measured in terms of fatalities per mile traveled, airplanes are indeed some 15 times safer than cars (and 176 times safer than walking, we might add). But this number masks the fact that 68 percent of aircraft accidents happen on takeoff and landing, and these operations occupy only 6 percent of flight time. It is presumably this fact that quite sensibly makes people nervous whenever they find themselves approaching an airport.

DISCUSSION QUESTIONS

1. Is it possible to be too safe? Explain what you mean by "too safe."

2. Many automobile manufacturers routinely advertise the safety of their cars, yet airlines generally do not even mention safety in their advertising. Can you suggest an explanation for this difference?

3. Many economists would argue that private companies are likely to be more efficient than the government in operating airlines. Yet many economists would also argue that there is a valid reason for government to regulate the safety of those same airlines. Can you explain why (or why not) the government might be good at ensuring safety, even though it might not be good at operating the airlines?

4. Professional football teams sometimes charter airplanes to take them to their "away" games. Would you feel safer riding on a United Airlines plane that had been chartered by the Washington Redskins rather than on a regularly scheduled United Airlines flight?

4

The Costs of Terrorism

On September 11, 2001, terrorists hijacked four U.S. commercial jetliners. The hijackers deliberately crashed two of the planes into the twin towers of New York's World Trade Center. Another was flown into the side of the Pentagon. The fourth plane crashed in a Pennsylvania field, and is believed to have gone down in the midst of a struggle for control between the passengers and hijackers. Three thousand people died in the attacks, a toll that exceeded even that of the Japanese attack on Pearl Harbor, some 60 years before.

The terrorists who planned and executed these attacks presumably hoped to accomplish at least two goals: (1) destroy symbols of American capitalist and military might; and (2) damage—perhaps cripple—the American economy. They largely succeeded in their first objective: Although the Pentagon survived and has been repaired, the Trade Center's twin towers are no more, and may never be rebuilt as they were. Yet despite the horrific human carnage, the economic significance of the September 11 attacks will almost surely turn out to be far less than the terrorists hoped.

The loss of physical capital due to the attack can be fairly easily translated into economic terms. Rental rates on office space in Lower Manhattan (the location of the Trade Center) are available in the market place, and the computers, furniture, and art that was destroyed (as well as the jetliners themselves) can also be readily valued based on market prices of comparable items. The destruction of the Trade Center buildings, including the smaller ones around the twin towers, cost perhaps $5 billion. The lost assets of the buildings' tenants, plus the clean-up costs, and the loss of the four planes add about $10 billion more to the physical destruction wrought by the terrorist attacks. Estimating the costs of the damage to the Pentagon is a bit tougher, in part because details of some damage is considered by the government to be classified information. Still, plausible estimates put the costs of the Pentagon damage at around $1 billion. Thus, the total physical damage due to the attacks was about $16 billion.

Far more important, however, in both human and economic terms, was the loss of life that resulted from the September 11 attacks. Overall, some 3,000 people were killed, including the passengers and crew of the four planes. Although economics makes no pretense of being able to address all of the emotional and other human impact of such losses, we can fairly readily make an estimate of the economic losses implied by the fatalities. We can do this by taking into account the behavior of people when they make choices about their own risks of death. Consider first the purchases people make. Smoke alarms and carbon monoxide detectors, for example, lower the risk of dying. If an individual spends $50 on such devices, and if the result is to lower her risk of death by 1 in 100,000, then we know that person must value her life as being worth at least $5,000,000 (= $50 × 100,000). Alternatively, consider the choices people make when they decide where to work. Some jobs (such fire fighting and coal mining) have higher fatality risks than do other jobs (such teaching). The people who work in high risk jobs implicitly insist upon a wage premium for accepting those risks, and economists have estimated the size of those premiums. Putting together data from these various sources, economists estimate that people place an average value of about $3-5 million on their lives.

Now, many of the people who died on September 11 were not average. In particular, the World Trade Center housed some of the most brilliant financial minds in the world. Add to this the legions of highly specialized securities lawyers, other types of lawyers, accountants, and computer technicians, and you come up with a staggering loss of intellectual horsepower. This intellectual horsepower is called **human capital** to contrast it from physical capital, such as buildings and equipment. It is not at all implausible that the economic value of the human capital lost in the September 11 attacks was on the order of $8 million per person. Given that 3,000 people were killed, this implies that the loss of human capital was perhaps $24 billion—an amount much greater than the value of the physical capital lost.

Totaling up the damages due to the loss of the planes, the buildings destroyed, the clean-up costs, and the human capital lost in the attacks, we can thus estimate that the wealth of the United States dropped in the matter of a few hours by about $40 billion—although given the uncertainties of the estimates, the total might actually range from $30 to $50 billion. The total direct economic costs of the Japanese attack on Pearl Harbor (expressed in terms of today's dollars) were significantly less. Indeed, it now seems clear that the terrorist attack of September 11 was probably the most costly one-day event in the history of the United States.

It is important, however, to put these losses into context. The U.S. as well as other countries have suffered serious natural disasters as well as political upheavals. For example, in 1992, Hurricane Andrew cut a huge swath through south Florida. Although far fewer people were killed than in the September 11 terrorist attacks, the economic damage of the storm was estimated to be about $25 billion (perhaps $30 billion in today's terms). Although some of the affected neighborhoods still have a storm-ravaged appearance, overall the economy of the area seems to be fully recovered. Looking abroad, the Japanese city of Kobe suffered an earthquake in 1995 that destroyed more than a thousand buildings and left hundreds of thousands homeless. Six thousand people died. The economic loss was estimated to be $114 billion, which represented perhaps one-quarter of one percent of the entire wealth of Japan. Nonetheless, it took only a year before economic activity in the Kobe region returned to its pre-earthquake levels.

The American economy is—by a considerable margin—the largest in the world. As we noted above, the cost of the immediate destruction due to the terrorist attacks is between $30 billion and $50 billion. At the time of the attack, total physical assets in the U.S. were worth about $30 trillion. When human capital is added, the total assets of the U.S. amounted to about $100 trillion. A maximum $50 billion economic loss due to the September 11 attacks means that at most 0.05 percent (that's one-twentieth of one percent) of the total productive assets in the U.S. were lost. The point is not that the September 11 attacks were unimportant, nor that the human tragedy of that day should be forgotten. The point is rather that the U.S. economy has both the size and the strength to recover: The very capitalist machine that apparently helped stimulate the attacks is what will make it possible for us to survive and quickly repair the economic damage.

One key feature that distinguishes the September 11 attacks from hurricanes or earthquakes is the new information it delivered—and bad news it was, too. To a degree never before imagined, we shall have to take measures to protect ourselves against future attacks, including the immediate military actions in Afghanistan, future military actions, and added airport and other security measures. All of these are costs that will continue for many years, and they must implicitly be reckoned as part of the damage done by the original attacks.

The 6,000-plus commercial airplanes in the U.S. carry nearly 700 million people some 500 billion passenger miles every year. Prior to every one of the 11 million takeoffs each year, passengers and baggage now must be scrutinized with a heightened degree of care. Not only does this call for added resources to implement, but all of those passengers have to spend countless added hours in airports waiting for it to take place. Moreover, cockpit doors have had to be strengthened, bomb-sniffing dogs employed, and air marshals added to many flights.

In the short run, the complications are enormous. Yet the likely economic costs are smaller than one might imagine. Economists Gary Becker and Kevin Murphy of the University of Chicago estimate that increased airport security will cost about $4 per passenger per flight segment. When they add increased flight delays and security checks, they still only come up with the total cost of $10 billion per year. This represents a very small fraction of an American economy that generates $10 trillion per year in economic activity.

Researchers Becker and Murphy also have estimated the cost of continuing terrorist attacks in the United States, including downed planes and property losses, to be about $15 billion per year. Even accounting for all of the likely future costs, at worst they believe that the total impact of the added security at airports and on planes, plus the damages due to successful terrorist attacks, will only reduce annual national income by about three-tenths of one percent. This does not mean we should be complacent about the likelihood of nor necessity to defend against future attacks. Rather, Becker and Murphy simply note that we are a country with huge supplies of physical and human capital, blessed with a population that exhibits tremendous innovative skills. The events of September 11 have made us poorer, but they have not made us poor.

Although most of our discussion of the costs of terrorism have been in monetary terms, it is important to recognize that dollars are but a convenient way of summarizing the market value of what we have really lost—the goods, services, and peace of mind that were taken away by the attacks. This point brings home a simple but important point: Some commentators argued that the attacks had a hidden "bright side" because they put to work so many people cleaning up the wreckage and defending against future attacks. This view is erroneous, for all of those people and other resources could have been put to other uses had the attacks not occurred. The construction workers who removed debris from the Trade Center rubble could have been building homes instead. The dogs who will be trained to detect bombs in luggage could have become companions to the blind or the disabled. The cleanup, recovery, and security measures will make their way into measured national income, but only at the expense of other activities that all of us would truly have preferred before the events of September 11. This, together with the human tragedy, is the real cost of that day.

DISCUSSION QUESTIONS

1. America responded to the September 11 attacks by launching attacks against the Taliban government of Afghanistan, which had been harboring the people who were believed to have financed and organized the hijackings. This was followed by anti-terrorist U.S. military activity elsewhere in the world, including the Philippines. Can economic principles suggest how far the U.S. should carry its anti-terrorist policies? Should the objective be to eliminate any possibility of future attacks? Or should there be some other goal?

2. As America prepared to improve future air travel safety, a debate erupted over the future employment status of airport security screening personnel. Some people wanted them to remain private sector employees, while others wanted them to be employees of the federal government. Do you think the level of safety would be greater with screeners as federal employees or private sector employees? Under which circumstances would the cost of achieving any given level of security likely have been lower? (Hint: Take a look at the discussion in Chapters 2 and 3.)

3. The stock market was closed for four days after the September 11 attacks. What do you think happened to the value of stocks when the market reopened? How would information about this change help us estimate the costs of the attack? Is it possible that some stocks went up while others went down—that is, might there have been winners as well as losers as a result of the attacks?

4. Suppose the onset of a major snowstorm forces a bakery owner to put his bakers to work all day shoveling snow off the roof of his building instead of making pies. If the bakers get paid what they would have been paid anyway, what has been the economic loss—if any—as a result of the storm? How does this help us understand the economic losses of the September 11 attacks?

Part Two

Supply and Demand

INTRODUCTION

The tools of demand and supply are the most basic and useful elements of the economist's kit. Indeed, many economists would argue that the **law of demand**—the lower the price of a good, the greater the quantity of that good demanded by purchasers—is the single most powerful proposition in all of economics. Simply stated, the law of demand has the capacity, unmatched by any other proposition in economics, to explain an incredibly diverse range of human behaviors. For example, the law of demand explains why buildings are taller in downtown areas than in outlying suburbs, and also why people are willing to sit in the upper deck of football stadiums even though lower deck seats are clearly superior. The great explanatory power of the law of demand is almost matched by that of the **law of supply,** which states that the higher the price of a good, the greater will be the quantity of that good supplied by producers. The law of supply helps us understand why people receive a premium wage when they work overtime, as well as why parking places at the beach are so much more expensive during the summer months than they are during the winter.

When the laws of demand and supply are combined, they illuminate the enormous **gains from trade** that arise from voluntary exchange. In Chapter 5, "Sex, Booze, and Drugs," we examine what happens when the government attempts to prohibit the exchanges that give rise to these gains. The consequences are often surprising, always costly, and—sadly—sometimes tragic. We find, for example, that when the federal government made alcoholic beverages illegal during the era known as Prohibition, Americans responded by switching from beer to hard liquor and by getting drunk a larger proportion of the times when they drank. We also show that the government's ongoing efforts to prevent individuals from using drugs such as marijuana and cocaine cause the drive-by shootings that occur in many major cities, and also encourage drug overdoses among users. Finally, we explain why laws against prostitution help to foster the spread of acquired immune deficiency syndrome (AIDS).

In Chapter 6, "Is Water Different?", we dispel the myth that the consumption of some goods does not conform to the law of demand. Here, we examine the demand for water, that "most necessary of all necessities," and find that—lo and behold—when the price of water is raised, people consume less of it—exactly as predicted by the law of demand. One important conclusion of this chapter is that the water shortages and water crises that afflict various parts of the nation are not the result of droughts, but in fact are caused by government officials who are unwilling or unable to accept the reality of the law of demand.

It is surely distasteful to think in terms of the supply and demand for human beings; yet that is what developments half a world away compel us to do in Chapter 7, "Slave Redemption in Sudan." Nearly a century after human slavery was abolished there by British troops, the slave trade has reemerged in Sudan, the largest nation in Africa. Following in the tracks of the slave raiders are slave redemptionists, who seek to alleviate the human suffering in Sudan by purchasing freedom for thousands of enslaved individuals. Yet the efforts of these well-intentioned individuals are having consequences surely not intended by them. Indeed, attempts to reduce slavery in Sudan actually have encouraged the slave trade and even may have resulted in more—not fewer—people in bondage. And so we see that sometimes the consequences of well-intentioned actions are not merely unexpected but tragic as well.

Medical matters form the focus of our analysis in Chapter 8, "Choice and Life," where we look at an issue seemingly unrelated to economics—abortion. Although the debate between a woman's right to choose and a fetus's right to live is usually cast in highly charged, emotional terms, we demonstrate that the dispassionate reasoning of the economist can illuminate some of the issues at stake. Economics can never be the ultimate arbiter of whether abortion should be legal or illegal, but it can help us understand more about what our choices cost.

The cost of a pack of cigarettes in the United States has more than doubled over the last few years, importantly because the federal and state governments have sharply increased cigarette taxes. These tax increases have reduced the supply of cigarettes and so pushed up prices. As we see in Chapter 9, "Smoking and Smuggling," this has led to a host of other developments. The number of smokers and the amount of smoking are both down, as would readily be predicted by the law of demand. Nevertheless, for people who continue to smoke in the face of higher taxes, things are worse: Not only is a larger share of their income going to the "evil weed"; they are also smoking stronger, more carcinogenic cigarettes. At the market level, higher cigarette taxes have also led to much more widespread smuggling of cigarettes, as consumers seek to minimize the costs of the higher taxes. On a variety of fronts, then, we see that the basic tools of supply and demand enable us to understand the sometimes unintended and often surprising economics of public issues.

5

Sex, Booze, and Drugs

Prior to 1914, cocaine was legal in this country; today it is not. Alcohol (of the intoxicating variety) is legal in United States today; from 1920 to 1933 it was not. Prostitution is legal in Nevada today; in the other forty-nine states it is not.[1] All these goods—sex, booze, and drugs—have at least one thing in common: The consumption of each brings together a willing seller with a willing buyer; there is an act of mutually beneficial exchange (at least in the opinion of the parties involved). Partly because of this property, attempts to proscribe the consumption of these goods have (1) met with less than spectacular success, and (2) yielded some peculiar patterns of production, distribution, and usage. Let's see why.

When the government seeks to prevent voluntary exchange, it generally must decide whether to go after the seller or the buyer. In most cases—and certainly when sex, booze, or drugs have been involved—the government targets sellers, because this is where the authorities get the most benefit from their enforcement dollars. A cocaine dealer, even a small retail pusher, often supplies dozens or even hundreds of users each day, as did speakeasies (illegal saloons) during Prohibition; a hooker typically services anywhere from three to ten tricks per day. By incarcerating the supplier, the police can prevent several—or even several hundred—transactions from taking place, which is usually much more cost-effective than going after the buyers one by one. It is not that the police ignore the consumers of illegal goods; indeed, sting operations—in which the police pose

---

[1] These statements are not quite correct. Even today, cocaine may be legally obtained by prescription from a physician. Prostitution in Nevada is legal only in those counties that have, by virtue of local option, chosen to proclaim it as such. Finally, some counties in the United States remain dry, prohibiting the sale of beer, wine, and distilled spirits.

as illicit sellers—often make the headlines. Nevertheless, most enforcement efforts focus on the supply side, and so shall we.

Law enforcement activities directed against the suppliers of illegal goods increase the suppliers' operating costs. The risks of fines,
jail sentences, and possibly even violence become part of the costs
of doing business and must be taken into account by existing and
potential suppliers. Some entrepreneurs will leave the business,
turning their talents to other activities; others will resort to clandes-
tine (and costly) means to hide their operations from the police; still
others will restrict the circle of buyers with whom they are willing to
deal to minimize the chances that a customer is a cop. Across the
board, the costs of operation are higher, and at any given price, less
of the product will be available. There is a reduction in supply, and
the result is a higher price for the good.

This increase in price is, in a sense, exactly what the enforcement officials are after, for the consumers of sex, booze, and drugs
behave according to the law of demand: The higher the price of a
good, the lower the amount consumed. So the immediate impact of
the enforcement efforts against sellers is to reduce the consumption
of the illegal good by buyers. There are, however, some other effects.

First, because the good in question is illegal, people who have a
comparative advantage in conducting illegal activities will be attracted to the business of supplying (and perhaps demanding) the
good. Some may have an existing criminal record and are relatively
unconcerned about adding to it. Others may have developed skills
in evading detection and prosecution while engaged in other criminal activities. Some may simply look at the illegal activity as another
means of thumbing their noses at society. The general point is that
when an activity is made illegal, people who are good at being criminals are attracted to that activity.

Illegal contracts usually are not enforceable through legal channels (and even if they were, few suppliers of illegal goods would be
stupid enough to complain to the police about not being paid for
their products). Thus, buyers and sellers of illegal goods frequently
must resort to private methods of contract enforcement—which
often means violence.[2] Hence, people who are relatively good at

---

[2] Fundamentally, violence—such as involuntary incarceration—also plays a key role in
the government's enforcement of legal contracts. We often do not think of it as violence,
of course, because it is usually cushioned by constitutional safeguards, procedural rules,
and so on.

violence are attracted to illegal activities and are given greater incentives to employ their talents. This is one reason why the murder rate in America rose to record levels during Prohibition (1920–1933) and then dropped sharply when liquor was again made legal. It also helps explain why the number of drug-related murders soared during the 1980s, and why drive-by shootings became commonplace in many drug-infested cities. The Thompson submachine gun of the 1930s and the MAC-10 machine gun of the 1980s were, importantly, just low-cost means of contract enforcement.

The attempts of law enforcement officials to drive sellers of illegal goods out of business have another effect. Based on recent wholesale prices, $50,000 worth of pure heroin weighs about two ounces; $50,000 worth of marijuana weighs about twenty pounds. As any drug smuggler can tell you, hiding two ounces of contraband is a lot easier than hiding twenty pounds. Thus, to avoid detection and prosecution, suppliers of the illegal good have an incentive to deal in the more valuable versions of their product, which for drugs and booze mean the more potent versions. Bootleggers during Prohibition concentrated on hard liquor rather than beer and wine; even today, moonshine typically has roughly twice the alcohol content of legal hard liquor such as bourbon, scotch, or vodka. After narcotics became illegal in this country in 1914, importers switched from the milder opium to its more valuable, more potent, and more addictive derivative, heroin.

The move to the more potent versions of illegal commodities is enhanced by enforcement activities directed against users. Not only do users, like suppliers, find it easier (cheaper) to hide the more potent versions, there is also a change in relative prices due to user penalties. Typically, the law has lower penalties for using an illegal substance than for distributing it. Within each category (use or sale), however, there is commonly the same penalty regardless of value per unit. For example, during Prohibition, a bottle of wine and a bottle of more expensive, more potent hard liquor were equally illegal. Today, the possession of one gram of 90 percent pure cocaine brings the same penalty as the possession of one gram of 10 percent pure cocaine. Given the physical quantities, there is a fixed cost (the legal penalty) associated with being caught, regardless of value per unit (and thus potency) of the substance.

Hence, the structure of legal penalties raises the relative price of less potent versions, encouraging users to substitute more potent versions—heroin instead of opium, hashish instead of marijuana, hard liquor instead of beer.

Penalties against users also encourage a change in the nature of usage. Prior to 1914, cocaine was legal in this country and was used openly as a mild stimulant, much as people today use caffeine. (Cocaine was even included in the original formulation of Coca-Cola.) This type of usage—small, regular doses over long time intervals—becomes relatively more expensive when the substance is made illegal. Extensive usage (small doses spread over time) is more likely to be detected by the authorities than is intensive usage (a large dose consumed at once), simply because possession time is longer and the drug must be accessed more frequently. Thus, when a substance is made illegal, there is an incentive for consumers to switch toward usage that is more intensive. Rather than ingesting cocaine orally in the form of a highly diluted liquid solution, as was commonly done before 1914, people switched to snorting or even injecting it. During Prohibition, people dispensed with cocktails before dinner each night; instead, on the less frequent occasions when they drank, they more often drank to get drunk. The same phenomenon is observed today. People under the age of twenty-one consume alcoholic beverages less frequently than do people over the age of twenty-one. But when they do drink, they are more likely to drink to get drunk.

Not surprisingly, the suppliers of illegal commodities are reluctant to advertise their wares openly; the police are as capable of reading billboards and watching TV as are potential customers. Suppliers are also reluctant to establish easily recognized identities and regular places and hours of business, because to do so raises the chance of being caught by the police. Information about the price and quality of products being sold goes underground, often with unfortunate effects for consumers.

With legal goods, consumers have several means of obtaining information. They can learn from friends, advertisements, and personal experience. When goods are legal, they can be trademarked for identification. The trademark may not legally be copied, and the courts protect it. Given such easily identified brands, consumers can be made aware of the quality and price of each. If their experience does not meet expectations, they can assure themselves of no further contact with the unsatisfactory product by never buying that brand again.

When a general class of products becomes illegal, there are fewer ways to obtain information. Brand names are no longer protected by law, so falsification of well-known brands ensues. When products do not meet expectations, it is more difficult (costly) for consumers to punish suppliers. Frequently, the result is degradation of and uncertainty about product quality. The consequences for consumers of the illegal goods are often unpleasant, sometimes fatal.

Consider prostitution. In those counties in Nevada where prostitution is legal, the prostitutes are required to register with the local authorities, and they generally conduct their business within the confines of well-established bordellos. These establishments advertise openly and rely heavily on repeat business. Health officials test the prostitutes weekly for venereal disease and every month for AIDS. Contrast this with other areas of the country, where prostitution is illegal. Suppliers generally are streetwalkers, because a fixed, physical location is too easy for the police to detect and raid. Suppliers change locations frequently, to reduce harassment by police. Repeat business is reported to be minimal; frequently, customers have never seen the prostitute before and never will again.

The difference in outcomes is striking. In Nevada, the spread of venereal disease by legal prostitutes is estimated to be almost nonexistent; to date, none of the 9000 registered prostitutes in Nevada has tested positive for AIDS. By contrast, in some major cities outside Nevada the incidence of venereal disease among prostitutes is estimated to be near 100 percent. In Miami, one study found that 19 percent of all incarcerated prostitutes tested positive for AIDS; in Newark, New Jersey, 52 percent of the prostitutes tested were infected with the AIDS virus, and about half of the prostitutes in Washington, D.C., and New York City are also believed to be carrying the AIDS virus. Because of the lack of reliable information in markets for illegal goods, customers frequently do not know exactly what they are getting; as a result, they sometimes get more than they bargained for.

Consider alcohol and drugs. Today, alcoholic beverages are heavily advertised to establish their brand names and are carried by reputable dealers. Customers can readily punish suppliers for any deviation from the expected potency or quality by withdrawing their business, telling their friends, or even bringing a lawsuit. Similar circumstances prevailed before 1914 in this country for the hundreds of products containing opium or cocaine.

During Prohibition, consumers of alcohol often did not know exactly what they were buying or where to find the supplier the next day if they were dissatisfied. Fly-by-night operators sometimes adulterated liquor with methyl alcohol. In extremely small concentrations, this made watered-down booze taste like it had more kick; in only slightly higher concentrations, the methyl alcohol blinded or even killed the unsuspecting consumer. Even in "reputable" speakeasies (those likely to be in business at the same location the next day), bottles bearing the labels of high-priced foreign whiskeys were refilled repeatedly with locally (and illegally) produced rotgut until their labels wore off.

In the 1970s, more than one purchaser of what was reputed to be high-potency Panama Red or Acapulco Gold marijuana ended up with low-potency pot heavily loaded with stems, seeds, and maybe even oregano. Buyers of cocaine must worry about not only how much the product has been cut along the distribution chain, but also what has been used to cut it. In recent years the purity of cocaine at the retail level has ranged between 10 percent and 95 percent; for heroin, the degree of purity has ranged from 5 percent to 50 percent. Cutting agents can turn out to be any of various sugars, local anesthetics, or amphetamines; on occasion, rat poison has been used.

We noted earlier that the legal penalties for the users of illegal goods encourage them to use more potent forms and to use them more intensively. These facts and the uncertain quality and potency of the illegal products yield a deadly combination. During Prohibition, the death rate from acute alcohol poisoning (i.e., due to an overdose) was more than thirty times higher than today. During 1927 alone, 12,000 people died from acute alcohol poisoning, and many thousands more were blinded or killed by contaminated booze. Today, about 3000 people per year die as a direct result of consuming either cocaine or heroin. Of that total, it is estimated, roughly 80 percent die from (1) an overdose caused by unexpectedly potent product, or (2) an adverse reaction to the material used to cut the drug. Clearly, caveat emptor (let the buyer beware) is a warning to be taken seriously if one is consuming an illegal product.

We noted at the beginning of the chapter that one of the effects of making a good illegal is to raise its price. One might well ask, by how much? During the early 1990s, the federal government was spending about $2 billion a year in its efforts to stop the importation of cocaine from Colombia. One recent study concluded that these efforts had hiked the price of cocaine by 4 percent (yes, 4 percent) relative to what it would have been had the federal government done nothing to interdict cocaine imports. The study estimated that the cost of raising the price of cocaine an additional 2 percent would be $1 billion per year.[3]

The government's efforts to halt imports of marijuana have been more successful, presumably because that product is easier to detect than cocaine. Nevertheless, suppliers have responded by cultivating marijuana domestically instead of importing it. The net effect has been an estimated tenfold increase in potency due to the superior farming techniques available in this country, as well as the use of genetic bioengineering to improve strains.

We might also consider the government's efforts to eliminate the consumption of alcohol during the 1920s and 1930s. They failed so badly that the Eighteenth Amendment, which put Prohibition in place, was the first (and thus far the only) constitutional amendment ever to be repealed. As for prostitution—it is reputed to be "the oldest profession," and by all accounts continues to flourish today, even in Newark and Miami.

The government's inability to halt the consumption of sex, booze, or drugs does not in and of itself mean that those efforts have failed. Indeed, the "successes" of these efforts are manifested in their consequences—ranging from tainted drugs and alcohol to disease-ridden prostitutes. The message instead is that when the government attempts to prevent mutually beneficial exchange, even its best efforts are unlikely to meet with spectacular success.

---

[3] Federal attempts to prevent cocaine from entering the country are, of course, supplemented by other federal, as well as state and local, efforts to eradicate the drug once it has crossed our borders. To date, there are no empirical estimates of the extent to which these other efforts have increased prices.

DISCUSSION QUESTIONS

1. The federal government currently taxes alcohol on the basis of the 100-proof gallon. (One-hundred-proof alcohol is exactly 50 percent pure ethyl alcohol; most hard liquor sold is 80 proof, or 40 percent ethyl alcohol, whereas wine is usually about 24 proof and most beer is 6 to 10 proof.) How would alcohol consumption patterns be different if the government taxed alcohol strictly on the basis of volume rather than taking into account its potency as well?

2. During Prohibition, some speakeasy operators paid bribes to ensure that the police did not raid them. Would you expect the quality of the liquor served in such speakeasies to be higher or lower than in speakeasies that did not pay such bribes? Would you expect any systematic differences (e.g., with regard to income levels) among the customers patronizing the two types of speakeasies?

3. When comparing the markets for prostitution in Nevada and New Jersey, there are two important differences: (1) Prostitutes in New Jersey face higher costs because of government efforts to prosecute them; and (2) customers in New Jersey face higher risks of contracting diseases from prostitutes, because the illegal nature of the business makes reliable information about product quality much more costly to obtain. Given these facts, would you expect the price of prostitution services to be higher or lower in New Jersey, compared to Nevada? Which state would have the higher amount of services consumed (adjusted for population differences)?

4. According to the Surgeon General of the United States, nicotine is the most addictive drug known to humanity, and cigarette smoking kills perhaps 300,000 to 400,000 people per year in the United States. Why isn't tobacco illegal in the United States?

6

Is Water Different?

Mono Lake has gotten a reprieve. Over a fifty-year period, this California lake—our country's oldest lake and one of its most beautiful—shrank from more than 80 square miles in area to about 60. Why? Because in 1941, most of the eastern Sierra mountain water that once fed Mono Lake began disappearing down a 275-mile-long aqueduct, south to Los Angeles, where it was used to wash cars, sprinkle lawns, and otherwise lubricate the lifestyle of southern California. Environmentalists cried out that the diversion of water from Mono Lake must stop. Los Angelenos, who pay $350 per acre-foot for the water, claimed there were no viable alternative sources. Central California farmers, who pay but $12.50 per acre-foot for subsidized water from the western side of the Sierras, feared that diverting their own "liquid gold" to save Mono Lake would dry up their livelihood. Meanwhile, this migratory rest stop for hundreds of thousands of birds was disappearing.

Finally, prodded by the California Water Resources Control Board and aided by special funds voted by the state legislature, the City of Los Angeles agreed to drastically curtail its usage of Mono Lake water. Under the water-trading plan agreed to, Los Angeles will cut its usage of Mono Lake water by more than 80 percent until the lake's water level has risen sixteen feet. Even after that elevation has been reached, the city will limit its usage of Mono Lake water to less than half of its long-term average usage. To replace the water it is losing, Los Angeles will buy water from elsewhere, using state funds appropriated for this purpose.

The issues that have arisen over the future of Mono Lake are surfacing in hundreds of locations throughout the United States.

Conservationists are increasingly concerned about the toxic contamination of our water supply and the depletion of our underground water sources. Extensive irrigation projects in the western states use more than 150 *billion* gallons of water a day—seven times as much water as all the nation's city water systems combined. The Ogallala aquifer (a 20-million-acre lake beneath the beef-and-breadbasket states of Colorado, Kansas, Nebraska, New Mexico, Oklahoma, and Texas) has been dropping by three feet per year because 150,000 wells are pumping water out faster than nature can replenish it.

Water problems are not confined to the United States. In China, water is being siphoned away from farmlands surrounding Beijing in order to meet rising urban and industrial demands, and some 400 Chinese cities are now estimated to face water **shortages.** In the arid Middle East, water is a constant source of friction, and schemes to add to the region's supplies have included floating plastic bags of water southward across the Mediterranean, and stirring the sea in the summer in the hopes of causing more rain to fall in the winter. In the island city-state of Singapore, half of the total land area of 247 square miles is set aside for collecting and storing water. Because there is no more room for additional reservoirs, Singapore is now building desalination plants to convert seawater into drinking water. The result will be more water, but the cost of fresh water produced in such a manner is seven to eight times higher than the current cost of treated water.

The common view of water is that it is an overused, precious resource and that we are running out of it. The economic analysis of the water "problem," however, is not quite so pessimistic, nor so tied to the physical quantities of water that exist on our earth and in the atmosphere. Rather, an economic analysis of water is similar to an analysis of any other scarce resource, revealing that water is fundamentally no different from other scarce resources.

The water industry is one of the oldest and largest in the United States, and the philosophy surrounding it merits examination. Many commentators believe that water is unique and that it should not be treated as an **economic good,** that is, a scarce good. Engineering studies that concern themselves with demand for residential water typically use a so-called requirements approach. The forecaster simply predicts population changes and then multiplies those estimates by data showing the average amount of water currently used per person. The underlying assumption of such a forecast is that, regardless of the price charged for water in the future, the same quantity will be demanded per person. Implicitly, then, both the short- and long-run price elasticities of demand are assumed to be zero.

But is this really the case? Perhaps not. To see why, let's look at a study of water prices in Boulder, Colorado, conducted by economist Steve Hanke. Boulder was selected by Hanke because a number of years ago the water utility in that city installed water meters in every home and business that it supplied. Prior to that time, Boulder, like many other municipalities in the United States, had charged a flat monthly rate for water. Each household paid a specified amount per month no matter how much (or how little) water was used. In essence, the previous flat-fee system meant that a zero price was being charged at the margin (for any incremental use of water). The introduction of usage meters meant that a positive price for the marginal unit of water was now imposed.

Hanke looked at the quantity of water demanded both before and after the meters were installed in Boulder. He began by computing an index of water usage, relative to what he called the "ideal" use of water. (The term *ideal* implies nothing from an economic point of view. It merely indicates the minimum quantity of water required to maintain the aesthetic quality of each resident's lawn, taking into account such factors as average temperature, the effect of rainfall, and so forth.) An index value of 100 meant that usage was exactly equal to the hypothetical ideal. A value of, say, 150 meant that residents were using 50 percent more than the ideal, whereas an index of 75 meant that usage was 25 percent less than Hanke's ideal figure of 100.

From the data in Table 6–1, which compares water usage in Boulder with and without metering, we find that individuals used much more water under the flat-rate system than they did under the metered-rate system. Column 1 shows the meter route numbers of the eight routes studied by Hanke. Column 2 shows the index of water usage for each of the routes during the unmetered period when a flat rate was charged for water usage. The data in column 3 show water usage on each route for the one-year period after the metering system was put into effect. Note that under the flat-rate system every route used substantially more than the ideal amount of water, whereas under the metered system six of the eight routes used less than the hypothetical ideal. Moreover, water usage dropped substantially on every route when metering was intro-

TABLE 6–1   Comparing Water Usage With and Without Metering of Actual Usage

(1)	(2)	(3)
Meter Routes	Index of Water Usage (Flat-Rate Period)	Index of Water Usage (Metered-Rate Period)
1	128	78
2	175	72
3	156	72
4	177	63
5	175	97
6	175	102
7	176	105
8	157	86

Source: Adapted from Steve Hanke, "Demand for Water Under Dynamic Conditions," *Water Resources Research*, vol. 6, no. 5, October 1970.

duced, and each user was being charged for the actual amount of water used. Because less water is used in the presence of metering (which raises the price of incremental water), Hanke's data indicate that the quantity of water demanded is a function of the price charged for water. Hanke also found that for many years after the imposition of the metered-rate pricing system for water, the quantity of water demanded not only remained at a lower level than before metering but continued to fall slightly. That, of course, means that the long-run **price elasticity of demand** for water was greater than the short-run price elasticity of demand.

Would attaching a dollar sign to water help solve problems of recurring water shortages and endemic waste? Many economists feel it would. It is well known, for example, that much of the water supplied by federal irrigation projects is wasted by farmers and other users because they have no incentive to conserve water and curb overconsumption. The federal government, which has subsidized water projects since 1902, allots water to certain districts, communities, or farmers on the basis of previous usage "requirements." This means that if farmers in a certain irrigation district were to conserve on water usage by, say, upgrading their irrigation systems, their water allotment eventually would be reduced. As a result, a "use it or lose it" attitude has prevailed among users of federal water. Water supplied by federal water projects is also inexpensive. The Congressional Budget Office has estimated that users pay only about 19 percent of the total cost of the water they get.

One would think that with growing worldwide concern over water conservation, the federal government would be trying to do its part to reduce waste. Let's first consider toilets—or water closets, as they are often called in the industry—a major source of residential water usage. In 1992, Congress mandated that all new water closets installed in the U.S. be "low-flow" models, which discharge only 1.6 gallons per flush, about half the rate per flush of regular toilets. The idea, it was claimed, was that low-flow toilets would reduce the amount of water that people "wasted" when they flushed. There were some problems with Congressional reasoning on this issue. First, the basic low-flow toilet simply doesn't work very well when attempting to dispose of some forms of waste, requiring that the user flush them twice or even three times to accomplish the task. This, of course, eliminates all of the supposed water-conservation advantages of the low-flow mode—and may also help explain why some people have taken to smuggling regular toilets in from Canada. Now, it is possible to re-engineer toilets to make them work better with less water, including the addition of a compressed air power assist. Such toilets cost up to ten times what regular water closets cost, however, and the power assist models have one additional problem—their operation produces a noise level comparable to that of a loud vacuum cleaner. Just as importantly, Congress apparently failed to recognize that when water is flushed down the drain, it is not vaporized or sent into outer space. It is simply moved someplace else. The earth is a closed system and flushing more water or more often simply moves water from one place to another more rapidly. Regular toilets may require that we devote more resources to treating wastewater, but they don't destroy the water. Indeed, many (although not all) cities actually return the treated water to the lake or river from which it was originally drawn, and cleaner than it originally started.

The year after it gave us low-flow toilets, Congress authorized completion of the Central Utah Project (CUP). This project includes a series of dams, aqueducts, tunnels, and canals designed to collect water from the Colorado River drainage in Utah and transport it to the Great Basin. The cost of delivering this water to farmers for irrigation is estimated to be $400 per acre-foot. The water will be used to produce additional crops yielding enough revenue to make the water worth $30 per acre-foot to the Utah farmers who receive it. But these farmers will pay only $8 per acre-foot for the water—that is, only *2 percent* of the cost of delivering the water to them!

Economists have suggested that raising the price of federal water would lead to more efficient and less wasteful water consumption. For example, a study by B. Delworth Gardner, an economist now at Brigham Young University, concluded that a 10 percent rise in prices could reduce water use on some California farm crops by as much as 20 percent. Support for such a price increase is politically difficult, however, because federal law stipulates that ability to pay, as well as cost, must be considered when determining water prices.

An alternative solution involving the trading and sale of water rights held by existing federal water users has been proposed by some economists. Such a solution, it is felt, would benefit the economy overall because it could help curb water use, prevent water shortages, and lessen the pressure for costly new water projects. Trading and sales of water rights have already taken place in California, Oregon, and Utah. In addition, environmentalists were instrumental in helping to arrange the water trading plan for Mono Lake. Despite these modest successes, numerous federal and state laws have, to date, made such trading very difficult.

Until recent years, it had been thought that there was so much water we simply did not have to worry about it—there was always another river or another well to draw on if we ran short. Putting a price tag on water would require a substantial change in the way we have traditionally thought about water. Is this possible or even desirable? Well, events half a world away from Mono Lake may shed some light on this. In the Chinese capital of Beijing, an extended period of dry weather in a recent year caused the water levels in the city's reservoirs to drop sharply. The municipal State Council responded by raising the price of water for home use to $110 per acre-foot from its previous level of $80. For industrial and government users, the price hike was to $160 per acre-foot from the previous $125. Why were these actions taken? According to Liu Hangui, deputy director of the Beijing Water Conservancy Bureau, "the price adjustments were introduced to relieve the water shortage." Even communism, it would seem, is not enough to make water different.

DISCUSSION QUESTIONS

1. In your opinion, do the data presented in Table 6–1 refute the "water is different" philosophy?

2. How much water does your neighbor "need"? Is your answer the same if you have to pay your neighbor's water bill?

3. Evaluate the following: "Although taxpayers foot the bill for federal water sold to farmers at subsidized prices, they also eat the crops grown with that water. Because the crops are cheaper due to the subsidized water, taxpayers get back exactly what they put in, and so there is no waste from having subsidized water for farmers." Would you give the author of this quote an A or an F in economics?

4. During the drought that plagued California in the late 1980s and early 1990s, farmers in California were able to purchase subsidized water to irrigate their crops, even though many California homeowners had to pay large fines if they watered their lawns. Can you suggest an explanation for this difference in the treatment of two different groups of citizens within the state of California?

7

Slave Redemption
in Sudan

Sudan is Africa's largest nation. Located immediately south of
Egypt, it encompasses nearly one million square miles and is home
to 36 million people. It is also home to poverty, disease, civil war—
and the emergence of modern-day slavery. The slave trade, in turn,
has given rise to a new humanitarian movement, whose adherents
seek to alleviate Sudan's misery by buying freedom for its slaves.
Well-intentioned though they are, these humanitarian efforts may
be making things worse.

Slavery is a centuries-old practice in Sudan, one that colonial
British rulers finally managed to halt during World War I. The
Sudanese gained independence in 1956 but, despite ensuing periods
of civil war, the slave trade initially remained a piece of history. This
changed in 1989, when the National Islamic Front (NIF) took control of the government. The NIF quickly began arming the Muslim
Baggara tribe in the northern part of the country to fight against the
rebellious Christian tribes of the south. The Baggara previously had
made a regular practice of enslaving members of the southern
Dinka tribe, and once armed by the NIF the Baggara resumed the
slave raids the British had suppressed. This activity was further
aided by the government, which supplied horses to the Baggara and
permitted slave markets to open in the cities controlled by the NIF.
Perhaps as many as 20,000 Dinkas, mostly women and children,
were enslaved and taken north, selling for as little as $15 each. The
slaves were branded with the names of their owners and put to
work as cooks, maids, field hands, and concubines.[1]

---

[1] See Richard Miniter, "The False Promise of Slave Redemption," *The Atlantic
Monthly*, July 1999, pp. 63–70.

Within a few years, word of the revived slave trade began filtering out of Sudan. In response, a variety of humanitarian groups from other nations began buying slaves in large batches and setting them free. The process is called "slave redemption," and its purpose—one hopes—is to reduce the number of people who are enslaved.

Raising money for slave redemption soon became big business, spreading rapidly among public schools and evangelical churches. A middle school in Oregon, for example, raised $2500 to be used for slave redemption. Even more impressive was an elementary school class in Colorado: After the children's efforts caught the media's eye, the class raised more than $50,000 for slave redemption.

The largest of the humanitarian groups involved in slave redemption is Christian Solidarity International (CSI). This group says it has freed thousands of slaves since 1995, most at prices of about $50 each. In 1999 alone, for example, CSI purchased the freedom of nearly 3000 slaves. Several other groups also purchased the freedom of several hundred slaves that year, sometimes at prices of up to $100 each.

Per capita income in Sudan is about $500 per year, which makes slave prices of $50 to $100 apiece quite attractive to the Baggara slave raiders. This is particularly true when the redeemers are buying in the south, where the targeted Dinkas live, and prices in the north, the traditional market for slaves, are as low as $15 apiece. In fact, says one individual who used to be active in slave redemption, "We've made slave redemption more profitable than narcotics." What are the consequences of such profitability?

There have been two sets of responses. First, on the demand side, the higher prices for slaves make it more costly for owners in the north to hold slaves. So rather than own slaves, some of them have offered their slaves to the redeemers. This, of course, is exactly the effect the slave redemption movement has desired. But there is also a supply response: When the market value of slaves rises due to an increase in demand (the demand of the slave redeemers), we expect an increase in the quantity supplied. That is, we expect the raiders who produce slaves by capturing them to engage in more of that activity. This is exactly what has happened in Sudan.

Slave redemption began in earnest in 1995 and, according to local authorities, the number of slave raids has grown sharply since.

Moreover, the size of a typical raiding party rose from roughly 400 attackers to more than 2500. Why the increase? Slaves used to be traded in relatively small batches, but the redeemers prefer to buy in large lots—1000 or more at a time. Collecting and assembling the number of slaves required to satisfy the redemption buyers thus requires considerably more manpower. Hence, the slave trade has been transformed from a cottage industry into a large-scale business enterprise. Overall, it is estimated that the number of slaves captured in raids each year is greater now than at the inception of slave redemption.

Initially, it is likely that the impact of slave redemption was chiefly on the demand side; that is, the first slaves redeemed were almost surely "freed from slavery" in the sense that we would normally use that terminology. But once the stock of slave holdings in the north had adjusted downward in response to the newly elevated equilibrium price, there was only one place for the slave traders to get the slaves demanded by the redemption buyers. This was from the raiders who were now taking slaves for one purpose only—sale to the redeemers. Thus, once the stock of slaves in the north is adjusted to its lower equilibrium level, *all* of the slaves subsequently "freed" by the redeemers are in fact individuals who never would have been enslaved had the redeemers not first made a market for them. In addition, because large numbers of new slaves now spend some time in captivity awaiting redemption, it is even possible that the total number of people in slavery at any point in time is actually *higher* because of the well-intentioned efforts of the slave redeemers.

As unpleasant as such reasoning is, it agrees with the opinions of people who observe the slave trade firsthand. As a local humanitarian worker says, "[G]iving money to the slave traders only encourages the trade. It is wrong and must stop. Where does the money go? It goes to the raiders to buy more guns, raid more villages. . . . It is a vicious circle." In a similar vein, the chief of one village that has been targeted by the slave raiders says, "Redemption is not the solution. It means you are encouraging the raiders."

In addition to encouraging the capture of new slaves, redemption also reduces any incentive for owners to set free their less productive slaves. Prior to 1995, about 10 percent of all slaves, chiefly older women and young children, were allowed to escape or even told to go home, because the costs of feeding, clothing, and housing them exceeded their value to their owners. Now slaves who would have been freed on their own are instead held in captivity until a trader can be found to haul them south for sale to the redeemers.

The final effect of redemption has been to create a trade in fictitious slaves—individuals who are paid to pose as slaves for the purposes of redemption, and who are then given a cut of the redemption price after they are "freed." Although redemption groups obviously try to avoid participating in such deals, observers familiar with the trade consider them a regular part of the redemption business.

Is there another way to combat slavery in Sudan? On the demand side, the U.S. government has long refused to negotiate with terrorists or pay ransom to kidnappers, simply because it believes that such tactics encourage terrorism and kidnapping. It recognizes that paying a ransom increases the profits of kidnapping, thus enticing more individuals into the trade.

On the supply side, the British were originally successful in ending the slave trade in Sudan and elsewhere in their empire by dispatching soldiers to kill or disarm slave raiders, and by sending warships to close off maritime slave-trading routes. Sudan, of course, is an independent sovereign nation today; both the United Nations and the British electorate would likely oppose unilateral military action by the British government against Sudanese slave raiders. Yet even the people who used to be subject to British colonial rule have mixed feelings. When asked to compare the colonial British policies to the redeemers' policies of today, a schoolmaster in the affected area remarked, "If the colonial government were standing for election, I would vote for them." So too might the victims of the slave trade in Sudan.

DISCUSSION QUESTIONS

1. Is there anything in the historical British experience with the slave trade that suggests how the international community of today could reduce slavery in Sudan?

2. It appears that the actions of the slave redeemers have raised the equilibrium price of slaves. What does this mean has hap-

pened to the number of slaves held by private owners in northern Sudan—as long as the demand for slaves is downward sloping? What does the higher profitability and volume of slave trading today imply about the number of slaves held in inventory in the south for trading purposes, compared to the number that used to be held there?

3. How does the cost of "backhauling" a slave from the north down to the south, where the redeemers are purchasing, affect the extent to which the efforts of the redeemers cause slaves to be released from the existing stock in the north, compared to causing new slaves to be produced in the south?

4. Suppose the redeemers had succeeded in buying slaves without causing the equilibrium price of slaves to change at all. What would this imply about the elasticity of supply of new slaves? What would it imply about the number of slaves actually released from slavery in the north?

8

Choice and Life

The Supreme Court is back in the abortion business. For sixteen years, the Court refused to tamper substantively with its 1973 *Roe* v. *Wade* decision legalizing abortion. But in 1989, in *Webster* v. *Reproductive Health Services,* the Court upheld the constitutionality of a Missouri law restricting, but not eliminating, a woman's right to have an abortion. Then, in a 1992 case, *Planned Parenthood* v. *Casey,* the Supreme Court upheld most of a Pennsylvania law that discourages, but does not prohibit, abortion. Since the *Webster* decision, citizens on both sides of the abortion issue have engaged in legislative battles and sometimes violent public protests over the issue of a woman's right to choose versus a fetus's right to live. Thus far most of the legislative battles have been won by the proponents of legal abortions, but the legal battles and protests continue. It thus seems certain that the Supreme Court will be deciding abortion cases long after you have finished reading this book.

Very few of the major issues of our time are purely economic, and abortion is no exception. Economics cannot answer the question of whether life begins at conception, at twenty-four weeks, or at birth, nor can economics determine whether abortion should be permitted or proscribed. Economics cannot (as yet) even predict how the Supreme Court may ultimately rule on such issues. What economics can do, however, is demonstrate the striking and sometimes surprising implications of the Court's decisions on abortion—whatever those decisions may be.

Pregnancy termination has been practiced since ancient times, and any legal bars to abortion seem to have been based on the father's right to his offspring. English common law allowed abortion before quickening (when fetal movement is first evident), and there is some doubt whether abortion even after quickening was considered a crime. The American colonies retained the tradition of English common law until the changeover to state statutes at the adoption of the Constitution. In 1828, New York enacted an antiabortion statute that became a model for most other states. The statute declared that abortion before quickening was a misdemeanor and abortion after quickening, second-degree manslaughter. In the late nineteenth century, the quickening distinction disappeared and the penalties for all abortions were increased.

Except under extreme circumstances (such as to protect the life of the mother), abortion remained illegal in this country until about 1960, when a few states began to ease the conditions under which it was legal to perform an abortion. The gradual process of liberalization that state legislatures seemed to be following was suddenly disrupted in 1973 with the landmark Supreme Court decision in *Roe* v. *Wade*, which overruled all state laws prohibiting abortion before the last three months of pregnancy. In effect, the Court ruled that a woman's right to an abortion was constitutionally protected except during the last stages of pregnancy. There matters stood until the Supreme Court's 1989 decision in *Webster* v. *Reproductive Health Services.*

Strictly speaking, the Court's decision in *Webster* was narrowly focused; its direct impact has been to permit states to restrict the circumstances under which abortion is legal. Although the *Webster* decision stops far short of overturning *Roe* v. *Wade,* both the subsequent *Planned Parenthood* decision and numerous legislative actions at the state level have further restricted abortion. Examination of the market for abortions during the period prior to *Roe* v. *Wade* will help clarify the economic consequences of these developments.

Consider first the factors of cost and risk. During the early 1970s, an illegal but otherwise routine abortion by a reputable physician in the United States typically cost a minimum of $3500 (in 2003 dollars) and could run $5000 in a major East Coast City.[1] Following *Roe* v. *Wade*, these prices dropped sharply, and by the time of *Webster*, a routine legal abortion performed during the first

---

[1] All of the dollar amounts mentioned in this chapter are adjusted for **inflation** and expressed in terms of 2003 dollars, for purposes of comparison.

three months of pregnancy cost only about $350.[2] Prior to the legalization of abortion, more than 350,000 women were admitted annually to American hospitals with complications resulting from abortions, and it is estimated that more than 1000 women per year died from improperly performed pregnancy terminations. Following the Court's 1973 decision, complications and deaths from pregnancy termination dropped sharply. In recent years, it is estimated that significant physical complications occur in less than 1 percent of all legal abortions, and deaths due to legal abortions are virtually unknown. In short, the legalization of abortion was associated with a drastic reduction in both the monetary costs and physical dangers of pregnancy termination. Why was such an association observed?

Let us begin by looking at who might be willing to perform an illegal abortion and the price at which she or he would be willing to perform it. A physician convicted of performing an illegal abortion faced not only criminal prosecution (and the associated costs of a legal defense) but also expulsion from the medical profession and the consequent lifetime loss of license and livelihood. In addition, the doctor may have had to endure ostracism by a community that regarded abortion as a criminal act. In short, the costs to a doctor of such a criminal conviction were enormous, and the greatest portion of the fee for an illegal abortion was simply compensation for bearing this potential cost.

It must be acknowledged, of course, that there were physicians who had strong moral convictions regarding a woman's right to abortion. Some were willing to absorb the risks of performing an illegal abortion at a substantially reduced fee. Nevertheless, such physicians were a small minority and not easy to find. Consequently, most women were faced with the choices of paying $3500 or more for an abortion, paying $700 to $900 to an unlicensed abortionist operating under unsanitary conditions, or simply doing without. For those choosing back-alley abortionists, the consequences could include infection, hospitalization, sterility, or death.

The illegality of abortions, of course, increased the cost both of supplying and obtaining information about them; in turn, this made decisions about whether to have an abortion and who should per-

---

[2] More complicated abortions, performed as late as the fifth or sixth month of pregnancy, cost $1200 to $1400 if done on an outpatient basis in a clinic, and $1600 to $2000 if performed in a hospital.

form it more difficult, and increased the chances of an undesirable outcome. Information is never free, even in legalized activities, because there are costs to acquaint potential buyers with the location, quality, and price of a good or service. But, as mentioned in Chapter 5, in the case of an illegal activity the provision of information is even more expensive. Abortionists could not advertise, and the more widely they let their availability be known, the more likely they were to be arrested. Although some doctors unwilling to perform abortions did refer patients to other, more willing physicians, the referral was itself illegal and therefore risky. Women seeking an abortionist thus were not able to inform themselves of all of the possibilities without spending large amounts of money and time; and even having done so, many were left facing enormous uncertainty about the best path. Some ended up spending too much money; others exposed themselves to unnecessary risks. Some might even have chosen not to have an abortion had they been fully informed of the potential risks.

The situation confronting women during the years prior to the legalization of abortion can be usefully categorized by considering three examples. Although the settings are stylized, they are representative of the nature of the choices involved and the costs and risks of each.

First, there is a wealthy entertainer who visits a travel agency that arranges a package tour of Japan. Included is round-trip airfare, an essentially risk-free abortion procedure in that country (where abortions are legal), and several days of subsequent sightseeing. The price tag: $7500.

Next, let's look at how a young attorney earning $48,000 per year resolves her dilemma. She goes to her physician, who on the quiet refers her to a doctor willing to perform an illegal abortion in his office for $3500. The expense forces the attorney and her husband to delay the purchase of their first home, but then so would the cost of having the baby.

Finally, there is a blue-collar couple making $24,000 a year. Surreptitiously asking around, the wife finds out from an acquaintance someone who will do the abortion in a back room for $900— aspirins, but not antibiotics, included.

For the wealthy entertainer, both the risk and the financial burden are negligible; to be sure, the money could have been spent on an expensive bauble, but at least there was a trip to Japan in return. For the young lawyer, the financial burden is considerable; if unpaid law school debts preclude either the physician-performed abortion or the cost of completing the pregnancy, the only alternative is the risk of the backroom abortionist. The blue-collar couple gets the worst of both worlds: The abortionist's fee pushes them over their already tight budget, and the woman risks hospitalization or worse.

The pattern suggested by these examples was borne out in the years preceding the legalization of abortion. Relatively few women had the resources permitting travel to a foreign country where abortion was both safe and legal, nor did many have access to the information needed to learn about and arrange such an undertaking. Somewhat more women had established relationships with physicians who either would perform abortions or could refer them to other, willing doctors; these women had the option of choosing between the higher expense of the physician or the greater risk of the unlicensed abortionist. For many women, however, the lack of readily available information about alternatives, combined with the high costs of a physician-performed abortion, meant that the backroom quack, with the attendant risks, was the only realistic means of terminating a pregnancy.

The statistics for New York City in the early 1960s support this argument: Private hospitals performed abortions on 1 pregnant patient in 250; municipal hospitals, 1 in 10,000. The rate for whites was five times that for nonwhites and thirty times that for Puerto Ricans. Lower-income women simply were not having as many abortions performed by qualified physicians in suitable surroundings as were upper-income women; as we noted earlier, the result was hundreds of thousands of abortion-related complications, plus more than 1000 deaths each year.

The legalization of abortion in 1973 brought a relatively swift end to such outcomes. No longer faced with the risk of losing liberty and livelihood, thousands of physicians became willing to perform abortions. Even those who, for moral or religious reasons, were unwilling to terminate pregnancies could refer patients to other physicians without legal risk to themselves. Within a short time, properly equipped abortion clinics were established, and even in states requiring that abortions be performed in hospitals, women found a greatly increased range of options. Legalization thus produced an enormous increase in the supply of pregnancy termination services, which in turn had several consequences.

As in any market in which there is an increase in supply, the price of abortions fell drastically; holding quality and safety constant, the price reduction was as much as 90 percent. The decline in the price of physician-supplied abortions to levels at or below those charged by back-alley abortionists quickly drove most of the quacks out of business. As a result, the safety of abortions increased dramatically; serious infections and deaths due to abortion are estimated to have declined by 50 percent within a year of *Roe* v. *Wade* and have since become quite rare. Information about abortions, once available only "on the sly" and at considerable trouble and expense, became openly available. A woman considering pregnancy termination could call her physician's office or simply look in the telephone book for information about local services. Moreover, not only was knowledge about the price, quality, and safety of abortion openly available, so too were counseling services about the potentially adverse psychological or emotional consequences of what, for many women, was a difficult and trying decision.

As would be expected, the lower price of abortion and the more widely available information about the procedure combined to bring about a large increase in the number of abortions performed in this country. During 1973, slightly over 700,000 legal abortions were performed in the United States, many of them in the aftermath of the Supreme Court's landmark decision. One early study concluded that of the legal abortions that took place in the year following *Roe* v. *Wade,* "well over half—most likely between two-thirds and three-fourths ... were replacements for illegal abortions."[3] By 1981, 1.6 million legal abortions per year were being performed in the United States. After holding steady at that rate until 1988, the number of abortions performed each year began a slow decline, reaching about one million in 2000.

What then have been the consequences of the Court's decision in *Webster*? In the short run, not much. To be sure, abortions in public facilities in Missouri are now illegal, and women in the later stages of pregnancy must undergo costly and risky tests regarding fetal viability before having an abortion. Thus the Court's decision has increased the costs of pregnancy termination in Missouri. The

[3] June Sklar and Beth Berkov, "Abortion, Illegitimacy, and the American Birth Rate," *Science*, vol. 185, September 13, 1974, pp. 914ff.

result has been fewer abortions, perhaps some illegal abortions, and the selection of more effective means of (prepregnancy) birth control. Nevertheless, there are good (albeit more expensive) substitutes available—abortions in private facilities or in neighboring states—so the magnitude of these effects has been small. Of more significance is that the Court's decision, combined with growing public opposition to abortion, has encouraged numerous states to restrict abortions. For example, at least seventeen states now have three or more abortion restrictions, up from three states in 1992. Indeed, in 1997 alone, states passed a record fifty-five abortion restrictions, ranging from parental consent laws to outright bans on certain forms of late-term abortions. Conditions thus are gradually moving toward those that prevailed before 1973: Abortions are becoming more expensive and more are probably being performed illegally and less safely. As was the case before 1973, the burden of these consequences will be borne largely by women in the middle- and lower-income brackets.

We emphasized at the beginning of this chapter that the issues raised by abortion go far beyond the economic consequences, and that economics cannot, in any event, determine whether abortion should be permitted or proscribed. What economics can do—as we hope we have shown—is to illustrate some of the consequences of the decision between "choice" and "life." Whether an understanding of those consequences can—or even should—play a role in making that decision is a matter we can leave only to the reader.

DISCUSSION QUESTIONS

1. Suppose you wished to predict which states would impose more restrictive conditions on abortions. What factors—for example, per capita income and average age of the population—would you take into account in making your predictions?

2. Before 1973, legal penalties generally were imposed on suppliers of abortion rather than on demanders. How might the effects of prohibiting abortion been different had legal penalties been imposed on demanders rather than on suppliers?

3. The discussion in this chapter focused solely on the economic consequences of prohibiting abortion. Do you think that legislatures base their decisions about abortion solely on the economic consequences? Can an understanding of the economic consequences of laws give us (and legislatures) any guidance about the "best" public policy on abortion?

4. As of 2002, it was up to the states to decide on public policy regarding abortion. Some people have argued that the federal government (perhaps through a Constitutional amendment) should decide on a uniform national policy regarding abortions. What are the advantages and disadvantages of having separate state policies rather than a uniform national policy?

9

Smoking and Smuggling

Cigarette taxes have been in the news lately, and for good reason: Federal taxes per pack jumped a nickel to 39 cents in 2002, and a majority of the states either have instituted their own tax increases or have such hikes on the legislative agenda. Indeed, higher federal and state taxes have helped double the average price of a pack of cigarettes in the United States since 1995.

A variety of motives is pushing the increase in tax rates. Partly, the higher taxes are an effort to reduce smoking, particularly among young people. Taxpayers often end up paying the tobacco-induced medical bills of smokers, through Medicare (for the elderly) and Medicaid (for the poor). Reducing the number of smokers, it is argued, will help cut these costs. In addition, given the current low state of public opinion about smoking, cigarette taxes are proving to be a politically palatable way of raising tax revenues. Sometimes (as in California) these receipts are used in part to fund antismoking advertising campaigns; other times cigarette tax receipts are seen as a source of funds for publicly provided health care initiatives.

Cigarette prices also have been pushed up by a second force. Several years ago, the major tobacco companies settled a series of lawsuits filed by state governments. The companies agreed to pay $246 billion over 25 years into a fund to be distributed to the states. The purpose of the fund was said to be to help states promote antismoking campaigns. In fact, thus far most of the states have spent most of the money on almost anything *but* antismoking campaigns. Roads have been paved, college scholarships funded, and—in the latest economic downturn—budgetary shortfalls have been made up. Nevertheless, the settlement has had an antismoking impact along a different dimension. In the aftermath of the settlement, cigarette companies hiked their wholesale prices by up to one dollar per pack. When added to state taxes that now range up to $1.42 (in the state of Washington), this helped push retail cigarette prices toward $5.00 per pack in some places. Many smokers have responded by becoming ex-smokers.

There is little doubt that, despite the addictive attributes of nicotine, higher cigarette prices make inroads on smoking—after all, the demand curve for cigarettes, like the demand curve for any other good, is downward sloping. For each 10 percent that taxes push up the retail price, the number of packs sold drops by 4 to 8 percent. Interestingly, however, although smokers respond to higher taxes by smoking fewer cigarettes, they also tend to smoke cigarettes that are longer and have higher nicotine and tar content. This effect is so pronounced among people aged 18 to 24 that the average daily tar intake among the young people who continue to smoke is actually higher when the tax rate is higher. Because tar is believed to be the principal carcinogenic substance in cigarettes, higher taxes probably lead to *more* adverse health consequences among young smokers.

Smoking tends to be concentrated among lower-income individuals, which means that the burden of cigarette taxes also tends to be concentrated in this segment of the population. For example, one survey several years ago revealed that only 19 percent of people earning more than $50,000 per year smoked, whereas 32 percent of those earning less than $10,000 smoked. As a result, cigarette taxes consumed 0.4 percent of the income of smokers in the high-income group but an amazing 5.1 percent of the income of the low-income smokers. Indeed, it is estimated that more than half the latest increases in federal taxes will be borne by people earning less than $25,000 per year.

Perhaps the most interesting consequence of changes in cigarette taxes, however, is the change in distribution channels that results. Cigarettes are both light and compact relative to their market value, and this becomes increasingly important when the taxes on them are raised. Thus, cigarettes are prime candidates for smuggling—and taxes are a prime stimulus to such smuggling. Worldwide, of the 1 trillion cigarettes exported in 2001 from producing nations, it is estimated that roughly 300 billion were sold by smugglers, up from 100 billion in 1989. The chief reason for this smuggling is that cigarette taxes vary enormously around the world, creating price differences across nations of several dollars per pack.

For example, in Britain, where cigarettes cost about $5.50 per pack, it is estimated that one-half of all British smokers consume at least some smuggled cigarettes each year. About one in four cigarettes consumed in Spain are illegal, 20 percent of Italian cigarettes are black market, and perhaps 40 percent of all cigarettes consumed in Hong Kong are contraband. In low-tax Luxembourg, it is estimated that only 15 percent of tobacco purchased is consumed in-country—with the rest being moved covertly to higher-tax locales elsewhere in Europe.

In 1991 the Canadian federal government raised cigarette taxes by 146 percent, yielding a price per pack of $3.50, compared to an average U.S. price of $1.00 at the time. Provincial governments soon followed suit with higher cigarette taxes of their own. By 1994, black market cigarette consumption in Canada had jumped to 25 percent of total consumption, up from about 2 percent. How did this happen? When Canadian cigarettes are exported, they are exempt from Canadian cigarette taxes. Soon after the higher federal and provincial taxes went into effect, there was a huge rise in (tax-exempt) exports to the United States, where the cigarettes were promptly—and illegally—reexported back to Canada. The federal and provincial governments ultimately were forced to slash their taxes down to about what they had been before the smuggling outbreak.

How big are the potential cigarette smuggling stakes in the United States? With an average $1.00-per-pack hike in combined state and federal taxes the potential net revenue to smugglers would be on the order of $3 billion to $6 billion per year, even if only a quarter of all smokers turned to the black market. And where would these smuggled cigarettes come from? Almost anywhere. Mexico, a transshipment point for much of America's illegal drug imports, is one possibility. Between 1989 and 1995, U.S. exports of cigarettes to Mexico went from 5 million packs a year to 150 million. Some of this surely was due to increased Mexican consumption, but a significant amount is believed to be due to reexports to California: In 1989 that state had raised cigarette generally taxes to 35 cents a pack from 10 cents a pack. Other likely sources of smuggled cigarettes are domestic U.S. military bases and Indian reservations, where cigarettes generally are tax-exempt. Both of these venues have been sources of bootleg cigarettes in the past, when combined federal and state taxes were far lower than they are now.

The potential problems facing states when they raise their cigarette taxes are magnified by the fact that other states represent potential sources of supply. Economists Daniel K. Benjamin and William R. Dougan of Clemson University have studied the role of bootleg cigarettes in shaping cigarette taxes around the country. They have found that cigarette smuggling is highly sensitive to interstate tax differentials of only a few cents per pack, and that state governments are thus forced to consider the taxing behavior of other states or suffer the consequences.[1] For example, the late 1940s saw an outbreak of smuggling when a significant number of states first began using cigarettes as a source of tax revenue. Another outbreak of smuggling occurred in the 1970s as states raised taxes to make up for other revenue losses caused by the recession of the early 1970s.

Recent experience in Michigan suggests that the latest round of state cigarette tax increases can be expected to produce yet another epidemic of interstate smuggling. In 1994 Michigan hiked its tax to 75 cents per pack from 25 cents. Within just over a year, 20 percent of the cigarettes consumed in Michigan were smuggled in, as smokers traveled to Ohio and Indiana to save more than $6.00 (about one-third) on the cost of a carton. There has been a sharp rise in organized, large-scale heists of cigarettes from convenience stores, and even a major law enforcement push against cigarette bootlegging seems unable to quell the onslaught of illegal imports.

None of these developments would be surprising to the British, who two centuries ago relied on import tariffs to fund much of their government spending and suffered the consequences. Between 1698 and 1758 the standard tariff rate went from 10 percent to 25 percent. After further increases in tariffs during the American Revolution, smuggled goods accounted for a full 20 percent of all imports to Britain. Tea was particularly popular and thus heavily taxed. Indeed, the tax rate reached 119 percent, and by 1784 it was estimated that two-thirds of all tea consumed in Britain was contraband. Given the direction that cigarette taxes are headed, cigarette smuggling seems headed the same way.

[1] Daniel K. Benjamin and William R. Dougan, "Efficient Excise Taxation: The Evidence from Cigarettes," *Journal of Law & Economics*, April 1997 pp. 113–136.

DISCUSSION QUESTIONS

1. Various state and federal laws specify that a pack of cigarettes contains twenty cigarettes, and that these cigarettes are limited in the total amount of tobacco they may contain. If such limits were not in place, when taxes per pack were raised, what would you expect to see happen to the number of cigarettes in a pack and the amount of tobacco in a cigarette?

2. In a world where transportation costs are positive, what effect would distance from the point of production be expected to have on the size of the tax that a state would find appropriate to levy on a pack of cigarettes?

3. In 1978, interstate trucking was deregulated in the United States, leading to greater competition in this industry and lower freight rates. In light of your answer to question 2, what effect would you expect trucking deregulation to have on the interstate pattern of cigarette taxes? In particular, what would happen to taxes in states distant from the major point of production in North Carolina, relative to taxes in states closer to North Carolina?

4. Cigarettes that are smuggled from North Carolina to New York must pass through Virginia, Maryland, Delaware, and New Jersey along the way. Suppose that authorities in Delaware decide to raise taxes in the hope of discouraging smoking. What impact would this Delaware tax hike have on cigarette taxes in New York and New Jersey, compared to cigarette taxes in Maryland and Virginia?

Part Three

Nonprice Rationing

INTRODUCTION

Although monetary prices are the most commonly used instrument of rationing in a market economy, they are not the only means. A key productive feature of government is its role in defining and enforcing property rights so that market prices can perform their role in allocating scarce resources. But sometimes—for any of a variety of reasons—government seeks to prevent monetary prices from doing their job. We still live in a world of scarcity, however, so rationing must still take place. A variety of instruments may perform the rationing functioning, and in this section we examine many of them. Along the way we find that nonprice rationing is both more costly and more complex than most people ever imagined.

Our first look at nonprice rationing comes in Chapter 10, "Bankrupt Landlords, from Sea to Shining Sea." Here we examine the effects of **rent control**—a legal ceiling on the rent that landlords may charge for apartments. As with many of the issues we consider in this book, the effects of rent controls are more surprising, and costly, than you might think. We find, for example, that legal ceilings on rents have increased the extent of homelessness in the United States, have led to a rise in racial discrimination, and have caused the wholesale destruction of hundreds of thousands of dwelling units in our nation's major cities. We cannot escape one simple fact: Politicians may pass legislation, and bureaucrats may do their best to enforce it, but the laws of demand and supply ultimately rule the economy.

Perhaps not surprisingly, many of the same people who argue that rent controls should be used to ensure "affordable housing" also advocate that the government should guarantee access to "affordable health care." Despite their laudable goals, it turns out that, once again, achieving them is rather more difficult than it might seem. As we see in Chapter 11, "Rationing Health Care," in response to the high cost of medical care, many nations have tried to remove health care from the marketplace. Yet the fundamental problems of scarcity remain: Producers must be rewarded for their efforts, and consumers' otherwise unlimited desires somehow must be rationed. In the market system, prices perform these functions. But under the systems of government-mandated, universal health care that now exist (or are likely to exist), suppliers are directed by government edict and prices no longer ration demand. Instead, these systems rely on another method of rationing, called "rationing by waiting" because people are forced to wait—weeks or even months—for whatever level of medical care is offered to them. Under such a system, the costs of health care are clearly different than they are under a market system, but it is not clear that they are any lower.

A "living wage" is yet another social goal that seems unassailable yet proves to be surprisingly elusive. In Chapter 12, we examine "The Effects of the Minimum Wage" and find once again that the effects of government actions are not always what they seem, nor are they usually what their proponents claim for them. The chief losers in minimum wage hikes are often the very people who can least afford those losses, while those who claim to support the law on altruistic grounds are in fact likely to be the biggest winners. The message of this chapter may well be this simple piece of advice: When someone claims to be doing something *for* you, it is time to ask what that person is doing *to* you.

Our final foray into nonprice rationing takes us to California, where in the summer of 2000 things started to get very strange in the electricity market. Wholesale electricity prices soared to ten times previous levels, even as retail prices stayed unchanged, pushing two of the state's three large electric utilities into financial ruin. Then the electric companies started turning the lights out—eliminating electricity services to blocks of customers for several hours each day. Plenty of people, in California and elsewhere, thought this mess was caused by a failure of the market system. In fact, as we see in Chapter 13, "Lights Out in California," the real culprit was the attempt by California's governor and legislature to circumvent market forces, by preventing electricity suppliers from raising prices when the firms' costs soared. A crucial function of market prices is to encourage consumers to alter their consumption patterns in response to changes in the true cost of goods. When the opportunity cost of goods rises, high prices will correctly induce consumers to use less; when the true cost of goods falls, low prices will correctly induce consumers to take advantage by using more. In this way we make the best use of our scarce resources. But in California, the legal limit on retail prices meant that when the wholesale cost of supplying electricity soared in 2000, consumers had no incentive to curtail their usage. With no other means of rationing customers, the utilities were compelled to resort to inefficient non-price rationing devices—in this case rolling power blackouts—that are commonplace when governments interfere with market prices.

10

Bankrupt Landlords, from Sea to Shining Sea

Take a tour of Santa Monica, a beachfront enclave of Los Angeles, and you will find a city of bizarre contrasts. Pick a street at random, and you will likely find run-down rental units sitting in disrepair next to homes costing $500,000. Try another street, and you will find abandoned apartment buildings adjacent to luxury car dealerships and trendy shops that sell high-fashion clothing to Hollywood stars. Sound strange? Not in Santa Monica—known locally as the People's Republic of Santa Monica—where stringent rent control laws once routinely forced property owners to leave their buildings empty and decaying rather than even bothering to sell them.

Three thousand miles to the east, rent control laws in New York City—known locally as the Big Apple—have forced landlords to abandon housing units because the owners no longer could afford the financial losses imposed by rent control. Largely as a result of such abandonments, the city government of New York owns thousands of derelict housing units—empty, except for rats and small-time cocaine dealers. Meanwhile, because the controls also discourage new construction, the city faces a housing gap of 200,000 rental units—apartments that easily could be filled at current controlled rental rates, if the units existed in habitable form.

From coast to coast, stories like these are commonplace in the 200 or so American cities and towns that practice some form of rent control—a system in which the local government tells building owners how much they can charge for rent. Time and again, the stories are the same: poorly maintained rental units, abandoned apartment buildings, tenants trapped by housing gridlock in apartments no longer suitable for them, bureaucracies bloated with rent control enforcers, and even homeless families that can find no one who will rent to them. Time and again, the reason for the stories is the same: legal limits on the rent that people may pay for a place to live.

Our story begins in 1943, when the federal government imposed rent control as a temporary wartime measure. Although the federal program ended after the war, New York City continued the controls on its own. Under New York's controls, a landlord generally could not raise rents on apartments as long as the tenants continued to renew their leases. Rent controls in Santa Monica are more recent. They were spurred by the inflation of the 1970s, which, combined with California's rapid population growth, pushed housing prices and rents to record levels. In 1979, the city of Santa Monica (where 80 percent of the residents were renters) ordered rents rolled back to the levels of the year before and stipulated that future rents could go up by only two-thirds as much as any increase in the overall price level. In both New York and Santa Monica, the objective of rent controls has been to keep rents below the levels that would be observed in freely competitive markets. Achieving this goal required that both cities impose extensive regulations to prevent landlord and tenant from evading the controls—regulations that are costly to enforce and that distort the normal operation of the market.

It is worth noting that the rent control systems in New York and Santa Monica are slowly yielding to decontrol. For a number of years, some apartments in New York have been subject only to "rent stabilization" regulations, which are somewhat less stringent than absolute rent controls. In addition, New York apartments going for over $2000 per month are deregulated when a lease ends. In Santa Monica, the state of California mandated that, effective in 1999, rent for newly vacant apartments could increase. Even so, in both cities, the bulk of the rental market is dominated by rent controls, and so we focus on the consequences of those controls.

In general, the unfettered movement of rental prices in a freely competitive housing market performs three vital functions: Prices allocate existing scarce housing among competing claimants; they promote the efficient maintenance of existing housing and stimulate the production of new housing, where appropriate; and they ration usage of housing by demanders, thereby preventing waste of scarce housing. Rent control prevents rental prices from effectively performing these functions. Let's see how.

Rent control discourages the construction of new rental units. Developers and mortgage lenders are reluctant to get involved in building new rental properties because controls artificially depress the most important long-run determinant of profitability—rents. Thus, in one recent year, 11,000 new housing units were built in Dallas, a city with a 16 percent rental vacancy rate but no rent control statute. In that same year, only 2000 units were built in San Francisco, a city with a 1.6 percent vacancy rate but stringent rent control laws. In New York City, the only rental units being built are either exempt from controls or are heavily subsidized by the government. Private construction of new apartments in Santa Monica also dried up under controls, even though new office space and commercial developments—both exempt from rent control—were built at a record pace.

Rent control leads to the deterioration of the existing supply of rental housing. When rental prices are held below free market levels, property owners cannot recover through higher rents the costs of maintenance, repairs, and capital improvements. Thus such activities are sharply curtailed. Eventually, taxes, utilities, and the expenses of the most rudimentary repairs—such as replacing broken windows—overwhelm the depressed rental receipts; as a result, the buildings are abandoned. In New York, some owners have resorted to arson, hoping to collect the insurance on their empty rent-controlled buildings before the city claims them for back taxes. Under rent controls in Santa Monica, the city insisted that owners wishing to convert empty apartment buildings into other uses had to build new rental units to replace the units they no longer rented. At a cost of up to $50,000 per apartment, it is little wonder that few owners were willing to bear the burden, choosing instead to leave the buildings empty and graffiti-scarred.

Rent control impedes the process of rationing scarce housing. One consequence of this is that tenant mobility is sharply restricted. Even when a family's demand for living space changes—due, for example, to a new baby or a teenager's departure for college—there can be substantial costs in giving up a rent-controlled unit. In New York City, landlords often charge "key money" (a large, up-front cash payment) before a new tenant is allowed to move in. The high cost of moving means that large families often stay in cramped quarters whereas small families, or even single persons, reside in very large units. In New York, this phenomenon of nonmobility came to be known as *housing gridlock*. In Santa Monica, many homeowners rented out portions of their houses in response to soaring prices in the 1970s and then found themselves trapped by their tenants, whom they could not evict even if they wanted to sell their homes and move to a retirement community.

Not surprisingly, the distortions produced by rent control lead to efforts by both landlords and tenants to evade the rules. This in turn leads to the growth of cumbersome and expensive government bureaucracies whose job is to enforce the controls. In New York, where rents can be raised when tenancy changes hands, landlords have an incentive to make life unpleasant for tenants or to evict them on the slightest pretense. The city has responded by making evictions extremely costly for landlords. Even if a tenant blatantly and repeatedly violates the terms of a lease, the tenant cannot be evicted if the violations are corrected within a "reasonable" time period. If the violations are not corrected—despite several trips to court by the owners and their attorneys—eviction requires a tedious and expensive judicial proceeding. For their part, tenants routinely try to sublet all or part of their rent-controlled apartments at prices substantially above the rent they pay the owner. Because both the city and the landlords try to prohibit subletting, the parties often end up in the city's Housing Courts, an entire judicial system developed chiefly to deal with disputes over rent-controlled apartments.

Strict controls on monthly rents force landlords to use other means to discriminate among prospective tenants. Simply to ensure that the rent check comes every month, many landlords rent only to well-heeled professionals. As one commentator put it, "There is no disputing that Santa Monica became younger, whiter, and richer under rent control." The same pattern occurred under the rent control laws of both Berkeley, California, and Cambridge, Massachusetts.

There is little doubt the bureaucracies that evolve to administer rent control laws are cumbersome and expensive. Between 1988 and 1993 New York City spent $5.1 billion rehabilitating housing confiscated from private landlords. Even so, derelict buildings continued piling up at a record rate. The overflow and appeals from the city's Housing Courts clog the rest of New York's judicial system, impeding the prosecution of violent criminals and drug dealers. In Santa Monica, the Rent Control Board began with an annual budget of $745,000 and a staff of twenty people. By the early 1990s, the staff had tripled in size and the budget was pushing $5 million. Who picked up the tab? The landlords did, of course, with an annual special assessment of $200 per unit levied on them. And even though the 1999 state-mandated changes in the law meant that apartment rents in Santa Monica can be increased when a new tenant moves in, the new rent is then controlled by the city for the duration of the tenancy. Indeed, the Rent Control Board conveniently maintains a Web site where one can go to learn the Maximum Allowable Rent on any of the tens of thousands of rent-controlled residences throughout Santa Monica.

Ironically, the big losers from rent control—in addition to landlords—are often low-income individuals, especially single mothers. Indeed, many observers believe that one significant cause of homelessness in cities such as New York and Los Angeles is rent control. Often, poor individuals cannot assure the discriminating landlord that their rent will be paid on time—much less paid—each month. Because controlled rents generally are well below free-market levels, there is little incentive for apartment owners to take a chance on low-income individuals as tenants. This is especially true if the prospective tenant's chief source of income is a welfare check. Indeed, a significant number of the tenants appearing in New York's Housing Courts have been low-income mothers who, due to emergency expenses or delayed welfare checks, have missed rent payments. Often their appeals end in evictions and new homes in temporary public shelters or on the streets. Prior to the state-mandated 1999 easing of controls, some apartment owners in Santa Monica who used to rent one- and two-room units to welfare recipients and other low-income individuals simply abandoned their buildings, leaving them vacant rather than trying to collect artificially depressed rents that failed to cover operating costs. The disgusted owner of one empty and decaying eighteen-unit building had a friend spray-paint his feelings on the wall: "I want to tear this mess down, but Big Brother won't let me." Perhaps because the owner had escaped from a concentration camp in search of freedom in the United States, the friend added a personalized touch: a drawing of a large hammer and sickle, symbol of the former Soviet Union.

It is worth noting that the ravages of rent controls are not confined to capitalist nations. In a heavily publicized news conference several years ago, the foreign minister of Vietnam, Nguyen Co

Thach, declared that a "romantic conception of socialism" had destroyed his country's economy after the Vietnam War. Mr. Thach stated that rent control had artificially encouraged demand and discouraged supply, and that all of the housing in Hanoi had fallen into disrepair as a result. Thach concluded by noting, "The Americans couldn't destroy Hanoi, but we have destroyed our city by very low rents. We realized it was stupid and that we must change policy."

Apparently, this same thinking was what induced the state of California to compel changes in Santa Monica's rent control ordinance. The result of that policy change was an almost immediate jump in rents on newly vacant apartments, as well as a noticeable rise in the vacancy rate—both exactly what we would expect to occur. Interestingly enough, however, prospective new tenants were less enthusiastic about the higher rents than many landlords had expected. The reason? Well, twenty years of rent controls had produced that many years of reduced upkeep, and thus apartments that were, well, less than pristine. As one renter noted, "The trouble is, most of this area . . . [is] basically falling apart." And another complained, "I don't want to move into a place that's depressing, with old brown carpet that smells like chicken soup." Higher rents are gradually changing both the ambiance and the aroma of Santa Monica apartments—but only at the same rate that the market is allowed to perform its functions.

DISCUSSION QUESTIONS

1. Why do you think governments frequently attempt to control apartment rents but not house prices?

2. What determines the size of the key money payments that landlords demand (and tenants offer) for the right to rent a controlled apartment?

3. Who, other than the owners of rental units, loses as a result of rent controls? Who gains from rent controls? What effect would the imposition of rent controls have on the market price of an existing single-family house? What effect would rent controls have on the value of vacant land?

4. Why do the owners of rental units reduce their maintenance expenditures on the units when rent controls are imposed? Does their decision have anything to do with whether they can afford those expenditures?

11

Rationing Health Care

Americans spend a larger share of national income on health care—more than 14 percent—than any other people of the world. Moreover, for almost every one of the last twenty-five years, the price index for medical care has increased more rapidly than the price index for all goods and services in general. With spending on health care at record high levels, it is little wonder that some political leaders have labeled health care in the United States a "crisis," arguing we should implement government-mandated universal health care coverage. It is thus instructive to look at what has happened in other countries that have adopted some form of a national health care system.

We obviously cannot cover every aspect of health care here, nor can we demonstrate that one system of health care delivery is better than another one. What we can do, however, is to note the consequences of this critical point: In a world of scarcity, some form of rationing is inevitable. In the market system, that rationing is done by prices. Under the systems of government-mandated universal health care that now exist (or are likely to exist in the future), prices are not permitted to ration demands. Instead, these systems rely on another system of rationing: It is called *rationing by waiting,* because people are forced to wait—for weeks or months—for whatever level of medical care is offered them.

The most common form of government-mandated universal health care coverage found in the world today is the single-payer health care system that in essence offers universal health care to consumers at a money price of zero. (The term *single-payer* is used because the government writes the checks for the medical bills.)

Britain offers a typical example. The British National Health Service (NHS) has been in existence since 1948. Once touted as one of the world's best national health care examples, the NHS has deteriorated dramatically. Consider hospital beds: In 1948 there were ten hospital beds per thousand people. Today there are about five per thousand people. Since 1948 about 50 percent of Britain's hospitals have been closed for "efficiency" reasons—meaning that the British government cannot or will not afford to keep them open. Britain now has fewer hospital beds per capita than every Western European country except Portugal and Spain.

Because patients in Britain do not pay directly for the services they receive, some other means of rationing must be used. In Britain, the rationing device is waiting, and as the number of hospital beds and other medical facilities have been cut relative to the population, it is little surprise that waiting times have increased. Currently more than a million British patients are waiting for hospital admission. Many others do not show up on waiting lists because they simply do not apply, knowing that the wait is so long. In some London hospitals, individuals routinely spend more than 12 hours waiting to see a physician.

The total staff in the NHS has, in contrast, skyrocketed. Whereas in 1948 the staff-to-bed ratio was .73 to 1 for each hospital bed, today it is 3.1 to 1 for each hospital bed; even with the drop in beds per capita, there are now twice as many staff members for each patient as there were in 1948. One would expect this would enhance medical care. Unfortunately, however, the staff, for the most part, do not deal directly with the treatment of patients. Rather, they have become part of the NHS bureaucracy. This is because the government-run NHS adds a new department or committee for every new aspect of medicine that develops. The NHS consists of a bureaucratic network unknown in the decentralized medical system in the United States.

In fairness to the NHS, some of the changes in the system over the last fifty years have been mirrored in health care systems elsewhere. For example, improvements in surgical techniques and pharmaceuticals have shortened hospital stays in most nations, resulting in a reduced demand for hospital beds. This surely helps explain at least some of the sharp cuts in NHS beds per capita. Nevertheless, horror stories of bungled operations and patients left untended in hospital hallways have become a regular feature in British newspapers. Things got so bad by 2002 that Britain's Labor Party—the initial creator and steadfast supporter of the NHS—proposed that the poorest-performing NHS hospitals be handed over to the private sector.

The national health care system in Canada offers another example of the effects of nonprice rationing. In essence, under the Canadian system the government picks up the entire tab for all covered medical procedures. Currently, only 11 percent of Canada's national health care spending goes to administration, compared to 24 percent in the United States. Canada devotes 9.5 percent of its national income to health care, about a third less than in the United States. Perhaps because of the seemingly low cost of the Canadian system, many supporters of health care reform in the United States often point to Canada's system as one that the United States should emulate.

One impact of the lower level of spending in Canada is that their system does not provide the latest in medical technology. Although Canada ranks fifth highest among developed nations in health care spending as a share of income, it ranks in the bottom third of those countries in availability of technology. For example, compared to the United States, on a per capita basis Canada has far fewer CAT scan and magnetic resonance imaging (MRI) machines, critical in performing sophisticated, difficult diagnostics. Similarly, Canadian medical facilities have almost none of the medical devices needed to remove kidney stones without painful and dangerous surgery. Moreover, operating rooms in Canada operate on strict financial budgets and are allowed to continue operating only if they are within those monthly budgets. What happens if an operating room exhausts its budget on, say, the 20th of the month? It shuts down until the beginning of the next monthly budget cycle.

The costs to the users of the Canadian system show up in other ways as well. Two Canadian economists, Cynthia Ramsay and Michael Walker of The Fraser Institute in British Columbia, have studied the waiting times across a variety of medical specialties. They discovered that many Canadians each year were not permitted to enter the hospital when they or their physician deemed best; instead they had to wait until facilities became available. Moreover, Canadians typically were not even able to get in to see their doctors when they wanted. Ramsay and Walker measured the delay from

TABLE 11–1   Average Waiting Time for Treatment by a Specialist in Canada

(In Weeks)

Specialty	Shortest Wait	Longest Wait	Canada Average
Orthopedics	10.3	39.7	25
Plastic Surgery	9.1	40.5	19.8
Ophthalmology	8.1	39	22.3
Gynecology	5.5	27.2	13.1
Otolaryngology	8.3	26	14.4
Urology	8.2	29.2	12.6
Neurosurgery	10	31	17
General Surgery	6.2	22.3	9.2
Internal Medicine	4.6	7.2	6.4
Cardiovascular	12.5	31.5	17.9

Source: The Fraser Institute, Vancouver, BC, Canada.

the time that a primary care physician referred a patient until a specialist actually treated the patient; they found that the demand for health care was rationed by waiting. Listed in Table 11–1 are the average waiting times in weeks for the services of various medical specialists. The three columns show the waiting times for Canada as a whole and the waiting times in individual Canadian provinces that had, respectively, the shortest and longest waiting times.

Two facts are apparent from Table 11–1. First, it is common-place for Canadians to have to wait three or four months to receive health care that is anything beyond that offered by a nurse or primary care physician. Second, the Canadian system produces huge inequalities in the way people are treated, not only across illnesses, but also across provinces for the same illness. These long waits, and the extent of unequal treatment, have produced a regular stream of Canadians who come to the United States and spend their own money for medical care here, rather than await their fate at home. The waiting in Canada has gotten so bad that some provincial governments ship heart bypass patients and cancer patients needing radiation over the U.S. border to receive treatment. Although this is politically unpopular with the Canadian federal government, the alternative, it seems, is to let the patients die at home, waiting.

Another example of government-controlled health care involves the Netherlands. The government there decides on global budgets to control hospital expenditures. It also limits the number of doctors who may specialize in a given area and caps the number of patients they may see. In addition, the government controls physician fees. To help the government meet its budgets, many medical specialists have simply stopped working as much as they used to work. It is commonplace for highly trained surgeons to work only half days or to take weeks off at the end of the year. The result is that typically there is about a three-month waiting list for coronary bypass surgery. Over 15 percent of the patients on the waiting list die before the operation can be performed. Diabetics wait an average of three months to obtain laser treatment for retinal hemorrhaging—and risk blindness in the process. The average wait for removal of gallbladder stones and repairs of hernias is from four to eight weeks. Some forms of reconstructive surgery require waits of up to four years.

Under Dutch law, companies must pay employees' salaries for the first two to six weeks of an illness, depending on the size of the company. This has generated an interesting incentive: The companies have discovered that they can reduce their costs by renting hospital rooms that they keep open for their employees. The companies thus do not have to pay employee salaries while they wait—disabled—for treatment. Although the Dutch system is supposed to provide equal treatment for all, treatment in fact has come to depend on the size and influence of the company for which a person works.

Although our analyses have involved three foreign countries, we need go no further than our own Veterans Administration (VA) to find similar examples. The Veterans Administration operates a 100 percent government-owned and financed health care system. It is the largest health care system in our country and one of the largest in the world. It has 163 medical centers with over 80,000 beds. It operates 362 outpatient and community clinics that receive 43 million patient visits a year. In addition, it has 137 nursing homes with over 87,000 patients. All of the states, plus the District of

Columbia and Puerto Rico, have at least one VA medical center, and the VA boasts almost 250,000 employees nationwide.

The General Accounting Office (GAO) did a study of the VA a few years ago, concluding that the VA system faces a growing demand for "free" medical services. Herein lies the rub—the quantity demanded of most services at a zero price will almost always exceed the quantity supplied. Consequently, because price is not used as a rationing device, some other method must be used to ration the scarce resources. Fifty-five percent of the patients who use the VA for routine medical problems wait three hours or longer and sometimes an entire day in order to be seen for a few minutes by a VA general physician. Even among patients requiring urgent medical care, one in nine must wait at least three hours. Patients in need of specialized care cannot even be *seen* by a specialist for 60 to 90 days. They wait months more if surgery or other special procedures are required.

Whether the location is Britain, Canada, Holland, or even the U.S. Veterans Administration, when prices are prevented from clearing the market for medical care, waiting time is the most commonly used means of rationing demand. As one unidentified U.S. veteran told the GAO, "I pack a lunch and take a book." Another veteran, retired 69-year-old Army Major Elmer Erickson, stated, "Be prepared to spend the day there. You will eventually see a doctor."

DISCUSSION QUESTIONS

1. Suppose we had government-mandated universal access to food. How would the outcome likely differ from what is observed with health care systems of this type?

2. Under the Canadian system, those who are unhappy with the health care they receive can come to the United States for medical care if they can afford it. If the United States adopted a system similar to Canada's, where could Americans go if they were not satisfied with the medical care they were receiving?

3. Under the current U.S. health care system, insurance companies often perform the role performed by government agencies un-

der the British, Canadian, and Dutch systems—they pay the bills and they limit the care that people are able to consume. Why might health insurance companies be expected to do a better job in performing these functions than would a government agency?

4. How much health care do people "need"? Does this amount depend on the cost of providing it?

12

The Effects of the Minimum Wage

Ask workers if they would like a raise and the answer is likely to be a resounding yes. But ask them if they would like to be fired or have their hours of work reduced and they would probably tell you no. The effects of the minimum wage are centered on exactly these points.

Proponents of the **minimum wage**—the lowest hourly wage firms legally may pay their workers—argue that low-income workers are underpaid and unable to support themselves or their families. The minimum wage, they say, raises earnings at the bottom of the wage distribution, with little disruption to workers or businesses. Opponents claim that most low-wage workers are low-skilled youths without families to support. The minimum wage, it is said, merely enriches a few teenagers at the far greater expense of many others, who can't get jobs. Most important, opponents argue, many individuals at the bottom of the economic ladder lack the skills needed for employers to hire them at the federal minimum. Willing to work but unable to find jobs, these people never learn the basic job skills needed to move up the economic ladder to higher-paying jobs. The issues are clear—but what are the facts?

The federal minimum wage was instituted in 1938 as a provision of the Fair Labor Standards Act (FLSA). It was originally set at $0.25 per hour, about 40 percent of the average manufacturing wage at the time. Over the next forty years, the legal minimum was raised periodically, roughly in accord with the movement of market wages throughout the economy. Typically, its level has averaged between 40 percent and 50 percent of average manufacturing wages. In response to the high inflation of the late 1970s, the minimum wage was hiked seven times between 1974 and 1981, reaching $3.35 per hour—about 42 percent of manufacturing wages. Ronald Reagan vowed to keep a lid on the minimum wage, and by the time he stepped down as president, the minimum's unchanged level left it at 31 percent of average wages. Legislation passed in 1989 raised the minimum to $3.80 in 1990 and $4.25 in 1991. Five years later, at the urging of President Clinton, Congress raised it in two steps to $5.15 per hour. By the time you read this, it is likely that the minimum wage will have been increased again.

Nearly 4 million workers earn the minimum wage; another 2 million or so take home even less because the law doesn't cover them. Supporters of the minimum wage argue that it prevents exploitation of employees and helps them earn enough to support their families and themselves. Even so, at $5.15 per hour, a full-time worker earns less than 60 percent of what the government considers enough to keep a family of four out of poverty. In fact, to get a family of four with one wage earner up to the poverty line, the minimum wage would have to be over $8.00 per hour.

Yet those who oppose the minimum wage argue that such calculations are irrelevant. For example, two-thirds of the workers earning the minimum wage are single, and they earn enough to put them above the poverty cutoff. Moreover, about half of these single workers are teenagers, most of whom have no financial obligations, except possibly for their clothing and car insurance expenditures. Thus opponents argue that the minimum wage chiefly benefits upper-middle class teens who are least in need of assistance at the same time that it costs the jobs of thousands of disadvantaged minority youths.

The debate over the minimum wage intensified a few years ago when research by David Card and Alan Krueger suggested that a change in the New Jersey minimum wage had no adverse short-run impact on employment. Further research by other scholars focusing on Canada reveals more clearly what happens when the minimum wage is hiked. In Canada there are important differences in minimum wages both over time and across different provinces. This enabled researchers to distinguish between the short-run and long-run effects of changes in minimum wages. The short-run effects are indeed negligible, as implied by Card and Krueger. Nevertheless, the

Canadian research shows that in the *long run* the adverse effects of a higher minimum wage are quite substantial. In the short run, it is true that firms do not cut their workforce by much, if at all, in response to a higher minimum. But over time, the higher costs due to a higher minimum wage force smaller firms out of business, and it is here that the drop in employment shows up clearly.

The Canadian results are consistent with the overwhelming bulk of the U.S. evidence on this issue, which points to a negative impact of the minimum wage on employment. After all, the number of workers demanded, like the quantity demanded for all goods, responds to price: the higher the price, the lower the number desired. There remains, however, debate over *how many* jobs are lost due to the minimum wage. For example, when the minimum wage was raised from $3.35 to $4.25, credible estimates of the number of potential job losses ranged from 50,000 all the way up to 400,000. When the minimum was hiked to $5.15, researchers suggested that at least 200,000 jobs were at stake. With a workforce of 140 million persons, numbers like these may not sound very large. But most of the people who don't have jobs as a result of the minimum wage are teenagers; they comprise only about 5 percent of the workforce but bear almost all of the burden of foregone employment alternatives.

Significantly, the youths most likely to lose work due to the minimum wage are disadvantaged teenagers, chiefly minorities. On average, these teens enter the workforce with the fewest job skills and the greatest need for on-the-job training. Until and unless these disadvantaged teenagers can acquire these skills, they are the most likely to be unemployed as a result of the minimum wage—and thus least likely to have the opportunity to move up the economic ladder. With a teen unemployment rate better than triple the overall rate, and unemployment among black youngsters hovering above 30 percent, critics argue that the minimum wage is a major impediment to long-term labor market success for minority youth.

Indeed, the minimum wage has an aspect that its supporters are not inclined to discuss: It can make employers more likely to discriminate on the basis of sex or race. When wages are set by market forces, employers who would discriminate face a reduced, and thus more expensive, pool of workers. But when the government mandates an above-market wage, a surplus of low-skilled workers results, and it becomes easier and cheaper to discriminate. As former U.S. Treasury Secretary Lawrence Summers noted, the minimum wage "removes the economic penalty to the employer. He can choose the one who's white with blond hair."

Critics of the minimum wage also argue that it makes firms less willing to train workers lacking basic skills. Instead, companies may choose to hire only experienced workers whose abilities justify the higher wage. Firms are also likely to become less generous with fringe benefits in an effort to hold down labor costs. The prospect of more discrimination, less job training for low-skilled workers, and fewer fringe benefits for entry-level workers leaves many observers uncomfortable. As economist Jacob Mincer of Columbia University notes, the minimum wage means "a loss of opportunity" for the hard-core unemployed.

The last time Congress and the President agreed to raise the minimum wage, it was only after a heated battle lasting months. Given the stakes involved—an improved standard of living for some, a loss of job opportunities for others—it is not surprising that discussions of the minimum wage soon turn to controversy. As one former high-level U.S. Department of Labor official said: "When it comes to the minimum wage, there are no easy positions to take. Either you are in favor of more jobs, less discrimination, and more on-the-job training, or you support better wages for workers. Whatever stance you choose, you are bound to get clobbered by the opposition." When the Congress and the President face this issue, one or both parties usually feel the same way.

DISCUSSION QUESTIONS

1. Are teenagers better off when a higher minimum wage enables some to get higher wages but causes others to lose their jobs?

2. Are there methods other than a higher minimum wage that could raise the incomes of low-wage workers without reducing employment among minority youngsters?

3. Why do you think organized labor groups, such as unions, are supporters of a higher minimum wage, even though their members all earn much more than the minimum wage?

4. Is it possible that a higher minimum wage could ever *raise* employment?

13

Lights Out in California

In the summer of 2000 things started to get very strange in California's electricity market. First, wholesale electricity prices soared to ten times previous levels, even as retail prices stayed unchanged, pushing two of the state's three large electric utilities into financial ruin. Then the electric companies started turning the lights out—electricity services to large blocks of customers were simply turned off for several hours each day. And finally, the government of California decided to get into the electricity business, buying it on the wholesale market and selling it at retail for prices that didn't come close to covering costs. Plenty of people, in California and elsewhere, thought this mess was caused by a failure of the market system. In fact, nothing could be farther from the truth. The real culprit was the attempt by California's governor and legislature to circumvent market forces. Let's see why.

We must begin with a look back in time. Historically, electricity in this country has been supplied by **regulated monopolies**—firms that are granted the exclusive right to sell electricity in part or all of a state, but at prices that are regulated (decided upon) by an agency of the state government. The rationale for this arrangement has been technological constraints that led to **economies of scale** in the industry: costs have been lower when one firm supplied the electricity than when several firms competed to do so. But with only one firm in the market, there would be an incentive for it to raise prices well above costs. To ensure that the savings of the scale economies were achieved and passed on to consumers, states have thus allowed firms to be **monopoly** suppliers of electricity, but limited the prices they have been permitted to charge.

In recent years, rapidly advancing technology has virtually eliminated the huge economies of scale that once dominated this industry. Small plants can now generate electricity much more cheaply than before; efficient high-power transmission lines enable firms to compete effectively with those in other states; and communications and computer advances have made it possible to coordinate the production and distribution of electricity across dozens or even thousands of different firms across the country. As a result, interest has grown in reducing the amount of electricity regulation in the U.S., i.e., opening up markets to competition, in the hopes that electricity bills could be lowered as more firms competed for the business of consumers. This process, called "deregulation," was the path along which California seemed to start in the 1990s. Unfortunately, although California used the term deregulation to describe the actions it took, the label bore almost no resemblance to reality. In fact, the new rules imposed by the state are better described as "re-regulation."

What California called deregulation was a combination of three policies. First, the state cut legally permissible retail electricity prices by 9% and then forbade firms from raising prices to customers, regardless of costs. Second, in a move that actually did resemble true deregulation, the state allowed wholesale electricity prices to move freely in response to market forces. Because California electric companies were on balance net importers of electricity from producers in other states, this meant that the wholesale costs of California electric companies were free to fluctuate, even though their retail prices were fixed by law. The third component of California's plan was to require utilities to sell off much of their productive capacity and simultaneously prohibit them from using long-term contracts to buy electricity on behalf of their customers. Instead, California electric utilities were required to buy electricity on a day-ahead basis in so-called "spot" markets at whatever prices happened to be each day.

This odd combination of rules was cobbled together by California politicians in their efforts to get consumers and producers to agree to deregulation. Consumers, suspicious of the long history of monopolies in this market, wanted assurances they wouldn't get stuck with higher bills when deregulation went into effect; thus the state cut retail prices and locked them in at the lower level. Producers hoped that wholesale prices would go down and wanted to be able to capture all of the profits if they did so; hence, the state freed wholesale prices to move in accord with market forces. And finally, politicians and regulators in California wanted to encourage new firms to supply wholesale electricity to the state; to encourage utilities to buy from newcomers, the state forbade long-term contracts that might have discouraged new firms from trying to crack the market.

There was actually a chance this system could have worked— if things had gone just right. What the state needed was a combination of stable demand in California, to keep consumption from growing too much, and low wholesale electricity prices, to keep the utilities' costs down. Fortunately, for the first two years of the plan, these conditions were met. Unfortunately, in 2000 the state's luck ran out: as we'll see below, demand in California rose, supply was reduced, and the restrictions the legislature had imposed on the market prevented it from mitigating the effects of either. The result was catastrophe.

Electricity consumption is importantly affected by both weather and business conditions. In 2000 the California economy was booming, pushing up the demand for electricity, and adverse weather conditions in the state helped fuel demand even further. With retail prices fixed by law, there was nothing to choke off consumption. On the supply side, a substantial portion of the electricity in the West comes from hydroelectric sources, which of course ultimately rely on accumulated rainfall. Gas turbines burning natural gas are also used to produce electricity. As it turned out, drought in the Pacific Northwest combined with rising natural gas prices to produce a surge in wholesale prices.

Ordinarily, California suppliers would have purchased insurance against such an event by entering into long-term contracts at prices mutually agreed upon ahead of time—prices that weren't subject to the day-to-day fluctuations of the volatile spot market. But of course such contracts had been made impermissible in California, forcing the utilities to buy at wholesale prices up to ten times higher than their long-term average. Just as important, in a truly deregulated market, higher wholesale costs would have been partially passed on to consumers in the form of higher retail prices. This in turn would have reduced **quantity demanded** and also dampened the financial losses for the utilities. But of course retail prices were fixed by the state. Hence the utilities suffered huge losses; moreover, to mitigate those losses they started ra-

tioning consumers in the only way left to them—by turning out
the lights in a series of rolling power blackouts, literally not supplying successive blocks of customers with electricity for hours at
a time. Even so, two of the biggest utilities in the state were pushed
into financial ruin.

Faced with the prospect of having *no* utilities around to supply
electricity, the state decided to become a middleman itself. It began
buying wholesale electricity from outside the state and then selling
to California consumers at the below-cost retail prices it had mandated. The financial drain eliminated the state's budgetary surplus
and ultimately has saddled its citizens with $7 billion in debt.

Where did things go wrong? Almost everywhere, but there are
two elements of California's supposed deregulation that are particularly relevant. First there was the state's prohibition against
long-term contracts. Electricity consumption is highly sensitive to
weather and business conditions—both of which are subject to
considerable uncertainty. Private firms have strong incentives to
make the best possible forecasts of the future, because if they are
correct they earn large profits, which quickly turn into large losses
if they are wrong. Ordinarily, firms minimize their expected costs
by using a blend of measures: long-term contracts to guard against
price increases and spot contracts to take advantage of price reductions. California rules prevented utilities from doing this, driving up their risks and ultimately their costs.

Just as important was the legal ceiling on retail electricity
prices. A crucial function of market prices is to encourage consumers to alter their consumption patterns in response to changes
in the true cost of goods. Thus, when the opportunity cost of goods
rises, high prices will correctly induce consumers to use less.
Alternatively, when the true cost of goods falls, low prices will
correctly induce consumers to take advantage by using more. In
this way we make the best use of our scarce resources. But in
California, the upper limit on retail prices meant that when the
cost of supplying electricity soared in 2000, consumers had no incentive to curtail their usage. With no other means of rationing
customers, the utilities were compelled to resort to inefficient nonprice rationing devices—in this case rolling power blackouts—that
are commonplace when governments interfere with market prices.

Few things in life are without irony, and California's energy crisis was no exception. By the spring of 2001, the rains had returned

to the Pacific Northwest and natural gas prices had begun to fall, in both cases pushing wholesale electricity prices down sharply. But during the height of the crisis, the California state government had chosen to use *long-term* contracts to acquire the electricity it was selling to consumers—the very same long-term contracts it had prevented private firms from using. With the decline in wholesale prices in 2001, this left the state government buying power at far more than current spot market prices—and left the taxpayers paying for the failure of their politicians to truly deregulate.

DISCUSSION QUESTIONS

1. In the midst of California's crisis, Governor Gray Davis said, "If I wanted to raise prices, I could solve this problem in 20 minutes." Was the Governor correct in saying this? If so, why didn't he do it?

2. Are customers better off with low electricity prices most of the day and no electricity some of the day than they would be with high prices all day? How does your answer depend on (i) how long the electricity is off under a price control regime, and (ii) how high prices get when they are allowed to move up?

3. The events in California illustrate that the choice of making purchases through the spot market versus using long-term contracts can have important effects on profitability. Is there any reason to believe that private sector firms might do a better job of making this choice than would legislators or other government agents? Can you think of a way to test your conjecture?

4. Electricity prices are typically regulated so that electric utilities are limited in the amount of profits they can make. Does this limit on profits likely affect the way these companies do business? For example, would it affect how careful they were about choosing between spot market purchases and long-term contracts? Would it affect the unionization rate or the rate at which cost-saving technologies are introduced?

Part Four

Market Structures

INTRODUCTION

The competitive model employed in our discussion of demand and supply assumes that firms on both sides of the market satisfy the conditions of **pure competition**. For sellers of goods, this means the demand curve they face is **perfectly elastic**: Suppliers must take the market price as given, because any attempt by them to raise their price above the market price will result in the loss of all of their sales. Similarly, purchasers in the competitive model face a supply curve that is also perfectly elastic. The market price is given, and any attempt by them to purchase at less than that price will be unsuccessful—no one will sell to them.

The conditions of pure competition imply that buyers and sellers have no effect individually on market prices. Even a casual glance at the world suggests that the conditions of pure competition are not always met. Sometimes, as is the case for major corporations, the firms are large enough relative to the market that significant changes in their purchase or sale decisions clearly must have an effect on prices. In other cases, buyers or sellers are somehow "unique," in that no other buyer or seller offers exactly what they do. (Classic examples include the superstars of sports and entertainment, who will sell less of their services if they raise their prices, but will still sell some.) Sometimes firms that otherwise would be pure competitors join to form a **cartel**, acting as a single decision-making unit whose collective output decisions affect the market price.

When a seller's decisions affect the price of a good, economists usually call the firm a **monopoly**. Literally, this means "single seller," but what is actually meant is that the firm faces a downward-sloping demand curve for its output, so that its decisions affect the price at which its output is sold. When a buyer's decisions affect the market price, we term the firm a **monopsony**, or "single buyer." This just means that the firm faces a positively sloped supply curve, so that its purchasing decisions affect the price at which it buys goods. (Some economists use the term **price searcher** to mean any firm—buyer or seller—whose decisions affect market prices, and who must therefore search for (or decide on) the price that maximizes the firm's profits. Following this terminology, a pure competitor would be called a **price taker**, for such a firm takes the market price as given.)

The starting point for our examination of different market structures, Chapter 14, "The Internet Economy," provides a look at some implications of the growth of commercial activity on the Internet. Many economists initially believed that the Internet would become the home of **pure competition** at its finest. Instead, two forces are combining to make price searchers the dominant organizational form on the Web. First, there are important **network effects**: sites such as Monster.com and eBay are more valuable to a given user the larger the number of *other* people who are also using them. Second, for most sites there are also important **economies of scale**: average costs are lower when the sites are larger. On both counts, there are tremendous competitive pressures for firms to consolidate down to one or a few dominant entities in each line of business. This has led to growing calls for government action to limit the pricing behavior and other business practices of these large firms. Such calls for government action are accompanied by other requests for government action to prevent piracy of **intellectual property**. Digital information is a tempting target for those who would steal ideas, and the Internet is the ideal medium for distributing the fruits of that theft. Between government efforts to prevent such behavior and to monitor the pricing behavior of large firms, the virtual world of the Web is starting to look a lot like the non-virtual reality we inhabited before the advent of the Internet.

As we see in Chapter 15, "Contracts, Combinations, and Conspiracies," even when there are no technical factors tending to reduce the number of viable firms, the rigors (and low profits) of competition are such that firms often try to devise ways to avoid competing. One of the most popular is the **cartel**, which is simply a collective agreement by many or all firms in an industry to reduce total output so that the price of the product—and thus the profits of the cartel's members—may be raised. Cartels generally are illegal in the United States, but they sometimes are observed in international markets. Here we examine three such cartels, in the markets for oil, diamonds, and caviar. In each case we find that although the incentives to form cartels are great, even greater are the incentives to cheat on the cartels, almost as soon as they are formed. The overriding message of this chapter is that, despite their enormous profit potential, competitive pressures make cartels inherently unstable, and thus generally short-lived.

Whatever the degree of competition, firms are always seeking ways to raise profits. Often this means developing new products and striving to offer superior service. But sometimes, as we see in Chapter 16, "Coffee, Tea, or Tuition-Free?", it simply means adjusting prices on existing products. The practice of charging prices that differ across customers in ways not due to differences in the marginal costs of supplying them is called **price discrimination.** Although technically illegal in the United States, it is routinely observed, in markets ranging from airline travel to college financial aid. In the case of air travel, you are almost certainly the beneficiary of price discrimination, paying a lower price than you would if price discrimination were completely eliminated. But don't feel too smug: By the time you start traveling for business rather than pleasure, you are likely to be on the wrong end of the price discrimination, paying plenty so that the college kid in the seat next to can enjoy Spring Break in a sunny clime.

Yet another way that firms try to enhance profits is **product differentiation**—that is, developing new products or styles that catch the fancy of customers and pull business away from one's rivals. The story of product differentiation is usually told as a tale of great financial gain to the firms that do it, inflicted at sizeable cost on consumers, who don't really "need" the new products. In fact, as we see in Chapter 17, "The Perils of Product Differentiation," a careful look at the record suggests that the practice is neither so easy nor so profitable as it might seem at first glance. Instead, it appears that consumers are considerably more discriminating than they are usually given credit for. Moreover, if they are not interested in what is being offered, they'll reject it—at great cost to the firm that tries to inflict it upon them. Because of this, product differentiation is a risky business, fraught with potential losses and likely to succeed only if the firms doing it have something that is truly of value to consumers. Thus, product differentiation seems to be much like any other business venture—likely to be successful only if the product is valued by the consumer, and on average an activity that can be expected to yield only the competitive rate of return.

As we see in Chapter 18, "Keeping the Competition Out," enlisting the government to hamstring or exclude competitors is probably the most reliable means of ensuring that you are protected from the rigors of competition. Perhaps for this reason, the array of markets in which the government stifles competition is nothing short of remarkable. Here we examine just a handful, ranging from taxicabs to hair braiding, but the list could have gone on and on. In each case, the method is the same: Usually under the guise of "consumer protection," the government prevents entry by some firms into a market, thereby reducing supply in that market. The effect is much the same as that produced by a fully enforced cartel. Firms thus protected by the government enjoy both a higher price for their product and a larger market share. Consumers—supposedly "protected" by their government—are usually the big losers, due to higher product prices and reduced selection among suppliers.

14

The Internet Economy

It didn't sound like much—one penny of profit per share. That was the operating profit that Amazon.com announced for the last quarter of 2001, a grand total of $5 million for those three months. That penny per share made headlines all over the country, even though many other companies made far larger profits without getting any press coverage. Why did Amazon's tiny profit make big news?

The reason is simple: Amazon.com was the first major Internet retailing company to show *any* profit. Indeed, precious few Internet companies of any description have ever made money. It was this almost universal lack of profits that played a key role in the dot-com stock market meltdown of 2000–2001. When investors got tired of yearly financial losses, they punished the Internet firms by dumping shares of those stocks. The result? The NASDAQ, a stock market index heavily weighted toward Internet stocks, lost over 60 percent of its value from its high in March of 2000 to its low in September of 2001.

Does all this mean the Internet economy is dead? Will nothing be left of the on-line world? The answer is: Definitely not. The Internet world is here to stay and grow and thrive. But it surely will be much different than many people thought it would be just a few years ago.

In the 1990s, it seemed that the commercial development of the Internet was going to yield thousands—or even millions—of tiny new companies, each with the capacity to reach all over the world from their Web sites. The result, it was confidently forecast, was that competition in the marketplace would be revolutionized, as dot-com startups effectively competed with (and sometimes out-competed) large-scale, old-line brick and mortar companies. To be sure, the dot-com companies tried this, but most of them never made it, and for the very reasons that make the Internet itself what it is. Let's see why.

An essential element of the Internet, and indeed of computer systems in general, is the presence of **network effects**. If just one person has an email account, it is worthless. But if a second person gets an account, email now has some value, and it becomes increasingly valuable as more and more people get accounts. Similarly, job-hunting sites such as Monster.com and auction sites such as eBay become more valuable to *other* people each time someone uses the sites. The result is that combining, say, many job-hunting sites into one site creates a single entity that is far more valuable than the sum of the previous independent entities. Thus, from the very day commercial activity started on the Internet, there were tremendous incentives to consolidate firms into larger and larger entities—and tremendous competitive pressure on any remaining smaller firms. The law of the jungle—eat or be eaten—soon took its toll.

There are also elements of the Internet that create **economies of scale**—that is, average costs that are lower when firms are larger. For example, to create a successful Web site, one must invest heavily in software development. But once the site is in existence, hundreds, thousands, or even millions of people can visit it without any additional new software. To be sure, more servers may have to be added, but many of the site's costs increase little as output rises, so average costs fall. This makes larger firms more formidable competitors, and creates an incentive for firms to consolidate, driving smaller competitors out of business.

Economies of scale are also referred to as **increasing returns,** a concept that is not new. The British economist Alfred Marshall discussed the notion back in the 1890s. He used as his examples the provision of electricity and gas to households and firms. At the time, the Standard Oil Trust in the United States was another real-world example of economies of scale. There was a big difference between then and now, however. At the beginning of the twentieth century Standard Oil, which was twice the size of its rivals, saw average costs fall by about 10 percent due to this size advantage. Such savings are tiny compared to what is possible in the knowledge economy of today. The reason is that once an idea is created, if the knowledge can be transformed into a digital string of zeros and ones, which is the case for movies, books, financial services, and software, then it can be reproduced and distributed via the Internet at a cost of almost zero. There are vast potential economies of scale with all knowledge-based products, importantly because of the Internet. The result is that a knowledge-intensive company that is twice as big as its rivals may have average costs that are 50 percent lower. This is the **natural monopoly** argument at its extreme—in the Internet economy, it is becoming more and more difficult for new entrants to break into the market because existing firms have already taken advantage of increasing returns to scale.

According to economist J. Bradford DeLong of the University of California at Berkeley and law professor A. Michael Froomkin of the University of Miami, the existence of factors such as these could prove to be the undoing of the Internet as we know it. These authors argue that the commercial aspects of the Net are going to be dominated by a few individual firms in each market sector. For example, there might be only a few major portals, such as Yahoo!, and a few auction sites, a few job-hunting sites, and so forth. Each of these major sites will be a monopoly or, at the very least an **oligopoly**, choosing prices well above marginal costs and enjoying freedom from substantial competition. DeLong and Froomkin suggest that in coming years, this could induce many consumers to clamor for government regulation of the prices and business practices of these companies. Ironically, the very medium that was originally envisioned to be the consummate example of pure competition may turn out to be merely one more haven for oligopolies—and one more venue for government regulation of private economic activity.

This pressure toward more government regulation of Internet firms will likely be intensified by another feature of the Internet economy—namely, its impact on the security of **intellectual property**. The total world value of intellectual property—movies, music, software, etc.—is at least as great as, and probably greater than, the total world value of physical property. Thus, what happens to intellectual properties is essential to economies around the world.

During the early days of the Internet, many observers felt that its most beneficial impact would be due to the instantaneous transmission of ideas it made possible. This, it was thought, would not merely enhance the current state of knowledge, but would also stimulate still more creative activity in the future. To some extent these predictions have been borne out, but there is another, darker side to this feature of the Internet.

Most intellectual property does not sell for the cost of reproduction plus a normal profit. Rather, intellectual property is sold at a higher price per unit that reflects the high fixed research costs involved in creating ingenious ideas. Any property that involves high research or development costs and low production costs is vulnerable to "piracy"—the unauthorized copying and use of the property. This is because to stay in business in the long run, the pirates don't have to cover the fixed costs of developing the good.

In the past, copying intellectual products was time consuming, and the pirated copies were worse than the originals. Even though the Xerox machine was vastly superior on both counts to transcription by hand, copying remained tedious and no copy was ever quite as good as the original. In today's on-line world, however, things have changed. Simply clicking a mouse can create millions of unauthorized copies, and pirated duplicates of copyrighted works obtained via the Internet are exactly the same as the originals—after all, they are digitized. Today, copyright law is based on national boundaries—but the Internet economy and its technology transcend those boundaries. Despite attempts to increase protection for intellectual property on a global level, countries vary widely in their implementation and enforcement of international agreements. The result is piracy on a widespread scale.

One example is file sharing, which has become a growing problem for intellectual property owners. Internet file sharing is accomplished through what is called peer-to-peer (P2P) networking. The concept is simple. Rather than going through a central Web server, P2P involves numerous personal computers (PCs) that are connected via the Internet. Others who are members of the same network can access files stored on one PC. Sometimes this is called a distributed network, because parts of the network are distributed all over the country or the world.

In all file-sharing arrangements, copyright issues abound. If you took this textbook to your local copy center and asked for fifty copies to resell to your classmates, you would be attempting to violate copyright law; the copy center would likely (we hope!) refuse your order. The materials in this text are copyrighted so that the authors and the publisher are rewarded for their efforts and so that the expense of publishing the text is covered. While Congress allows for "fair use," copying the entire book for resale (or even for distribution at no charge) would not fall under that exception to copyright law. File sharing over the Internet, when it involves copyrighted materials, is no different legally. Clearly, recording artists and their labels stand to lose large amounts of royalties and revenues if relatively few CDs are purchased and then made available on distributed networks, from which everyone can then get them for "free," which is to say, at a zero price to them and a zero return to the original creators. This is why many publishers, authors, and artists are concerned about unauthorized distribution of their works, and why the courts have so far taken a dim view of such activities.

Already some people are arguing that government should take a heavy hand in preventing intellectual piracy, including intensive (and intrusive) monitoring of who is doing what with their computers. After all, computer technologies developed to eavesdrop on international terrorists could be adapted to keep watch on domestic music fans. Moreover, one imagines, new government regulations could be devised that limit the hardware and software that individuals and firms are allowed to purchase. Although drastic measures such as these seem unbelievable to some, there is little doubt we will face a future ablaze with disagreements about whether Internet commerce should be subjected to the same kinds of governmental interventions that traditional firms have experienced. Thus, whether we are talking about product pricing or the protection of intellectual property, it seems the virtual world of the Web will probably end up looking a lot like the non-virtual reality we inhabited before the advent of the Internet.

DISCUSSION QUESTIONS

1. Suppose a firm invents a technology that reduces its costs so far that it can drive all of its competitors out of business, even though the price that maximizes the firm's profits is well above

its marginal cost. Would consumers be better off if this firm was forbidden from introducing its cost-saving technology?

2. Some music groups are in favor of allowing people to distribute their songs at no charge through P2P networks, while others are strongly opposed. Can you suggest why there are these differences of opinion?

3. Are the network effects present with the Internet fundamentally any different from those present with telephone systems or even from old-fashioned 3.5-inch disk drives and diskettes?

4. Some people argue that copyright protection and patent protection should be abolished, because the owners of patents and copyrights are effectively monopolists when it comes to supplying the goods for which they have these rights. What do you think would happen to the rate of innovation if patents and copyrights were abolished? What would be the likely impact on the well-being of consumers?

15

Contracts, Combinations, and Conspiracies

In December 2001, A. Alfred Taubman, chairman of the famous Sotheby's auction house, was convicted of masterminding an international price-fixing conspiracy with his firm's chief rival, Christie's. Taubman was convicted under the terms of the Sherman Act of 1890, which outlaws any "contract, combination, . . . or conspiracy, in restraint of trade or commerce" in the United States. Translated from the legalese, this means that firms in America may not lawfully join with competitors to form a **cartel** to raise prices above the competitive level.[1] Because successful cartels—like the alleged conspiracy between Sotheby's and Christie's—have the potential for great profits, there are strong incentives to form them. Usually, however, if the government discourages them, or even if it does not actively encourage them, cartels are difficult to keep together. This is because a cartel must meet four requirements if it is to be successful:

1. *Share*—It must control a large share of actual and potential output, so that other producers of the good it sells will not be able to depress prices by expanding output significantly.
2. *Substitutes*—Consumers must regard alternatives to the cartel's product as being relatively poor substitutes, and these substitutes must be few in number and relatively inelastic in

---

[1] Despite this, many American agricultural producers are legally permitted to collectively agree to raise their prices on products ranging from almonds to oranges. They do so under the umbrella of "marketing orders," which effectively are cartels approved and enforced by the U.S. Department of Agriculture.

supply; such factors all reduce the elasticity of demand facing the cartel, helping it to raise prices.

3. *Stability*—There must be very few outside factors that tend to disturb cost or demand conditions in the industry, so that the cartel is not continually having to make new price and output decisions in response to changing conditions.

4. *Solidarity*—It must be relatively easy for the cartel to maintain solidarity by identifying and punishing cartel members who cheat on the cartel agreement with price cuts.

All successful cartels have been able to meet these requirements to some extent. Conversely, it has been a breakdown in one or more of these factors that has been the downfall of each of them. In general, successful cartels are international in character. They are either effectively beyond (or exempt from) national laws forbidding them, or are encouraged by, or comprised of, governments themselves.

One of the most famous and successful cartels has been the Organization of Petroleum Exporting Countries (OPEC). Formed in 1960, its members have included many major oil producing countries, such as Algeria, Indonesia, Iran, Iraq, Kuwait, Libya, Nigeria, Saudi Arabia, and Venezuela. OPEC had little impact on the price of oil until the outbreak of the Middle East war in 1973 provided the impetus for cohesive action. Saudi Arabia, Kuwait, and several other Arab nations sharply reduced their production of oil; because the demand curve for oil is downward sloping, this reduction in supply pushed oil prices—and thus the profits of OPEC members—up sharply. On January 1, 1973, one could buy Saudi Arabian crude oil at $2.12 per barrel. Within one year, the price of crude had risen to $7.61 per barrel; by 1975, to $10.50; and by the end of the decade, the price of oil was $35 per barrel and rising.

Several forces combined to send oil prices in the opposite direction by the mid-1980s. At least partly in response to the high prices charged by OPEC, worldwide output of oil from other sources began to grow, led by rising production on Alaska's North Slope and by aggressive marketing of the oil flowing out of the Norwegian and British fields located in the North Sea. Eventually, this additional production significantly reduced the market share controlled by OPEC members, and helped reduce their stranglehold on price.

The most important problem for OPEC, however, as for so many cartels, has been cheating on the cartel agreement by its members. Whenever there are numerous firms or countries in a cartel arrangement, there will always be some that are unhappy with the situation, perhaps because they think they are not getting enough of the profits. They cheat by charging a slightly lower price than the one stipulated by the cartel, a move that will result in a very large increase in the cheater's revenues (and thus profits). The potential for cheating is a constant threat to a cartel's existence, and when enough of a cartel's members try to cheat, the cartel breaks up.

In the case of OPEC, war between the member nations of Iran and Iraq during the 1980s precipitated a major outbreak of cheating, as those two nations expanded production beyond their quotas, using the extra sales to finance heavy military expenditures. The price of crude oil plunged to $10 per barrel in 1986, when cheating on output quotas spread throughout the cartel. OPEC member Saudi Arabia, the world's largest producer of crude, finally restored order when it threatened to double its output if other OPEC members did not adhere to quotas. Although there have been short-lived price spikes since then (in 1990-91 and 2000-01) crude oil prices typically have hovered around $20 per barrel; after adjusting for inflation, this is more than 75 percent cheaper than in 1980.

The perils faced by cartels are also illustrated in the diamond market, where DeBeers Consolidated Mines, the famous diamond company, has controlled as much as 80 percent of the world supply. Although DeBeers itself produces only about 35 percent of the world's diamond output, it typically has directed the marketing of another 35–45 percent through a cartel called the Central Selling Organization, or CSO. The CSO has long restricted the sale of rough-cut diamonds to keep their prices at levels that maximize the profits of its members. After many years of profitable success, however, the diamond cartel hit rough times. Cartel profits spurred searches for new sources of supply, and major discoveries were made in Australia and Canada. Moreover, Russia, which accounted for about one-fourth of CSO's output, became a chronic cheater on CSO rules by permitting diamonds to "leak" into international markets. The combined effect of these forces has been substantial. In 1980, the wholesale price of investment-grade D-flawless diamonds—considered the most reliable measure of market conditions in the industry—was about $55,000 per carat. After adjusting for inflation, D-flawless diamonds recently have been worth 85 percent less.

Russians have had troubles with their own historically successful cartel, the one that controls—or controlled—the supply of fine caviar. The principal source of some of the world's best caviar is the Volga River Delta, where Kazakhstan and Russia (both former members of the Soviet Union) share a border at the northern end of the Caspian Sea. Both the temperature and salinity of the water in the Delta make it the ideal spawning ground for sturgeon, the long-nosed prehistoric fish whose eggs have for centuries been viewed as the world's finest caviar. Originally, the Russian czars and czarinas ran the show, eating what they wanted of the harvest, and then controlling the remaining supplies to their advantage.

Once the Bolsheviks disposed of the Romanovs in 1917, they quickly saw the potential profits to be had from cornering the market on caviar. Thus, for the next 75 years or so, a Soviet state-dominated cartel controlled the nation's caviar business from top to bottom. Although the Soviet sturgeon were considerate enough to produce an annual catch of some 2,000 tons of caviar, the communist cartel allowed only 150 tons out of the country. As a result, a state-supplied kilogram (2.2 pounds) of top-grade black caviar costing $5 or less on the Moscow black market, commanded $1000 or more in New York.

The demise of the Soviet Union spawned trouble, however, for competition reared its ugly head. As it turns out, the largest sturgeon fisheries fell under the jurisdictions of two different autonomous republics—Russia and Kazakhstan—each of which wanted to own and operate its own lucrative caviar business. Moreover, a variety of individuals, including enterprising Caspian Sea fishermen from these republics, staked private claims, and in some cases set up their own export channels (behavior officially termed "black market piracy"). The effect of this capitalist behavior was a 20-percent drop in the official caviar export price during the first year of autonomy, plus an escalation of competition since then.

Caviar consumers were pleased at this turn of events, but old-line suppliers were not quite so happy. "We don't need this kind of competition," complained one. "All of these small rivals mean that prices will fall and the market will be ripped apart. This is a delicacy—we need to keep it elite." Recent years have seen a sharp upswing in world caviar prices, although not because Russia and Kazakhstan have managed to get competition under control. Instead, it turns out that pollution from left-over Soviet industry in the area has helped sharply reduce the region's sturgeon population. The resulting decline in the amount of harvestable caviar drove costs and prices up, and profits even lower. Adding insult to injury, firms in America (whose costs are not affected by the Soviet pollution) have entered the caviar market in response to the higher prices, intensifying the price-cost squeeze that the former Soviet republics are suffering. And so, just as Soviet citizens found that communism wasn't all that it was cracked up to be, it appears some of them are now learning that capitalism may be more than they bargained for—but perhaps no less than Karl Marx warned them about.

DISCUSSION QUESTIONS

1. Why are all cartels inherently unstable?

2. Would it be easier to form a cartel in a market with many producers or one with very few producers?

3. What happens to the producers of caviar made from other types of fish eggs (such as salmon, whitefish, and trout) when the price of the finest sturgeon caviar changes? Would these firms ever have an incentive to help the governments of Russia and Kazakhstan re-establish the caviar cartel?

4. If the members of your class were to attempt to form a study-reduction cartel in which everyone agreed to study less, which individuals would have the greatest to gain from the cartel? Which ones would have the greatest incentive to cheat on the cartel?

16

Coffee, Tea, or Tuition-Free?

A few years ago, Internet retailing giant Amazon.com received some unwanted publicity when it was revealed that the company was charging different prices for movies sold to different customers. Amazon insisted that the price differences were random and amounted to an effort to simply test the market. But some customers complained that Amazon was using the practice to tailor prices to customer characteristics, charging more to people who were likely to be willing to pay more. The flap over Amazon's "market test" soon died out, but as time passes, Internet firms will find it almost irresistible to regularly charge different prices to different customers. The reason is simple: by tracking past buying habits, other sites visited, and so forth, firms can get a pretty good idea of how to engage in **price discrimination** among their customers, and thus increase their profits.

Now, price discrimination not only sounds like something that should be illegal, it *is* illegal, at least under some circumstances. Despite that, it is routinely practiced by businesses of all descriptions—and perhaps even by the college you attend. Interestingly, although price discrimination definitely benefits the firms (or colleges) that engage in it, you too may benefit. Let's see how.

First things first: Price discrimination is defined as the existence of price differences across customers for the same good that are not due to differences in the marginal costs of supplying the customers. Thus, price discrimination can occur when marginal costs are the same across customers, but prices are different, or when prices are the same, despite differences in marginal costs. An example of the former occurs when pharmacies or movie theaters charge lower prices to "senior citizens" than to other customers. An example of the latter can be found at "all-you-can-eat" buffets, where the price is the same to all diners, even though some eat much more food than others.

There are three conditions that must exist for a firm to engage in price discrimination. First, the firm must be, at least to some extent, a **price searcher**—that is, it must be able to raise price above marginal cost without losing all of its sales to rivals. Second, there must be identifiable differences across customers in their willingness (or ability) to pay different prices for the same good. Third, the firm must be able to prevent customers who pay lower prices from reselling the good to customers who otherwise would be charged higher prices—or else customers eligible for the lowest price will buy on behalf of all customers.

The objective of price discrimination is, of course, higher profits for the firm that engages in it. To see how this might work, consider a firm selling to two identifiable groups of customers, say, retirees and working people. Also suppose that the retirees have lower income, and so perhaps have a higher **price elasticity of demand** for the good; that is, they tend to be more sensitive to changes in price. In this case, it may be possible for the firm to reallocate sales among customer groups, lowering prices slightly to retirees and raising them somewhat more to working people, thereby getting more revenue at the same costs, and so earning higher profits. Of course to be able to accomplish this, it must be possible to distinguish between the two groups. (This is often approximated by offering the lower prices only to persons who can prove they are older, and thus more likely to be retired.) Moreover, the firm must be able to prevent resale from low-price buyers to other customers; in the case of prescription medicines, pharmacies are aided by federal and state laws that forbid such resale, while in the case of movie theaters, the person getting the lower price generally must attend the movie personally to get the lower price. (This helps explain why movie rental companies like Blockbuster are less likely to offer senior citizen discounts than are movie theaters: it would be too easy for seniors to rent movies

on behalf of other people who wish to avoid the higher prices ap-
plicable to them.)

If you have ever traveled on an airplane, you are likely to have
been a beneficiary of price discrimination (although your par-
ents—or their employers— may have been the victim of such discrimination, if they fly on short-notice business trips). Prior to
1978, the fares charged by airlines in the United States were regulated by the federal government, and so all airlines offered the
same government-approved fares; discounts were rare beyond
late-night ("red-eye") or weekend flights.[1] Once deregulation occurred, airlines quickly discovered there were large differences in
the price elasticity of demand across customers: business travelers
typically had a lower price elasticity of demand—and thus were
willing to pay higher fares—than leisure travelers. Fares charged
business travelers are now higher than they used to be, even
though leisure fares are significantly lower than they were in the
days of government regulation.

The precision and effectiveness with which the airlines engage
in price discrimination have been rising steadily over time, thanks
to a process known as "yield management." Combining sophisticated statistical techniques and massive historical databases, together with computerized up-to-the-minute bookings, the airlines
can predict with almost pinpoint accuracy how many business customers will want seats on a given flight—and how much they'll be
willing to pay. As a result, says one industry insider, "high fares get
higher and low fares get lower."

The process begins months before a flight ever departs, as the
airline divides the seats on a plane into as many as seven or more
different fare classes, or categories. Initial fares on a flight are established for each of the categories, and the yield-management
computers begin the process of monitoring the reservations, comparing them to historical patterns. If advance bookings are slow,
the airline will add seats to low-fare categories. But if business
travelers buy higher-priced, unrestricted tickets sooner than expected, the yield-management computer removes seats from dis-

---

[1] Those fares were also considerably higher on average than they are today, because the
federal government agency responsible for regulating the airlines also prevented them
from competing with one another on the basis of price.

count categories and holds them for last-minute business passengers that are predicted to show up.

A host of techniques are utilized to optimize the blend between filling the seats on a plane and getting the highest possible fare for each seat. In the weeks leading up to a flight, the level of fares assigned to each category may be adjusted up or down based on the latest moves by competitors, and as the flight date approaches, lower-priced categories are likely to be closed out altogether. Moreover, some people seeking reservations may be told a given flight is "sold out" even though passengers using that flight as a connector to another of the airline's routes may find ample seating—for a price, of course. The result of all this fine tuning is that passengers on the same flight from, say, Chicago to Phoenix, may pay round trip fares that vary by a factor of *five*—ranging, say, from $240 for the lowest-priced seats to $1400 for the top fares.

Interestingly, the same yield management techniques refined by the airlines are now being used by universities when they decide on financial aid packages offered to students. After all, given the nominal tuition at a university, a more generous financial aid offer can be thought of as a lower price, and students like everyone else behave according to the law of demand. Universities have found, for example, that they can offer less generous aid packages to students who apply for early admission, because such students are more anxious to attend; as one financial aid consultant notes, "those who have the most interest in the school are going to be less price sensitive." In a similar vein, some colleges have found that people who come for campus interviews are more interested in attending; the response has been to offer slightly less generous aid packages to such students, even though the colleges routinely recommend that students come for interviews.

In addition to these regular features of price discrimination in financial aid offers, universities also monitor their enrollment figures each year, just as the airlines watch bookings by fare category. If a school is getting, say, too many pre-med students and not enough in the humanities, financial aid offers will be adjusted accordingly, with bigger-than-usual aid offers being made to the students the school is trying to attract. Schools that are noted for excellence in one area but are trying to maintain a balanced mix of majors have become particularly adept at the financial aid game.

As the enrollment vice president for Carnegie Mellon University notes, without sophisticated adjustments to the blend of aid packages offered, "I'd have an institution full of engineers and computer scientists and I wouldn't have anybody in arts and design." Carnegie Mellon also recognizes the importance of competition in determining the prices it charges: After admitted students are notified of their aid offers in the spring, they are invited to fax the school any better offers they receive from other colleges. Using money from a special fund set aside for the purpose, the university generally meets competing offers received by desirable students.

Although price discrimination certainly profits the firms that practice it, there is an entirely different question—one that cannot be answered by economics—as to whether it is fair. Most college students who can stay over a Saturday night, or make reservations a month in advance, probably don't mind the lower fares made possible by price discrimination. But business travelers are far from pleased with the high fares they must pay to get where they want, when they want to, usually on short notice. "They've got you and they know it," says one executive. The flip side, of course, is that without the extra revenue generated by price discrimination, some companies or colleges would be hard-pressed to survive. Indeed, when asked about the equity of fine-tuning aid packages to willingness to attend rather than ability to pay, one financial aid official noted he had little choice in the matter: "I could make it very fair—and be out of business."

DISCUSSION QUESTIONS

1. First-class passengers generally pay higher fares than coach class passengers, even when they take advantage of advance purchase discounts. Is this price discrimination? (Hint: Seats in first class are generally leather rather than fabric, and are about 50 percent wider than coach seats. Also, there are more flight attendants per passenger in the first-class section.)

2. Is it price discrimination when a professional football team charges, say, $150 per ticket for 50-yard line tickets in the lower deck and $30 per ticket for upper deck tickets overlooking the end zone?

3. What factors other than income are likely to affect willingness to pay? How will differences in these factors among its customers affect the likelihood that a firm will engage in price discrimination?

4. Do you think price discrimination is fair? Does your answer depend on whether you get a lower price as a result? Does your answer depend on whether the company you work for— or own—would go out of business if it refrained from price discriminating?

17

The Perils of Product Differentiation

The story of **product differentiation** is usually told as a tale of great financial gain to the firms that do it, inflicted at sizeable cost on consumers, who don't really "need" the new products. Whether it is fast food, soft drinks, clothing styles, or automobile models, the reasoning seems to be this: Develop a catchy name or theme, design a slick advertising campaign to clearly differentiate your product from others on the market, and presto—instant wealth.

At first blush, the story seems eminently plausible. After all, are "Tommy Jeans" really any better than Levi's? Is a Whopper fundamentally different from a Big Mac? And does anybody believe the Gateway cows make the company's computers any faster? In each case, the firms that differentiated their product from those of their rivals profited handsomely. And in each case, it is remarkably difficult to come up with any objective evidence that one product is much different from another—much less any *better*. Product differentiation, it seems, is the sure road to financial success: Gullible consumers will buy almost anything, if it is just "positioned"—packaged and advertised—properly.

In fact, a careful look at the record suggests that product differentiation is neither so easy nor so profitable as it might seem at first glance. Instead, it appears that consumers are considerably more discriminating than they are usually given credit for. Moreover, if they are not interested in what is being offered, they'll reject it—at great cost to the firm that tries to inflict it upon them. Because of this, product differentiation is a risky business, fraught with potential losses and likely to succeed only if the firms doing it have something that is truly of value to consumers. The fact is that most new products fail—often spectacularly. Thus, product differentiation seems to be much like any other business venture—likely to be successful only if the product is valued by the consumer, and on average an activity that can be expected to yield only the competitive rate of return. A look back at history will suggest why this is so.

Our first episode takes us back nearly half a century and involves an icon of American industry—the Ford Motor Company. On September 2, 1957 amid pronouncements that "this product will raise the industry standard to a new level," Ford introduced a new automobile; its name was the Edsel. The car's unveiling culminated nearly ten years of research and development costing roughly $1.5 billion in today's terms. The company's official goal for first year sales of the Edsel was 200,000 vehicles. Little more than *half* this number were actually sold in the first *two* years of the model's existence. After several attempts to save the floundering wonder car (including a major reorganization of the Edsel division, and a complete redesign of the car) Edsel production was discontinued in November of 1959—just two years, two months, and fifteen days after its much-heralded introduction. The failure was so spectacular that the car became an object of derisive humor on a host of television shows, and one historian of the episode remarked that "compared with the Edsel, Custer's Last Stand was a victory." Overall, it appears that Ford lost more than $5 billion in today's terms—some 40 percent of the entire value of the company. The product that was supposed to restore it to industry leadership very nearly brought the company to it knees.

What went wrong? It certainly wasn't a lack of promotional efforts. By the time the Edsel was launched, Ford had recruited almost 1200 Edsel dealers to market and distribute the car. The advertising company handling the Edsel added sixty new employees to service the account and even opened a branch in Detroit, headquarters of Ford. The advertising campaign began in the fall of 1955, some two years before the Edsel hit the market. And the promotional effort was so intensive that, shortly before the car's 1957 unveiling, one Ford executive remarked that "When [consumers] find out it's got four wheels and one engine, just like the next car, they're liable to be disappointed."

And disappointed they were. Styling was one feature that Ford hoped would differentiate the Edsel from other cars, for it included a host of new features, including a vertically oriented grill with rounded corners. The problem, according to consumers, was that the car looked like "a Ford sucking a lemon." Perhaps the lemon analogy was appropriate, for within weeks of the Edsel's introduction, reports of manufacturing defects in the car became rampant—oil leaks, trunks that wouldn't open, inferior paint jobs, sagging springs, and incorrect rear axle ratios all became facts of life for Edsel buyers. The Edsel was different all right, and consumers quickly rejected it.

The Ford Motor Company is not the only corporate giant to have suffered at the hands of the consumers whom it supposedly controls. Consider the Coca-Cola Company, which on April 23, 1985 held a heavily publicized news conference to announce "the most significant soft drink marketing development in the company's history." Coca-Cola, the soft drink that had been the company's leading brand for nearly 100 years, was to be replaced with a formula (soon to be dubbed "new Coke") expected to be a more vigorous competitor for its chief rival, Pepsi. The announcement electrified millions across the country, and became the lead story on the evening's national news broadcasts. According to *Time* magazine, 81 percent of the U.S. population knew of the change in formula within 48 hours, more people than were aware in July 1969 that Neil Armstrong had walked on the moon. By June, fully 96 percent of Americans knew of new Coke. Indeed, Coca-Cola executives estimated that the news stories generated by the decision to change the formula were worth the equivalent of $150 million in advertising expenditures. It is difficult to find another product in history that has been launched with anything like the attention received by new Coke. Success—and profits—it seemed, were assured.

There was just one problem: the company's customers didn't like the new formula. Within a month, the company was getting 5,000 letters every week objecting to the change in formula, as well as that many complaining telephone calls every *day*. Perhaps more importantly, consumers backed up their complaints in the grocery stores and fast food restaurants, staying away from new Coke in droves. Company officials became increasingly concerned that their April decision had been a disastrous mistake, and on July 9 the Board of Directors decided to reverse that mistake:

Two days later, the original formula—newly dubbed "Coca-Cola Classic"—was back. By some estimates, the financial damage to the company was $1 billion in today's dollars.

It is tempting to think that mistakes such as those made by Ford and Coca-Cola are matters of history, unlikely to be repeated in the modern world of marketing focus groups and sophisticated computer-modeling of consumer behavior. The great Burger King french fry fiasco suggests otherwise. Although Burger King has long led the nation in taste tests of hamburgers, its larger rival, McDonald's, has remained top dog in the french fry department. This is a matter of some importance to all concerned, because with a profit margin as high as 80 cents on the dollar, fries are the most lucrative item on the fast food menu. Thus, after two years of intensive research and development, and armed with a $70 million marketing budget, Burger King launched a new line of french fries on January 2, 1998.

Burger King was determined to differentiate its product from McDonald's popular fry, hoping to do so with a special preparation that guaranteed extra crispiness. So exacting was the company that the specifications for preparing the new fries ran to 19 pages. And although the process was complicated, franchisees were excited. Said one, an owner of 41 Burger Kings, "This fry was supposed to be our salvation." For a while, it looked like it was. Intrigued by expensive Super Bowl advertising and a give-away of 15 million orders of fries on "Free Fryday," consumers swarmed into Burger Kings to try it out. By the middle of 1998, the company had sold 150 million more orders of fries than the same period the year before. But soon enough, consumers had enough: some said it was too salty, others too crispy. Some complained the fries clumped together, and others thought they were bitter. But whatever their words, their behavior said it all: they stayed away in droves, and by 1999 Burger King french fry sales were down 14 percent. Soon thereafter, the company pulled the plug: the fry that was to be salvation is no more. And although the company is tight-lipped on how much the fry fiasco cost, the president of Burger King's National Franchise Association made it clear how the franchisees felt: "The g— d— fry was bad—horrendous." Consumers, it seems, agreed.

Of course not all cases of product differentiation are like the disasters we have examined here. Indeed, if they were, no sensible business would seek to differentiate their goods from competitors'. The point instead is that product differentiation, for all of its oft-told stories of success, is far from being a road to riches. Like all economic endeavors, there are revenues, costs, and risks involved. There is no guarantee the profits will be positive, much less enough to warrant the risks. To hope to achieve even a competitive rate of return on differentiated products, companies must deliver to their customers a quality product at a reasonable price. This was a lesson that certainly made an impression on Donald Keogh, president of Coca-Cola in 1985. In announcing the return of the original formula to the shelves, Keogh apologized to consumers for the decision to launch new Coke. The episode, he said, had convinced him that "Our boss is the consumer." One guesses that Ford and Burger King would agree.

DISCUSSION QUESTIONS

1. If a firm can either devote resources to selling or improving an existing product, or to developing and differentiating a new product, what must be true about the profit rate on both activities in equilibrium?

2. Suppose that a large fraction of differentiated products fail. What will be true about the profit rate observed on differentiated products that happen to *succeed*? (Hint: Keep in mind your answer to Question 1.)

3. Suppose that product differentiation activity is much riskier than most other business ventures. What would you expect the profit rate for product differentiation to be, compared to the average profit rate on other business activities?

4. What parallels can you draw between the supposed "instant wealth" accessible to firms that differentiate products and the "instant wealth" that appeared to be available to anyone who started up a dot-com company in the 1990s? Does the experience of the dot-coms have any message here?

18

Keeping the Competition Out

Most competitors hate competition. And who can blame them? After all, if a firm can keep the competition out, profits are sure to rise. How high they will rise obviously varies by industry, but the lowly taxicab market gives some indication of what is at stake. In New York City, the number of taxicabs is limited by law—limited, in fact, to 12,187 cabs in a city of 8 million people. (That's about one cab for every 650 people, in a town where many people don't own cars.) To legally operate a taxi in New York, one must own a taxi medallion, a city-issued metal shield affixed to a cab's hood. After capping the number of medallions since 1937, the city offered 133 new ones for sale in 1996. Winning bidders paid about $175,000 for each medallion—that is, for the right to work seventy-hour weeks, subject to robbery, rude customers, and the erratic driving habits of other cabbies. And lest you think New York taxi drivers are crazy to pay such sums, keep this in mind: Because the city keeps the competition out, the taxi business is so lucrative that the medallions can be used as collateral to borrow money at favorable interest rates, and any cabby who wants to leave the business can immediately find a buyer for his medallion, usually at a price that will bring even more profit. And those new medallions that went for $175,000 in 1996? Well, by 1998 they had risen in value to over $250,000, but more recently their prices have dropped back to "only" $200,000.

Keeping the competition out works this way: Reducing the number of firms in an industry decreases the supply of the good, thus driving up its price. Firms that remain thereby enjoy both a higher price for their product and a larger market share. Consumers lose, however, suffering not only from higher prices but also from fewer alternative sources of supply from which to choose. Another group of losers is comprised of the firms who are excluded. They are forced to go into lower-paying pursuits for which they are not as well suited. The higher profits enjoyed by the firms that are protected from competition thus come at the expense of consumers and excluded competitors; the net result is also an overall loss to society as a whole, because the limit on competition reduces the total extent of mutually beneficial exchange.

Note we said that the number of taxi medallions in New York is limited by the government. This is typical. Even though many government agencies (for example, the Federal Trade Commission and the Department of Justice at the federal level) are supposed to promote competition, the most effective way to *prevent* competition is usually to get the government involved. Consider telephones. It used to be that both long-distance and local telephone markets were regulated by the federal government. In 1984 the long-distance market was deregulated, and AT&T had to begin competing with MCI and Sprint for customers. The result was a 40 percent drop in inflation-adjusted long-distance rates. Local telephone service continued to be regulated by the Federal Communications Commission (FCC), however, and over the same period of time, local phone rates have *risen* 40 percent in real terms—chiefly because the FCC has kept competition out of the local phone service market.

The government of Mexico has been even more successful in protecting phone giant Telmex from competition. Formerly a state-owned company, Telmex was privatized in 1990, with the understanding that the government would gradually but steadily end the firm's monopoly. The thought was nice, but the monopoly remains. Telmex has effectively been permitted to prevent potential entrants to the Mexican phone market from connecting through its dominant switching equipment. The result has been sky-high connection charges and virtually no new connections. Hence, there are now only 10 telephones per 100 inhabitants of Mexico. In Poland, the fellow member of the Organization of Economic Cooperation and Development with the next fewest number of lines, there are 20 telephones per 100 inhabitants. In addition to poor service, the lack of competition also shows up in prices, which sharply hampers

Mexican businesses. For example, a U.S. firm trying to drum up business in London would pay $5.40 to make five phone calls to Britain of four minutes each. Those same calls would cost its Mexican rival $25.40.

Many of the decision makers who work for the government agencies that limit competition are lawyers, so it is not surprising that competition among lawyers is limited. For example, in every state but one (California), the number of law schools is capped by state law, thereby restricting entry into the profession and driving up earnings. The high fees lawyers earn have in turn generated competition from lawyers' assistants, called paralegals. This competition—or rather, attempted competition—can be seen in the market for personal bankruptcies. Rising consumer debt, combined with less restrictive federal bankruptcy law, has produced a massive increase in personal bankruptcies. During the 1990s, the number of people declaring bankruptcy tripled. A typical personal bankruptcy case costs about $750 when done by a lawyer, but the procedure is a simple one, requiring only that some standard paperwork be filled out and filed with the relevant authorities. Thus, in come the paralegals (who, if working for a lawyer, would be doing the paperwork anyway), offering to perform the same services for, say, $269. Faced with competition like this, the legal profession struck back, gaining passage of Section 110 of the Bankruptcy Reform Act. This statute gives judges the power to cap the fees paralegals can charge. Thus far, imposed caps have run from $50 to $100 per case, which is low enough to force most paralegals out. Paralegals who charge more than the legal limit are subject to fines of up to $500 for each violation of the law. Lawyers are free to charge what they like, sometimes as much as $1500, now that they don't have paralegals to worry about.

Sometimes the government gets involved in some unlikely markets in its efforts to prevent the ravages of competition from taking their toll. Consider hair braiding. Some African Americans like to have their hair straightened in beauty shops, a procedure that requires a touch-up every four weeks, for an average monthly cost (excluding cutting and styling) of about $100. An alternative is to get one's hair braided at a braiding salon. There are now about 10,000 of these salons across the country, and they are growing in popularity. Braids need maintenance only once every ten weeks, cutting the cost to $50 per month. The same low cost and convenience that make braiding salons attractive to consumers also make them threatening to the conventional beauty shops that straighten hair, especially in fashion-conscious California. Claiming that they are seeking to protect consumers, agents of the California Barbering & Cosmetology Board have begun raiding the salons of unlicensed hair braiders. Not surprisingly, the hair braiders think the state is actually trying to protect state-licensed cosmetologists at beauty shops, who must spend $6000 for 1600 hours of training to get their licenses. Indeed, one of the braiders, Ali Rasheed, argues that the marketplace is better than state licensing boards at protecting consumers. "It's simple," he says. "If I mess up your hair, you don't come back. You spread the word. And very quickly I'd be out of business." Perhaps so, but it looks like the state of California doesn't want to give consumers that option.

Apparently, the government doesn't like competition, either. The U.S. Postal Service, a federal government corporation, faces potential competition from Federal Express, a privately owned express delivery company. Although the Postal Service has been unable to prevent FedEx from making considerable inroads on its parcel delivery service, it has had more luck in keeping FedEx out of the first-class mail business, by getting the U.S. Congress to mandate that anyone wishing to have a letter delivered by FedEx must affix postage stamps in addition to paying the FedEx delivery rates!

Back in New York, there is yet another example of the fact that the government likes to protect itself from competition. New York City is well known for its massive public transit system, comprising both subways and bus lines. What is not so well known is that mass transit in New York City started off as private enterprise. The first horsecars and elevated trains in the city were developed by private companies. Moreover, even though New York's first subway was partly financed by a loan from the city, it was otherwise a private operation, operated profitably at a fare of a nickel (the equivalent of less than a dollar today).

New York's politicians refused to allow fares to rise during the inflation of World War I, yielding financial losses for the private transit companies. Promising to show the private sector how to run a transit system efficiently, while simultaneously offering to protect the public from the "dictatorship" of the transit firms, the city took over the subway, merged it with the bus line, and promptly started raising fares. Despite fare increases double the inflation rate, however, costs have risen even faster, so that today, even though the basic fare is $1.50, the city *loses* $2 a passenger.

Enter the jitneys, privately owned vans that operate along regular routes, like buses, but which charge only a $1 a passenger and will make detours for pick-ups and drop-offs on request. Actually, we should have said "attempted entry" by the jitneys, because the New York City Council—at the insistence of the public transit system—has denied operating permits to almost all jitney operators who have applied. The Council says it is only seeking to prevent the vans from causing accidents and traffic problems, but even fully insured drivers who have met federal requirements for operating interstate van services are routinely denied permits. Thus most of the hundreds of jitneys operating in New York City do so illegally. Even the few jitneys that have managed to get licensed are forbidden from operating along public bus routes—all in the name of public safety, of course.

Transportation economists such as Daniel Klein of Santa Clara University have argued that public transit systems could once more be profitable—instead of losing sixty cents on the dollar—if the jitneys were given a chance. "Government has demonstrated that it has no more business producing transit than producing cornflakes. It should concentrate instead on establishing new rules to foster competition," says Klein. Unfortunately for the jitneys and their customers, however, that competition would come at the expense of New York's public transit system. Thus, for the foreseeable future, it seems the jitneys will have to compete only by breaking the laws, because like most competitors, the New York City mass transit system just hates competition.

DISCUSSION QUESTIONS

1. If you were operating a business, would you encourage competitors to start operating in your market? Would you attempt to use legal means to prevent them from competing with you?

2. Consider two different ways of beating your competition. One is to offer your customers lower prices and better service. The other is to get a law passed that raises your competitors' costs—for example, by imposing special operating requirements on them. Can you see any difference between these two, assuming that both succeed in keeping your competition out?

3. Although governments at all levels sometimes act to prevent some individuals from competing with others, the federal government is probably the most active in this role, state governments are less active, and local governments are the least active. Can you explain this pattern?

4. Is there any difference between prohibiting entry by a group of firms and levying a special tax on those firms?

Part Five

Political Economy

INTRODUCTION

The chief focus of economics has always been on explaining the behavior of the private sector. Yet dating back at least to the publication of Adam Smith's *Wealth of Nations* more than 200 years ago, economists have never missed an opportunity to apply their theories to additional realms of behavior. For the past thirty years or so, much of this effort has been devoted to developing theories that explain the actions of governments, as well as the consequences of those actions. This undertaking is often referred to as the study of political economy, for it often involves a mixture of politics and economics. As the selections in this section hint, economists do not yet have a unified theory of government. Nevertheless, they are making progress and are sometimes able to offer surprising insights.

One of the first things that economists had to learn about government decision making is that the costs of government policies are always higher than promised, and the benefits are always lower. This simple proposition forms the centerpiece of Chapter 19, "Killer Cars and the Rise of the SUV," which explores the implications of federal rules that specify the minimum fuel efficiency permitted for new cars sold in the United States. Sometimes the effects of the federal regulations are surprisingly pervasive—as they are when they induce one-third of American drivers to switch from cars to trucks in response to federal fuel economy rules. Sometimes the effects are at least moderately expensive—as they are when they induce companies to spend millions of dollars redesigning vehicles, not to make them more fuel efficient but solely to satisfy the peculiar accounting conventions of the regulations. And sadly, sometimes the effects of the regulations are tragic: Indeed, reliable estimates suggest that the federal fuel economy standards have forced automakers to downsize their cars to such an extent as to make them less crashworthy. It is estimated that 3000 Americans lose their lives in traffic accidents every year as a result of these particular regulations.

Many government regulatory programs are supposed to protect lives. For example, the federal Superfund program was implemented in 1980 with the avowed goal of protecting Americans from the hazards of toxic wastes. It was supposed to be a short-lived, speedy program to rid the nation of dangerous waste disposal sites, such as the notorious Love Canal in New York. It was to cost at most a few billion dollars, paid for by those firms whose pollution had posed the risks or caused the harms. *Not one* of these goals has been achieved: As we see in Chapter 20, "Superfund Follies," cleanup is slow, costs are astronomical, and much of the program's resources are diverted to activities that do little good. How could such a well intentioned program turn out to be such a "disaster" as one U.S. president has termed it? Perhaps not surprisingly, the answer is politics, and so the Superfund program is a fascinating, albeit sad, example of political economy in action.

Crime rates that have gone up hand-in-hand with prison populations, coupled with criminals who seem impervious to law enforcement, have led many people to ask a simple if disturbing question: Is there *any* effective way to fight crime? Although economic theory says the answer to this question is "yes," the empirical estimates obtained by economists have said, well, "maybe." Yet as we see in Chapter 21, "Crime and Punishment," new evidence is shedding light on the answer to this question. Indeed, it is increasingly clear that the two central tools of traditional law enforcement—police to apprehend the criminals and prisons to punish them—may be every bit as effective as their proponents claim in discouraging criminal activity. Two lessons that emerge from this chapter are that politicians are likely to continue pouring more money into law enforcement, and those resources are going to have a growing impact in reducing crime in America.

For thirty years America struggled with the baby-boom generation as it graduated from bassinets to BMWs. For the next thirty years, we shall have to grapple with the problems that arise as the boomers progress from corporate boardrooms to nursing homes. As we see in Chapter 22, "The Graying of America," our nation is aging at the fastest rate in our history. It will not be long before all of America looks much like Florida, the retirement capital of the world, looks today. As America ages, two major problems in political economy are emerging. First, we must face the issue of paying the Social Security and Medicare bills of the rapidly growing elderly portion of the population. Second, as increasing numbers of people retire, there will be fewer workers capable of bearing the growing tax burden. America must learn new ways of utilizing the productive capabilities of the elderly and accept the fact that—as much as we may wish otherwise—sometimes the elderly may simply have to fend for themselves; otherwise, today's college students will soon find the financial burden beyond their capacity.

Although much of what economists have to say about political economy is critical of the behavior of government, there is one area where there is general agreement that government potentially has an important productive role to play: This is in the provision of commodities called **public goods**. These are goods that have two characteristics: Consumption by one person does not diminish the amount available for others to consume, and it is extremely costly to prevent non-paying individuals from consuming the goods. These characteristics make it difficult for the private sector to provide the appropriate amount of such goods, meaning that the government sometimes should step in and do the job. In Chapter 23, "The Economics of Weather Prediction," we take a trip back in time to examine the costs and benefits associated with the founding of what was to become the U.S. Weather Service. Here the public good in question was information on weather storm warnings on the Great Lakes. Although it will never be known if the private sector could have done the job better, we find that the government's earliest attempts at weather forecasting were good enough to yield positive net gains to society—an important reminder that, sometimes at least, the actions of government raise our wealth.

19

Killer Cars and the Rise of the SUV

Things are not always what they seem.
—Phaedrus, circa A.D. 8

If there were a Murphy's Law of economic policy making, it would be this: *The costs are always higher than promised, and the benefits are always lower.* The federal law that regulates automobile fuel economy provides just one example of this fundamental principle and along the way demonstrates that what Phaedrus had to say two thousand years ago is true today.

Our story begins in the 1970s, when the United States was in the middle of a so-called energy crisis. The Organization of Petroleum Exporting Countries (OPEC), a cartel of major oil-producing countries, had succeeded in raising the prices of petroleum products (including gasoline) to record-high levels. Consumers reacted by conserving on their use of gasoline and other petroleum products, and Congress responded by enacting legislation mandating energy conservation as the law of the land. One of these laws, known as the corporate average fuel economy (CAFE) standard, requires that each auto manufacturer's passenger cars sold in this country meet a federally mandated fuel economy standard. The new car fleets for the year 2002, for example, had to average 27.5 miles per gallon (mpg) of gasoline. If an automaker sells a gas-guzzler that gets only 15 mpg, somewhere along the line it must also sell enough gas-sipping subcompacts so that the average fuel economy of the entire fleet of cars sold by the company works out to 27.5 mpg. If an automaker's average fuel economy is worse than 27.5 mpg, the corporation is fined $5 per car for each 0.1 mpg it falls short. For example, if General Motors were to fail to meet the CAFE standard by only one mpg, it could be subject to penalties of $200 million per year or more.

The CAFE standard was first introduced at a time when the price of gasoline, measured in terms of today's dollars, was about $3 per gallon. During the mid-1980s, price-cutting by members of the OPEC cartel, combined with a rise in oil production elsewhere, sent gasoline prices into free fall. By 2002, with gasoline less than half as expensive (in inflation-adjusted dollars) as it was in the 1970s, the legally mandated CAFE standard of 27.5 mpg almost certainly resulted in cars that didn't consume *enough* gasoline. This seems like a strange conclusion, so we want to be sure we understand why it is correct.

There is no doubt that conserving gasoline is a good thing, for gasoline is a scarce good. If we are able to accomplish the same objectives (such as making a trip to the grocery store) and use less gasoline in doing so, the money that would have been spent on the gas can now be spent on other goods. Yet conserving gasoline is itself a costly activity. In the extreme case, we could engage in 100 percent conservation of gasoline, but doing so would mean giving up automobiles altogether! Somewhat more realistically, reducing the amount of gasoline that cars burn requires that they be lighter, have smaller engines, and be smaller and sometimes less crash-resistant. To meet the CAFE standards, for example, automobile manufacturers had to switch to production techniques that are more costly, use materials (such as aluminum and high-tech plastics) that are more easily damaged in accidents and more costly to repair, and design engines that are less responsive and more difficult and costly to repair. Although these are all things that probably would make sense if the price of gas were $3 per gallon, many economists believe that at $1.50 per gallon the principal effect of the CAFE standard is to raise consumers' total transportation costs: The costs of conserving on gasoline exceed the savings from consuming less of it.

But the costs of the CAFE standard are measured not just in terms of the dollars and cents of reduced economic efficiency. They are also measured in terms of people whose lives are lost as the result of the law—thousands of lives every year.

The seemingly obvious way to respond to a law that requires enhanced fuel efficiency is to redesign engines so that they burn less fuel. Indeed, the automakers have done exactly this. But another highly effective means of reducing the fuel appetite of automobiles is to downsize them by making them smaller and lighter. A major study by Robert Crandall of The Brookings Institution and John Graham of Harvard found that the CAFE standard forced automakers to produce cars that are about 500 pounds lighter than they would have been without the law. A 500-pound weight reduction implies a 14 percent increase in the fatality risk for the occupants of a car involved in an accident. That translates into approximately 3000 additional deaths per year, plus another 15,000 or so serious nonfatal injuries each year.

Apparently, consumers have not been happy with the lighter and less powerful cars, nor with the higher attendant risk of death they imply. Fortunately, consumers have found a way out: Light trucks, which include vans, pickups, and sport utility vehicles (SUVs) have been subject to a less demanding fuel economy standard. In contrast to the standard for cars, established in 1978 at 18.0 mpg, and now at 27.5 mpg, the CAFE standard for light trucks, initially set in 1980 at 17.5 mpg, is currently 20.6 mpg. Hence, the CAFE standards initially were less stringent for light trucks than for cars, and they have been raised less sharply (up 17 percent for light trucks, versus up 53 percent for cars).

Frustrated—and safety-conscious—consumers have thus been able to substitute out of passenger cars and thereby escape some of the consequences that Congress otherwise would have inflicted on them. Indeed, according to research by economist Paul E. Godek, CAFE has induced millions of consumers to move away from small cars and into larger, higher-powered SUVs and other light trucks. Between 1975 and 1995, the light-truck share of passenger vehicles rose to 41.5 percent from 20.9 percent. Godek estimates that without CAFE the light-truck share would have been only 29.2 percent. Hence, about three-fifths of the rise in the light-truck market share has been induced by the CAFE standards. By the year 2002, the market share for SUVs and other light trucks had reached fully 50 percent of the 17 million passenger vehicles sold each year, a remarkable transformation in the market in less than 25 years.

The original goal of CAFE was (in part) to induce substitution from large cars to small ones. But the rise of the SUV has, to some extent, frustrated this intent. Two consequences have resulted. First, light trucks are less fuel-efficient than passenger cars, so fuel economy has risen less than if light-truck substitution had not been possible. A rough estimate of this effect is that it is probably fairly modest—reducing overall fuel economy by about 1.0 mpg.

More important are the consequences in the arena of passenger vehicle safety. Despite their name, light trucks are heavier than cars. Because there are more light trucks on the road with CAFE-lightened cars, drivers of those cars are now at increased risk of death in crashes involving light trucks. This effect has made national headlines from time to time, as people have worried about the adverse effects for the occupants of small cars that tangle with large SUVs.

But there is a second effect. The occupants of light trucks are protected by the very mass that is hazardous to the occupants of cars. This mass not only protects light-truck occupants from cars, it protects them from heavy trucks, trees, wildlife, and so on. This, in turn, tends to cut accident fatalities. Crandall and Graham's earlier work on the impact of vehicle weight on fatality rates suggests that the substitution toward light trucks may actually, on balance, have reduced overall fatalities—meaning that CAFE is not killing quite as many extra people each year as it would without the rise of the SUV.

There remains one mystery in the CAFE story, which is why the law was originally enacted. If the real objective of CAFE was fuel economy (and thus, in part, environmental protection), this could have been accomplished much more cheaply with a direct tax on gasoline. According to Godek, the structure of the law suggests a different congressional motive. CAFE treats domestic and imported cars separately. Manufacturers must meet the standard for both fleets, so they can't simply import fuel-efficient cars to bring up the average mileage of their domestic cars. Instead, they must make more small cars here in America. Thus, CAFE has protected the jobs of domestic auto workers—giving us one more example of a law supposedly enacted to achieve a high-minded goal that instead serves chiefly to insulate a U.S. industry from the rigors of competition.

So, the next time a minivan takes your parking place, or an oversized four-wheeler tailgates you, remember this: Their owners are just trying to prevent Congress from killing them to save jobs in Detroit.

DISCUSSION QUESTIONS

1. Why do you think Congress passed the CAFE standard?

2. Does your answer to question 1 imply either (1) consumers do not know what is in their own best interest, or (2) firms will not voluntarily provide the goods (including fuel economy) consumers want to purchase?

3. Suppose Congress really knows what the best average fuel economy for automobiles is. How do you think "best" is (or should be) defined? Do the costs and benefits of achieving a particular level of fuel economy play a role in determining that definition?

4. If Congress wanted to increase the average fuel economy of cars, could it accomplish this by imposing a tax on gasoline? What are the advantages and disadvantages of using taxes rather than standards to achieve an improvement in fuel economy?

20

Superfund Follies

Superfund has been a disaster.
—William Jefferson Clinton, 1993

In 1978 residents near Love Canal, an abandoned waste site in Niagara Falls, New York, found chemicals leaking into their homes. Fearing that these chemicals might be causing health problems in the neighborhood, the state of New York declared a public health emergency. Ultimately, the government ordered the neighborhood abandoned, and more than 200 houses and a school were bulldozed. Although no scientific study has produced any credible evidence that the chemicals at Love Canal harmed anyone, the episode had one other lasting and very costly result: It induced Congress in 1980 to establish the Superfund program.[1]

Superfund was supposed to be a short-lived, speedy program to rid the nation of dangerous waste disposal sites like Love Canal. It was to cost at most a few billion dollars, paid for by those firms whose pollution had posed the risks or caused the harms. *None* of those intentions have been achieved: Cleanup is slow, costs are astronomical, and much of the program's resources are diverted to activities that do little good.

Despite more than twenty years of spending, less than 10 percent of the nation's Superfund sites have been cleaned up. This slow pace is not because of any lack of resources: The Environmental

---

[1] The full name of the legislation that created Superfund is the Comprehensive Environmental Response, Compensation, and Liability Act (CERCLA).

Protection Agency (EPA), which is charged with administering the Superfund program, is devoting more than a billion taxpayer dollars a year to it. Private firms that are cleaning up sites are spending an additional $1.5 billion per year on this task. By the EPA's own accounting, the agency's overhead costs run about $450 for every hour of work performed by its contractors in cleaning up sites—and this number does not include the wage or overhead costs charged by the cleanup firm. Moreover, of the billions spent each year on Superfund, roughly one-third is squandered on legal and other transaction costs—activities that ultimately clean up nothing.

One estimate of the magnitude of the waste involved in Superfund cleanups is contained in a recent study by economists Kip Viscusi of Harvard and James Hamilton of Duke.[2] They found that EPA cleanups of Superfund sites cost an average of almost $12 billion for every cancer case prevented. Even more amazing is that virtually all—99.5 percent—of the cancer cases that will be averted by EPA efforts are prevented by the first 5 percent of the agency's expenditures. The remaining 95 percent of expenditures prevent only 0.5 percent of the cancer cases—at a cost per case of an astonishing $200 *billion*.

Cleanup at Superfund sites targets chemical pathways. These are the specific ways in which people are exposed to particular chemicals—such as breathing in contaminated dust or drinking water from a well that has been tainted by a toxic chemical seepage. When the pathways pose a high risk, cleanup is mandatory; cleanup of low-risk pathways is at the discretion of local EPA officials. Viscusi and Hamilton found that the forces pushing the extent of cleanup often vary markedly between these two types of sites. To cite just one example of EPA's inconsistency, in high-risk settings, the agency sets more stringent cleanup standards the greater the population density, a policy that seems sensible enough. But in low-risk settings, greater population density leads the EPA to choose *less* stringent standards—an outcome that is arguably foolish.

Overall, Viscusi and Hamilton found that "Superfund site [cleanup] decisions do not follow the expected pattern for efficient

[2] W. Kip Viscusi and James T. Hamilton, "Are Risk Regulators Rational? Evidence from Hazardous Waste Cleanup Decisions," *American Economic Review*, September 1999, pp. 1010–1027.

risk management." Because Congress directs the EPA to make Superfund decisions but does not order the agency to consider costs, this is perhaps not surprising. What is disturbing is the nature of the factors that replace cost-effectiveness in guiding EPA decisions: misplaced risk perceptions and political influence.

For example, a key ingredient in determining EPA cleanup stringency is the public notoriety of the chemicals at the site. Even after controlling for the known risks of the site, Viscusi and Hamilton found that the more times a chemical was mentioned in the popular press, the more stringent was the target (or permissible) risk chosen by the EPA. Thus, instead of cleaning up the most dangerous sites, the EPA is cleaning up the sites that might get the most bad press.

Sadly, the EPA does not seem to care whether the cleanup costs it incurs will actually benefit real people. That is, cleanup decisions generally are unaffected by whether the risks of the site are borne by people who live there today or are hypothetically borne by people who *might someday,* under a worst-case scenario, live near the site. Thus, many cancer cases "prevented" by EPA cleanups are purely hypothetical—benefits likely to materialize only in the minds of EPA employees, who have simply assumed that the Superfund site will one day be a housing subdivision.

The average cost per cancer case averted by the EPA expenditures—$11.7 billion per case—masks enormous variation from site to site. At the most efficiently cleaned-up site, the cost per cancer case averted was only $20,000, surely a good deal by anyone's standards. At the other end of the spectrum, the cost was $961 *billion.* Now, the EPA is not actually spending $961 billion anywhere; indeed, the largest amount spent on any one site was only $134 million. The problem is that the hundreds of millions of dollars poured into the least-efficient cleanups had so little impact that they were essentially a complete waste to society.

According to Viscusi and Hamilton, a key factor leading to the EPA's abysmal decision making is plain old politics. That is, political pressure pushes the EPA into more stringent cleanups, and does so in the worst possible manner. For sites where cleanup is relatively cost-effective, political forces actually have little effect. But at the most inefficient sites, where costs per cancer case averted are in the billions, political factors have their strongest and most wasteful effect.

Although Viscusi and Hamilton focused only on the costs of cancer prevention, the types of problems they discovered appear to be pervasive. Indeed, even Carol Browner, administrator of the EPA under President Bill Clinton, criticized the Superfund program as one that "frequently moves too slowly, cleans up too little, has an unfair liability scheme, and costs too much." How can such a well-intentioned program produce such abysmal results?

There are several reasons. For example, EPA expenditures on Superfund are funded out of special earmarked taxes, rather than from general revenues. Hence the expenditures do not have to pass through the regular congressional appropriation process and are not subject to the budgetary scrutiny that virtually all other federal expenditures must withstand. Moreover, although Superfund was originally sold to Congress—and the nation—on the principle that firms that created the hazards would pay for the cleanup, the industrial taxes that fund EPA's Superfund efforts flagrantly violate this principle. Indeed, chemical and petroleum firms (and certain other large firms in other industries) have to pay the taxes that finance Superfund *regardless* of whether they have ever contaminated an industrial site. Production, not pollution, is taxed to pay for Superfund, meaning that these Superfund taxes create no incentive for firms to operate in a cleaner manner.

In addition to cleanups conducted by the agency itself, the EPA routinely orders firms to clean up other Superfund sites. In these cases, EPA not only does not have to worry about the budgetary consequences of its actions; it also does not have to worry about many other things you might think it would. For example, when EPA orders a firm to clean up a site, it does not have to show that any harm or serious threat of harm has been committed. It only has to show that some harm *might* occur to someone, some time in the future. Similarly, the EPA does not have to show that any law was broken by firms ordered to conduct a cleanup. In fact, most Superfund cleanups are at sites where the environmental damages originally were the result of law-abiding behavior.

It is perhaps even more striking that a firm ordered to perform a cleanup does not even have to be the entity that caused the chemical contamination at the site. It is sufficient that the EPA declare the firm to be a "potentially responsible party"—for example, because the firm once owned the contaminated property. Moreover, in ordering the cleanup, the EPA need not show that the cleanup is either necessary or reasonable, nor that the costs of doing it are reasonable; in fact, the EPA does not have to consider costs at all. As long as the EPA simply follows the procedures it wrote for itself, its decisions have the force of law.

So the problem with the Superfund program is neither bad intentions nor bad people. The problem is a set of institutions, created by Congress, that in turn creates bad incentives. Anyone—private sector, government, or perhaps even a saint—facing similar incentives would likely behave in exactly the manner the EPA does. Thus, if the Superfund program is be improved, the institutions that govern it must be changed. Otherwise, the Superfund follies will continue unabated.

DISCUSSION QUESTIONS

1. If you did not have to bear the costs of your actions, would your behavior be different than it is now? Do you think your behavior would be efficient, that is, would it equate the marginal social costs to the marginal social benefits?

2. If the EPA's Superfund cleanup expenditures were funded out of general revenues, how would competition from other possible uses of those funds likely affect the amount of money going to EPA?

3. If we want to minimize the total cost of preventing a particular number of cancers at Superfund sites, how should we allocate resources across those sites? If we want to maximize the number of cancer cases averted for a given expenditure of resources, how should we allocate resources across Superfund sites? If the EPA fails to meet these criteria for efficient cancer prevention, in what sense can the agency be said to be *causing* cancer?

4. Health and safety are "normal" goods, in the sense that people demand more of them as their income or wealth rises. If we waste resources and this reduces our wealth, what happens to the demand for health and safety—and thus to the amount of health and safety we enjoy? Is it then correct to say that wasteful programs have the effect of killing people?

21

Crime and Punishment

The city of Detroit, Michigan, has twice as many police per capita as Omaha, Nebraska, but the violent crime rate in Detroit is four times as high as in Omaha. Does this mean police are the source of violent crime? If that sounds like an odd question, consider this: Between 1970 and 2000 the number of Americans in prison nearly quadrupled as a share of the population, even as the violent crime rate doubled and the property crime rate rose 30 percent. Does sending people to prison actually encourage them to commit crimes?

Few people would answer either of these questions with a yes, but there is still a widespread concern that crime pays and that there seems to be little that policy makers can do about it. In a nation in which more than 20 percent of all households can expect to be victimized by a serious crime in any given year, it is little wonder that people are asking some tough questions about law enforcement. Do harsher penalties really discourage people from committing crimes? Will longer prison sentences reduce the crime rate? Are more police the answer, or should we try something else? Given that crime costs its victims more than $200 billion every year in America, even as we are spending roughly $100 billion per year in public monies to prevent it, answers to questions such as these are clearly important.

There is one thing we can be sure of at the start: Uniformly heavy punishments for all crimes will lead to a larger number of *major* crimes. Let's look at the reasoning. All decisions are made at the margin. If theft and murder will be punished by the same fate, there is no marginal deterrence to murder. If a theft of $5.00 is met with a punishment of ten years in jail and a theft of $50,000 incurs the same sentence, why not go all the way and steal $50,000? There is no marginal deterrence against committing the bigger theft.

To establish deterrents that are correct at the margin, we must observe empirically how criminals respond to changes in punishments. This leads us to the question of how people decide whether to commit a crime. A theory as to what determines the supply of criminal offenses needs to be established.

Adam Smith, the founder of modern economics, once said

> The affluence of the rich excites the indignation of the poor, who are often both driven by want, and prompted by envy, to invade his possessions. It is only under the shelter of the civil magistrate that the owner of that valuable property, which is acquired by the labour of many years, or perhaps by many successive generations, can sleep a single night in security. He is at all times surrounded by unknown enemies, whom, though he never provokes, he can never appease, and from whose injustice he can be protected only by the powerful arm of the civil magistrate continually held up to chastise it. The acquisition of valuable and extensive property, therefore, necessarily requires the establishment of civil government. Where there is no property, or at least none that exceeds the value of two or three days' labour, civil government is not so necessary.[1]

Thus, Smith concluded, theft will be committed in any society in which one person has substantially more property than another. If Smith is correct, we can surmise that the individuals who engage in theft are seeking income. We can also suppose that, before acting, a criminal might be expected to look at the anticipated costs and returns of criminal activity. These could then be compared with the net returns from legitimate activities. In other words, those engaging in crimes may be thought of as doing so on the basis of a cost/benefit analysis in which the benefits to them outweigh their costs. The benefits of the crime of theft are clear: loot. The costs to the criminal would include, but not be limited to, apprehension by the police, conviction, and jail. The criminal's calculations are thus analogous to those made by an athlete when weighing the cost of

---

[1] Adam Smith, Book V, Chapter 1, *An Inquiry into the Nature and Causes of the Wealth of Nations,* 1776.

possible serious injury against the benefits to be gained from participating in a sport.

If we view the supply of offenses in this manner, we can come up with ways in which society can lower the net expected benefit for committing any illegal activity. That is, we can figure out how to reduce crime most effectively. Indeed, economists have applied this sort of reasoning to study empirically the impact of punishment on criminal activity. The two areas on which they have focused are: (1) the impact of increasing the probability that criminals will be detected and apprehended, for example by putting more police on the street; and (2) the role of punishment, for example through imprisonment.

Surprisingly, at least to an economist, the empirical answers to these questions came back rather mixed in early research studies. For example, the estimated impact of imprisonment on crime rates appeared quite small, indeed often little different from zero. Moreover, a substantial majority of the early studies that attempted to estimate the impact of police on the crime rate found either no relationship or found that having more police on the force appeared to *increase* the crime rate!

The problem researchers have encountered in estimating the impact of police or prison terms on criminal activity is quite simple in principle but a difficult one to correct: Because people who live in areas with higher crime rates will want to take measures to protect themselves, they are likely to have larger police forces and to punish criminals more severely. Thus even if more police and more severe penalties actually do reduce crime, this true effect may be masked or even seem to be reversed in the data, because high crime areas will tend to have more police and higher prison populations.

Important new research has begun to unravel these influences, however, offering us the clearest picture yet of the likely effects of police and imprisonment on the crime rate. In a series of articles, Steven Levitt of the University of Chicago has looked for factors that strongly influence the number of police in a community or the size of a state's prison population but do not otherwise affect the crime rate. He has found such factors, and in so doing has revealed a much clearer picture of the true deterrence effect of law enforcement.

Levitt finds the strongest deterrent effect of police on violent crime, such as murder, rape, and assault. In fact, he estimates the **elasticity** of violent crime with respect to police to be about –1.0. Thus, for example, a 10 percent increase in a city's police force can be expected to produce about a 10 percent decrease in the violent crime rate in that city. With regard to property crimes, such as burglary, larceny, and auto theft, the impact of having more police is smaller but still significant. In this case, the estimated elasticity is about –0.3, meaning a 10 percent increase in the police force will yield about a 3 percent reduction in property crimes. The implications for a city like Detroit are quite striking. Increasing the police force by 10 percent would mean adding about 440 officers. Levitt's estimates imply that, as a result, the city could expect to suffer about 2100 fewer violent crimes each year and about 2700 fewer property crimes.

Levitt also has been able to isolate the role of imprisonment on deterring crime. He finds once again that the effects are strongest for violent crime: A 10 percent decrease in a state's prison population can be expected to increase the violent crime rate in that state by about 4 percent. In the case of property crime, a 10 percent decrease in prison population will yield about a 3 percent rise in burglaries, larcenies, and auto thefts in the state. Perhaps not surprisingly, many states have been constructing new prisons.

In separate research, Levitt has found that juvenile criminals respond to incentives, just as their adult counterparts do. From the mid-1970s to the mid-1990s, juvenile crime soared relative to adult crime, which has led many commentators to worry about a generation of juveniles who are seemingly undaunted by the threat of imprisonment. In fact, it appears soaring juvenile crime was largely the result of changes in the incentives faced by juveniles: Over this same period of time, violent crime imprisonment rates for juveniles fell 80 percent relative to those for adults. Hence, the chances of violent young criminals being jailed dropped to only about half that of violent adult criminals. Moreover, the change in penalties that occurs as youths become subject to adult laws (usually age 18) has a strong effect on their behavior. In states tough on youth but easy on adults, violent crime rates rise 23 percent at age 18, but in states that are easy on juveniles and tough on adults, such crime drops 4 percent at age 18. Incentives, it seems, still matter.

Are the growing expenditures on crime prevention worth it? According to Levitt's results, the answer is yes. Adding another person to the prison population costs about $30,000 per year but can be expected to yield benefits (in terms of crime prevention) of more than $50,000 per year. Although adding an officer to the police force has an expected cost of about $80,000 per year, that officer can be expected to produce crime prevention benefits of almost $200,000. If these numbers are anywhere close to being correct, we can expect further increases in spending on crime prevention in the years to come and perhaps even some noticeable reductions in the crime rate.

DISCUSSION QUESTIONS

1. The analysis just presented seems to make the assumption that criminals act rationally. Does the fact they do not necessarily do so negate the analysis?

2. In many cases, murder is committed among people who know each other. Does this mean that raising the penalty for murder will not affect the number of murders committed?

3. Consider the following prescription for punishments: "Eye for eye, tooth for tooth, hand for hand, foot for foot. . . ." Suppose our laws followed this rule, and further suppose we spent enough money on law enforcement to apprehend everyone who broke the law. What would the crime rate be? (*Hint:* If the penalty for stealing $10 was $10, and if you were certain you would be caught, would there be any expected gain from the theft? Would there be an expected gain from the theft if the penalty were only, say, $1.00, or if the chance of being caught were only 10 percent?)

4. In recent years, the penalty for selling illegal drugs has been increased sharply. How does that affect the incentive to sell drugs? For the people who decide to sell drugs anyway, what do the higher penalties for dealing do to their incentive to commit other crimes (such as murder) while they are engaged in selling drugs?

22

The Graying of America

America is aging. The 78 million baby boomers who pushed the Beatles and the Rolling Stones into stardom are entering middle age. Indeed, the future of America is now on display in Florida, where one person in five is over sixty-five. In thirty years, almost 20 percent of all Americans will be sixty-five or older. Just as the post–World War II baby boom presented both obstacles and opportunities, so too does the graying of America. Let's see why.

Two principal forces are behind America's "senior boom." First, we're living longer. Average life expectancy in 1900 was forty-seven. Today it is seventy-seven and is likely to reach eighty within the next decade. Second, the birth rate is near record low levels. Today's mothers are having far fewer children than their mothers had. In short, the old are living longer and the ranks of the young are growing too slowly to offset that fact. Together, these forces are pushing up the proportion of the population over sixty-five; indeed, the population of seniors is growing at twice the rate of the rest of the population. In 1970, the **median age** in the United States—the age that divides the older half of the population from the younger half—was twenty-eight; by 2002 the median age was thirty-six and rising. Compounding these factors, the average age at retirement has been declining as well, from sixty-five in 1963 to sixty-two currently. The result is more retirees relying on fewer workers to help ensure that their senior years are also golden years.

Why should a person who is, say, college age be concerned with the age of the rest of the population? Well, old people are expensive. In fact, people over sixty-five now consume over one-third of the federal government's budget. Social Security payments to retirees are the biggest item, now running over $300 billion a year. Medicare, which pays hospital and doctors' bills for the elderly, costs over $200 billion a year and is growing rapidly. Moreover, fully a third of the $150-billion-a-year budget for Medicaid, which helps pay medical bills for the poor of all ages, goes to those over the age of sixty-five.

Under current law, the elderly will consume 40 percent of all federal spending within fifteen years: Medicare's share of Gross Domestic Product (GDP) will double, as will the number of very old—those over eighty-five and most in need of care. Within thirty years, probably *one-half* of the federal budget will go to the old. In a nutshell, senior citizens are the beneficiaries of an expensive and rapidly growing share of all federal spending. What are they getting for our dollars?

To begin with, the elderly are already more prosperous than ever. Indeed, the annual discretionary income of those over sixty-five averages 30 percent higher than the average discretionary income of all age groups. Each year, inflation-adjusted Social Security benefits paid new retirees are higher than the first-year benefits paid people who retired the year before. In addition, for nearly thirty years, cost-of-living adjustments have protected Social Security benefits from inflation. The impact of Social Security is evident even at the lower end of the income scale: The poverty rate for people over sixty-five is much lower than for the population as a whole. Retired people today collect Social Security benefits that are two to five times what they and their employers contributed in payroll taxes, plus interest earned.

Not surprisingly, medical expenses are a major concern for many elderly. Perhaps reflecting that concern, each person under the age of sixty-five in America currently pays an average of roughly $1500 per year in federal taxes to subsidize medical care for the elderly. Indeed, no other country in the world goes to the lengths that America does to preserve life. Some 30 percent of Medicare's budget goes to patients in their last year of life. Coronary bypass operations—costing over $30,000 apiece—are routinely performed on Americans in their sixties and seventies. For those over sixty-five, Medicare picks up the tab. Even heart transplants are now performed on people in their sixties and paid for by Medicare for those over sixty-five. By contrast, the Japanese offer no organ transplants. Britain's National Health Service generally will not provide kidney dialysis for people over fifty-five. Yet Medicare subsidizes dialysis for more than one hundred thousand people, half of them over sixty. The cost: over $3 billion a year. Overall, the elderly receive Medicare benefits worth five to twenty times the payroll taxes (plus interest) they paid for this program.

The responsibility for the huge and growing bills for Social Security and Medicare falls squarely on current and future workers, because both programs are financed by taxes on payrolls. Thirty years ago, these programs were adequately financed with a payroll levy of less than 10 percent of the typical worker's earnings. Today, the tax rate exceeds 15 percent of median wages and is expected to grow rapidly.

By the year 2020, early baby boomers, born in the late 1940s and early 1950s, will have retired. Late baby boomers, born in the 1960s, will be nearing retirement. Both groups will leave today's college students, and their children, with a staggering bill to pay. For Social Security and Medicare to stay as they are, the payroll tax rate may have to rise to 25 percent of wages over the next twenty years. And a payroll tax rate of 40 percent is not unlikely by the middle of the twenty-first century.

One way to think of the immense bill facing today's college students, and their successors, is to consider the number of retirees each worker must support. In 1946, the burden of one Social Security recipient was shared by forty-two workers. By 1960, nine workers had to foot the bill for each retiree's Social Security benefits. Today, roughly three workers pick up the tab for each retiree's Social Security, plus his or her Medicare benefits. By 2030, only two workers will be available to pay the Social Security and Medicare benefits due each recipient. Thus a working couple will have to support not only themselves and their family, but also someone outside the family who is receiving Social Security and Medicare benefits.

Paying all the bills presented by the twenty-first century's senior citizens will be made more difficult by another fact: Older workers are leaving the workplace in record numbers. We noted earlier that the average retirement age is down to sixty-two and declining. Only 30 percent of the people age fifty-five and over hold jobs today, compared with 45 percent in 1930. Thus even as the elderly are making increasing demands on the federal budget, fewer of them are staying around to help foot the bill.

Part of the exodus of the old from the workplace is due simply to their prosperity. Older people have higher disposable incomes than any other age group in the population and are using it to consume more leisure. Importantly, however, the changing work habits of older individuals have been prompted—perhaps inadvertently—by American businesses. Career advancement often slows after age forty—over 60 percent of American corporations offer early retirement plans, whereas only about 5 percent offer inducements to delay retirement. Looking ahead to career dead-ends and hefty retirement checks, increasing numbers of older workers are opting for the golf course instead of the morning commute.

Recently, however, the private sector has begun to realize that the graying of America requires that we rethink the role of senior citizens in the workforce. Some firms are doing more than just thinking. For example, a major chain of home centers in California has begun vigorously recruiting senior citizens as salesclerks. The result has been a sharp increase in customer satisfaction: The older workers know the merchandise better and have more experience in dealing with people. Moreover, turnover and absenteeism have plummeted. People with gray hair, it seems, are immune to "surfer's throat," a malady that strikes younger Californians before sunny weekends.

Other firms have introduced retirement transition programs. Instead of early retirement at age fifty-five or sixty, for example, older workers are encouraged to simply cut back on their work-week while staying on the job. Often, it is possible for workers to get the best of both worlds, collecting a retirement check even while working part-time at the same firm. Another strategy recognizes the importance of rewarding superior performance among older workers. At some firms, for example, senior technical managers are relieved of the drudgery of mundane management tasks and allowed to spend more time focusing on the technical side of their specialties. To sweeten the pot, a pay hike is often included in the package.

Apparently, programs such as these are beginning to pay off. In one recent survey, more than 70 percent of the four hundred businesses queried gave their older workers top marks for job performance; over 80 percent of the seniors received ratings of excellent or very good for their commitment to quality. Moreover, many firms are finding that the retention of older workers cuts training and pension costs sharply and, because older workers are less likely to have school-age children, even reduces health insurance outlays.

Congress and the president thus far seem unwilling to face the pitfalls and promises of an aging America. Although the age of retirement for Social Security purposes is legislatively mandated to rise to sixty-seven from sixty-five, the politicians in Washington, D.C., appear unable to do anything else but appoint commissions to "study" the problems we face—problems that rapidly worsen as the studies pile up. And all the while, there are some solutions out there. Chile, for example, faced a national pension system with even more severe problems than our Social Security system. Its response was to transform the system into one that is rapidly (and automatically, as time passes) converting itself into a completely private pension system. The result has been security for existing retirees, higher potential benefits for future retirees, and lower taxes for all workers. Americans could do exactly what the Chileans have done—if we chose to do so.

Many experts believe that significant changes in America's immigration laws could offer the best hope of dealing with the tax burdens and workforce shrinkage of the future. About a million immigrants come to America each year, the largest number in our nation's history. Yet more than 90 percent of new immigrants are admitted based on a selection system unchanged since 1952, under which the right of immigration is tied to family preference. As a result, most people are admitted to the United States because they happen to be the spouses, children, or siblings of earlier immigrants, rather than because they have skills or training highly valued in the American workplace. Both Canada and Australia have modified their immigration laws to expand opportunities for those immigrants who possess skills in short supply, with results that are generally regarded quite favorably in both nations. Unless Congress manages to overhaul America's immigration preference system, new immigrants are unlikely to relieve much of the pressure building due to our aging population.

In the meantime, if Social Security and Medicare are kept on their current paths, and older workers continue to be taxed out of the workforce, the future burden on those who are today's college students is likely to be unbearable. If we are to avoid the social tension and enormous costs of such an outcome, the willingness and ability of older individuals to retain more of their self-sufficiency must be recognized. To do otherwise is to invite a future in which the golden years are but memories of the past.

DISCUSSION QUESTIONS

1. How do the payroll taxes levied on the earnings of workers affect their decisions about how much leisure they consume?

2. When the government taxes younger people so as to pay benefits to older people, how does this affect the amount of assistance that younger people might voluntarily choose to offer older people?

3. When the government taxes younger people so as to pay benefits to older people, how does this affect the size of the bequests that older people are likely to leave to their children or grandchildren when they die?

4. In general, people who are more productive earn higher incomes and thus pay higher taxes. How would a change in the immigration law that favored more highly educated and skilled individuals affect the future tax burden of today's American college students? Would the admission of better-educated immigrants tend to raise or lower the wages of American college graduates? On balance, would an overhaul of the immigration system benefit or harm today's college students?

23

The Economics of Weather Forecasting

Every government action has costs and generates benefits. Figuring out which of these—the costs or the benefits—is bigger in any given situation is often problematic. Data on the cost side usually are not too difficult to establish. After all, the direct budgetary costs typically are a matter of public record, and economists have developed ways to convert these budgetary data into numbers that correspond fairly closely with the relevant economic concepts of cost.

The real trouble comes when we try to determine the benefits of government action. For example, what is the economic benefit of having an antiballistic missile system, or the U.S. State Department, or, for that matter, the Weather Service? Surely these things are valuable, but just as surely, as with many things the government does, there is no marketplace that helps us establish what people are willing to pay for such services. In cases such as these, the government is producing services that are (or are close to being) public goods. This means that the goods have two characteristics. First, the consumption of the goods is nonrivalrous: the quantity available for you to consume does not fall when we consume more. An antiballistic missile system, for example, simultaneously can protect us all. Second, the consumption of these goods is (or is close to being) nonexcludable: it is extremely costly to provide the goods only to people who pay for them, while at the same time preventing or excluding nonpayers from obtaining them. Thus, even if you refuse to pay for the missile system, it continues to protect you from attack.

The nonexcludable aspect of public goods makes it difficult to get the private sector interested in providing these goods, because it is so hard to make a profit from them. This in turn means that either the government gets involved, or the good doesn't get produced at all. But because there is no market—and thus no market prices—for such goods, it is difficult to properly value them to compute the benefits of having the government provide them.

Every once in awhile, however, it is possible to estimate these benefits through fairly ingenious indirect means. Researcher Erik Craft did just that in studying the first twenty years of what was to become the modern-day U.S. Weather Service.[1] He concluded that the agency's collection of weather data and the dissemination of storm warnings across the Great Lakes region did in fact yield substantial, positive net benefits to society. These benefits included both averted economic losses due to shipwrecks, and fewer lives lost at sea.

The U.S. Congress established a national weather organization in 1870 when it instructed the Secretary of War to collect meteorological observations and issue storm warnings on the Great Lakes. If severe weather forecasts were a valuable transportation input, one would expect several consequences after the service was introduced in the early 1870s. Specifically, the collection and dissemination of weather information should have caused a clearly measurable decline in shipping losses on the Great Lakes. This also should have manifested itself in predictable changes in shipping rates and insurance premiums. Because fall weather on the Great Lakes is considerably more turbulent and destructive than summer weather, the beneficial impact of the storm warning system should have been much greater in the fall than in the summer.

After controlling for a host of other factors that might influence the analysis—including year-to-year fluctuations in weather conditions and the transition from sail to steam power during this period—Craft found clear evidence that storm warnings sharply re-

---

[1] Strictly speaking, weather information today probably satisfies only the first criterion (nonrivalrous consumption) for being a public good. With today's technology for encrypting data, it is entirely possible to exclude nonpayers from consuming weather information, and there is indeed a large market in privately produced weather forecasts purchased by airlines, ocean shipping companies, and interstate truckers. But 130 years ago, before the advent of wireless radio, it was far more difficult to exclude nonpayers from weather forecasts made for ships: the forecasts were broadcast by means of shore-based flags and semaphores visible to everyone.

duced shipping losses on the Great Lakes. Measured in terms of today's dollars, the storm warning system as a whole generated benefits of $20 million per year during the early years, rising to nearly $90 million per year during the late 1880s, the end of the study period. These benefits, resulting from fewer shipwrecks and reduced cargo losses, were achieved at an annual cost of under $20 million per year. It also appears that the storm warning system played a key role in saving fifty to seventy seamen's lives annually during this period, a benefit on top of the reduced shipping and cargo losses.

Because the Weather Service led to significant declines in shipping losses, the result should have been lower costs for firms offering shipping services, and also for companies insuring the ships and their cargo. Moreover, because the storm warning information was much more useful during stormy fall months, the differences between insurance and shipping rates in the peaceful summer months and the turbulent fall months should have diminished. The evidence is consistent with these predictions. The fall shipping price premium shrank by 50 percent due to the storm warning stations, and the ratio of fall-to-summer insurance premiums declined as well. Overall, the social rate of return from the expenditures on weather collection and dissemination during this period was at least 64 percent.

A one-year reduction in the Army Signal Service budget in fiscal year 1883 due to an embezzlement scandal conveniently provided an additional means of discerning the beneficial effects of the Weather Service. The budget cut forced a temporary reduction in the number of storm warning stations by nearly one-half. The result was a natural experiment: The apparently beneficial effects of the Weather Service should have been sharply curtailed during the period of budget austerity, only to return to their former levels with the restoration of the agency's full funding. This was precisely the pattern observed.

The 1883 budget cut saved about $2.5 million. But shipping losses that year soared from $30 million to about $55 million, returning to about $30 million when the funding was restored. Moreover, it appears that the sharp rise in shipping losses was accompanied by a corresponding increase in fatalities.

None of this evidence means, of course, that the timing of the establishment of the Weather Service was necessarily optimal. Nor does it imply that the government provision of weather information was necessary. Indeed, at the time the U.S. Weather Service was launched, one entrepreneur already had begun organizing the resources necessary to offer privately provided storm warnings to Great Lakes shipping companies. In fact, the scientist he was going to use as chief meteorologist was the man tapped to head the government effort. Once the government began offering storm warnings at no direct charge to shipping companies or insurers, the private effort collapsed. Today, although the National Weather Service offers its forecasts at no charge, there are many private weather forecasting services that profit handsomely by providing (presumably superior) forecasts to a host of consumers, including agribusinesses, airlines, America's Cup sailing teams, power utilities, ski areas, and trucking companies, to name but a few.

Whether private-sector weather forecasting and storm warnings could have beaten government's performance in protecting Great Lakes shipping during the nineteenth century is unknown. But in a world in which it seems all too easy to find examples of the waste generated by government policies, it is of some comfort to find an episode in which the government contributed positively to the well-being of the public it is supposed to serve.

DISCUSSION QUESTIONS

1. Consumption of many goods, including television shows and sporting events, is nonrivalrous, in the sense that when one person enjoys the performance it does not diminish the quantity or quality of performance available for others to consume. What makes it feasible for such goods to be provided by the private sector?

2. Consider a good for which the consumption is rivalrous, but which is nonexcludable. For example, suppose the government made it illegal for apartment owners to exclude (by charging a positive monthly rental) people from living in their apartments. Do you think apartments would continue to be provided by the private sector? Do the answers to this and question 1 reveal whether it is the rivalrous or the excludable features of goods

that determine whether the private sector is able to profitably supply them?

3. Suppose that the job done by the U.S. Weather Service in the late nineteenth century was actually inferior to the job that would have been done by a private-sector firm. Is it still possible that the private-sector firm would find it impossible to compete against the Weather Service? Is it possible that ship owners might prefer the inferior government service over the superior private service?

4. The next time you see a sporting event on television, watch carefully for an announcement specifying restrictions on your rights to rebroadcast the event or distribute it commercially. Why are these restrictions imposed on you and other viewers? What would be the likely consequences if the government prohibited sports leagues from imposing such restrictions?

Part Six

Property Rights and the Environment

INTRODUCTION

We saw in Part Four that monopoly produces outcomes that differ significantly from the competitive outcome and so yields gains from trade that fall short of the competitive ideal. In Part Six we see that when externalities are present—that is, when there are discrepancies between the private costs of action and the social costs of action— the competitive outcome differs from the competitive ideal. Typically, the problem in the case of externalities is said to be *market failure,* but the diagnosis might just as well be termed *government failure.* For markets to work efficiently, property rights to scarce goods must be clearly defined, cheaply enforceable, and fully transferable, and it is generally the government that is believed to have a comparative advantage in ensuring that these conditions are satisfied. If the government fails to define, enforce, or make transferable property rights, the market generally will fail to produce socially efficient outcomes, and it becomes a moot point as to who is at fault. The real point is this: What might be done to improve things?

As population and per capita income both rise, consumption rises faster than either, for it responds to the combined impetus of both. With consumption comes the residue of consumption, also known as plain old garbage. Many of us have heard of landfills being closed because of fears of groundwater contamination, or of homeless garbage scows wandering the high seas in search of a place to off-load; all of us have been bombarded with public service messages to recycle everything from aluminum cans to old newspapers. The United States, it seems, is becoming the garbage capital of the world. This is no doubt true, but it is also true that the United States is the professional football capital of the world—and yet pro football teams seem to have no problem finding cities across the country willing to welcome them with open arms. What is different about garbage? You probably are inclined to answer that football is enjoyable and garbage is not. True enough, but this is not why garbage sometimes piles up faster than anyone seems willing to dispose of it. Garbage becomes a problem only if it is not priced properly; that is, if the consumers and businesses that produce it are not charged enough for its removal, and the landfills where it is deposited are not paid enough for its disposal. The message of Chapter 24, "The Trashman Cometh," is that garbage really is not different from the things we consume in the course of producing it. As long as the trashman is paid, he will cometh, and as long as we have to pay for his services, his burden will be bearable. We will still have garbage, but we will not have a garbage problem.

We noted earlier that the property rights to a scarce good or resource must be clearly defined, fully enforced, and readily transferable if that resource is to be used efficiently—that is, in the manner that yields the greatest net benefits. This is true whether the resource in question is space in a landfill, water in a stream, or, as we see in Chapter 25, "Bye, Bye, Bison," members of an animal species. If these conditions are satisfied, the resource will be used in the manner that benefits both its owner and society the most. If these conditions are not satisfied—as they were not for American bison on the hoof or passenger pigeons on the wing—the resource generally will not be used in the most efficient manner. And in the case of animal species that are competing with human beings, this sometimes means extinction. What should be done when a species becomes endangered? If our desire is to produce the greatest net benefit to humanity, the answer in general is not to protect the species at *any* possible cost, for this would be equivalent to assigning an infinite value to the species. Instead, the proper course of action is to devise rules that induce people to act as though the members of the species were private property. If such rules can be developed, we shall not have to worry about spotted owls or

African elephants becoming extinct any more than we currently worry about parakeets or cocker spaniels becoming extinct.

In Chapter 26, "Smog Merchants," property rights are again the focus of the discussion as we look at air pollution. We ordinarily think of the air around us as being something that we all own. The practical consequence of this is that we act as though the air is owned by none of us—for no one can exclude anyone else from using our air. As a result, we overuse the air in the sense that air pollution becomes a problem. This chapter shows that it is possible to define and enforce property rights to air, which the owners can then use as they see fit—which includes selling the rights to others. Once this is done, the users of clean air have the incentive to use it just as efficiently as they do all of the other resources (such as land, labor, and capital) utilized in the production process.

Air—or more generally, the atmosphere as a whole—reappears as the topic of Chapter 27, "Greenhouse Economics." There is a growing body of evidence that human action is responsible for rising concentrations of so-called greenhouse gases in the earth's atmosphere, and that left unchecked this growth may produce costly increases in the average temperature of our planet. Given the nature of the problem—a **negative externality**—private action taken on the individual level will not yield the optimal outcome for society. Thus the potential gains from government action, in the form of environmental regulations or taxation, are substantial. The key word here is potential, for government action, no matter how well-intentioned, does not automatically yield benefits that exceed the costs. As we seek solutions to the potential problems associated with greenhouse gases, we must be sure that the consequences of premature action are not worse than those of first examining the problem further. If we forget this message, greenhouse economics may turn into bad economics—and worse policy.

24

The Trashman Cometh

Is garbage really different? To answer this question, let us consider a simple hypothetical situation. Suppose a city agreed to provide its residents with all of the food they wished to consume, prepared in the manner they specified, and delivered to their homes for a flat, monthly fee that was independent of what or how much they ate. What are the likely consequences of this city food delivery service? Most likely, people in the city would begin to eat more, because the size of their food bill would be independent of the amount they ate. They would also be more likely to consume lobster and filet mignon rather than fish sticks and hamburger because, once again, the cost to them would be independent of their menu selections. Soon the city's food budget would be astronomical, and either the monthly fee or taxes would have to be increased. People from other communities might even begin moving (or at least making extended visits) to the city, just to partake of this wonderful service. Within short order the city would face a food crisis as it sought to cope with providing a rapidly growing amount of food from a city budget that could no longer handle the financial burden.

If this story sounds silly to you, just change "food delivery" to "garbage pickup"; what we have just described is the way most cities in the country historically have operated their municipal garbage collection services. The result during the late 1980s and early 1990s was the appearance of a garbage crisis—with overflowing landfills, homeless garbage scows, and drinking-water wells polluted with the runoff from trash heaps. This seeming crisis—to the extent it existed—was fundamentally no different from the food crisis described above. The problem was not that (1) almost nobody wants garbage, nor that (2) garbage can have adverse environmental effects, nor even that (3) we had too much garbage. The problem lay in that (1) we often do not put prices on garbage in the way we put prices on the goods that generate the garbage, and (2) a strange assortment of bedfellows used a few smelly facts to make things seem worse than they were.

First things first. America is producing garbage at a record rate: In 2001 we generated about 230 million tons of household and commercial solid waste that either had to be burned, buried, or recycled. (That works out to about 1600 pounds per person.) About 40 percent of this was paper, whereas yard waste (such as grass trimmings) accounted for another 12 percent. Plastics amounted to about 20 percent of the volume of material that had to be disposed of, but because plastic is relatively light, it comprised only about 10 percent of the weight. More than 60 million tons of this trash was recycled.

Landfills are the final resting place for most of our garbage, although incineration is also widely used in some areas, particularly in the Northeast, where land values are high. Both methods began falling out of favor with people who lived near these facilities (or might eventually), as NIMBY (not-in-my-backyard) attitudes spread across the land. Federal, state, and local regulations also made it increasingly difficult to establish new waste disposal facilities, or even to keep old ones operating. The cost to open a modern 100-acre landfill rose to an estimated $70 million or more, and the permit process needed to open a new disposal facility soared to seven years in some states. Meanwhile, environmental concerns forced the closure of many landfills throughout the country and prevented others from ever beginning operations. By 1992, all but five states were exporting at least some of their garbage to other states. Today, most of the garbage from some densely populated states in the Northeast ends up in other people's backyards: New Jersey ships garbage to ten other states, while New York keeps landfill operators busy in thirteen different states. Across the country, some Americans have wondered where all of the garbage is going to go.

Although the failure of America's cities to price garbage appropriately led to an inefficient amount of the stuff, much of the appearance of a garbage crisis has been misleading. Rubbish first hit the headlines in 1987 when a garbage barge named *Mobro*, headed south with New York City trash, couldn't find a home for its load. As it turns out, the barge operator hadn't nailed down a satisfactory disposal contract before he sailed; when he tried to conduct negotiations over the radio while under way, operators of likely landfills (mistakenly) suspected he might be carrying toxic waste rather than routine trash. When adverse publicity forced the barge back to New York with its load, many people thought it was a lack of landfill space, rather than poor planning by the barge operator, that was the cause. This notion was reinforced by an odd combination of environmental groups, waste management firms, and the Environmental Protection Agency (EPA).

The Environmental Defense Fund wanted to start a major campaign to push recycling, and the *Mobro* gave things the necessary push. As one official for the organization noted, "An advertising firm couldn't have designed a better vehicle than a garbage barge." Meanwhile, a number of farsighted waste management companies had begun loading up on landfill space, taking advantage of new technologies that increased the efficient minimum size of a disposal facility. Looking to get firm contracts for filling this space, the trade group for the disposal industry started pushing the notion that America was running out of dump space. State and local officials who relied on the group's data quickly bought into the new landfills, paying premium prices to do so. The EPA, meanwhile, was studying the garbage problem but without accounting for the fact that its own regulations were causing the efficient scale of landfills to double and even quadruple in size. Thus the EPA merely counted landfills around the country and reported that they were shrinking in number. This was true enough, but what the EPA failed to report was that because landfills were getting bigger much faster than they were closing down, total disposal capacity was *growing* rapidly, not shrinking.

For a while, it seemed that recycling was going to take care of what appeared to be a growing trash problem. In 1987, for example, old newspapers were selling for as much as $60 per ton, and many municipalities felt that the answer to their financial woes and garbage troubles was at hand. Yet as more communities began putting mandatory recycling laws into effect, the prices of recycled trash began to plummet. Over the next five years, 3500 communities in more than half the states had some form of mandatory curbside recycling; the resulting increase in the supply of used newsprint meant that communities soon were having to pay to have the stuff carted away. For glass and plastics, the story is so far much the same: The market value of the used materials is below the cost of collecting and sorting it. About a dozen states have acted to increase the demand for old newsprint by requiring locally published newspapers to utilize a minimum content of recycled newsprint. Even so, many experts believe that no more than 60 to 70 percent of all newsprint can be recycled, and we are already recycling 52 percent of it, up from 33 percent in 1988.

Just as significantly, recycling raises significant issues that were often ignored during the early rush to embrace the concept. For example, the production of a hundred tons of de-inked fiber from old newsprint produces about forty tons of sludge that must be disposed of somehow. Although the total volume of material is reduced, the concentrated form of what is left can make it more costly to dispose of properly. Similarly, recycling paper is unlikely to save trees, for most virgin newsprint is made from trees planted expressly for that purpose and harvested as a crop: If recycling increases, many of these trees simply will not be planted. In a study done for Resources for the Future, A. Clark Wiseman concluded, "The likely effect of [newsprint recycling] appears to be smaller, rather than larger, forest inventory." Moreover, most virgin newsprint is made in Canada, using clean hydroelectric power. Makers of newsprint in the United States (the primary customers for the recycled stuff) often use higher-polluting energy such as coal. Thus one potential side effect of recycling is the switch from hydroelectric power to fossil fuels.

Some have argued that we should simply ban certain products. For example, Styrofoam cups have gotten a bad name because they take up more space in landfills than do paper hot-drink cups, and because Styrofoam remains in the landfill forever. Yet according to a widely cited study by Martin B. Hocking of the University of Victoria, the manufacture of a paper cup consumes 36 times as much electricity and generates 580 times as much wastewater as does the manufacture of a Styrofoam cup. Moreover, as paper degrades underground, it releases methane, a greenhouse gas that contributes to warming of the atmosphere. In a similar vein, consider disposable diapers, which have been trashed by their opponents because a week's worth generates 22.2 pounds of post-use waste, whereas a week's worth of reusable diapers generates only 0.24 pound. Because disposable diapers already amount to 2 percent of the nation's solid waste, the edge clearly seems to go to reusable cloth diapers. Yet the use of reusable rather than disposable diapers consumes more than three times as many BTUs (British thermal units) of energy and generates ten times as much water pollution. It would seem that the trade-offs that are present when we talk about "goods" are just as prevalent when we discuss "bads" such as garbage.

It also appears that more government regulation of the garbage business is likely to make things worse rather than better, as may be illustrated by the tale of two states: New Jersey and Pennsylvania. A number of years ago, to stop what was described as price-gouging by organized crime, New Jersey decided to regulate waste hauling and disposal as a public utility. Once the politicians got involved in the trash business, however, politics very nearly destroyed the business of trash. According to Paul Kleindorfer of the University of Pennsylvania, political opposition to passing garbage disposal costs along to consumers effectively ended investment in landfills. In 1972 there were 331 landfills operating in New Jersey; by 1988 the number had fallen to 13, because the state-regulated fees payable to landfill operators simply didn't cover the rising costs of operation. Half of New Jersey's municipal solid waste is now exported to neighboring Pennsylvania.

Pennsylvania's situation provides a sharp contrast. The state does not regulate the deals that communities make with landfill and incinerator operators; the market takes care of matters instead. For example, despite the state's hands-off policy, tipping fees (the charges for disposing of garbage in landfills) are below the national average in Pennsylvania, effectively limited by competition between disposal facilities. The market seems to be providing the right incentives; in one recent year, there were thirty-one pending applications to open landfills in Pennsylvania, but only two in New Jersey, despite the fact that New Jersey residents are paying the highest disposal rates in the country to ship garbage as far away as Michigan, Illinois, Missouri, and Alabama.

Ultimately, two issues must be solved when it comes to trash. First, what do we do with it once we have it? Second, how do we reduce the amount of it that we have? As hinted at by the Pennsylvania story and illustrated further by developments elsewhere in the country, the market mechanism can answer both questions. The fact of the matter is that in many areas of the country, population densities are high and land is expensive. Hence a large amount of trash is produced, and it is expensive to dispose of locally. In contrast, there are some areas of the country where there are relatively few people around to produce garbage, where land for disposal facilities is cheap, and where wide-open spaces minimize the potential air pollution hazards associated with incinerators. The sensible thing to do, it would seem, is to have the states that produce most of the trash ship it to states where it can be most efficiently disposed of—for a price, of course. This is already being done to an extent, but residents of potential recipient states are (not surprisingly) concerned, lest they end up being the garbage capitals of the nation. Yet Wisconsin, which imports garbage from as far away as New Jersey, is demonstrating that it is possible to get rid of the trash without trashing the neighborhood. Landfill operators in Wisconsin are now required to send water table monitoring reports to neighbors and to maintain the landfills for forty years after closure. Operators also have guaranteed the value of neighboring homes to gain the permission of nearby residents and in some cases have purchased homes to quiet neighbors' objections. These features all add to the cost of operating landfills, but as long as prospective customers are willing to pay the price and neighboring residents are satisfied with their protections—and so far these conditions appear to be satisfied—then it would seem tough to argue with the outcome.

Some might still argue that it does not seem right for one community to be able to dump its trash elsewhere. Yet the flip side is this: Is it right to *prevent* communities from accepting the trash, if that is what they want? Consider Gilliam County, Oregon (pop. 1,950), which wanted Seattle's garbage so badly it fought Oregon state legislators' attempts to tax out-of-state trash coming into Oregon. Seattle's decision to use the Gilliam County landfill generated $1 million per year for the little community—some 25 percent of its annual budget and enough to finance the operations of the county's largest school.

Faced with the prospect of paying to dispose of its garbage, Seattle quickly had to confront the problem of reducing the amount of trash its residents were generating. Its solution was to charge householders according to the amount they put out. Seattle thus began charging $16.10 per month for each can picked up weekly. Yard waste that has been separated for composting costs $4.25 per month, and paper, glass, and metal separated for recycling are hauled away at no charge. In the first year that per-can charges were imposed, the total tonnage that had to be buried fell by 22 percent. Voluntary recycling rose from 24 percent of waste to 36 percent—a rate almost triple the national average at the time. The "Seattle Stomp" (used to fit more trash into a can) became a regular source of exercise, and the city had trouble exporting enough garbage to fulfill its contract with Gilliam County.

The Seattle experience is paralleled by a similar program in Charlottesville, Virginia. A few years ago, this university town of 40,000 began charging $0.80 per 32-gallon bag or can of residential garbage collected at the curb. The results of the city's new policy suggest that people respond to garbage prices just as they do to all other prices: When an activity becomes more expensive, people engage in less of it. In fact, after controlling for other factors, the introduction of this unit-pricing plan induced people to reduce the volume of garbage presented for collection by 37 percent.

Where did all of the garbage go? Well, some of it didn't go anywhere, because many residents began practicing their own version of the Seattle Stomp, compacting garbage into fewer bags. Even so, the total weight of Charlottesville's residential garbage dropped by 14 percent in response to unit pricing. Not all of this represented a reduction in garbage production, because some residents resorted to "midnight dumping"—tossing their trash into commercial dumpsters or their neighbors' cans during late-night forays. This sort of behavior is much like the rise in gasoline thefts that occurred in the 1970s when gas prices jumped to the equivalent of $3 to $4 per gallon. But just as locking gas caps ended most gas thefts, there may be a simple way to prevent most midnight dumping. Economists who have studied the Charlottesville program in detail suggest that property taxes or monthly fees could be used to cover the cost of one bag per household each week, with a price per bag applied only to additional bags. According to these estimates, a one-bag allowance would stop all midnight dumping by most one-person households and stop almost half the dumping by a hypothetical three-person household. Moreover, such a scheme would retain most of the environmental benefits of the garbage pricing program.

The message slowly beginning to emerge across the country then, is that garbage really is not different from the things we consume in the course of producing it. As long as the trashman is paid, he will cometh, and as long as we must pay for his services, his burden will be bearable.

DISCUSSION QUESTIONS

1. How do deposits on bottles and cans affect the incentives of individuals to recycle these products?

2. Why do many communities mandate recycling? Is it possible to induce people to recycle more without requiring that all residents recycle?

3. How do hefty per-can garbage pickup fees influence the decisions people make about what goods they will consume?

4. A community planning on charging a fee for trash pickup might structure the fee in any of several ways. It might, for example, charge (1) a fixed amount per can; (2) an amount per pound of garbage; or (3) a flat fee per month, without regard to amount of garbage. How would each of these affect the amount and type of garbage produced? Which system would lead to an increase in the use of trash compactors? Which would lead to the most garbage?

25

Bye, Bye, Bison

The destruction of animal species by humans is nothing new. For example, the arrival of human beings in North America about 12,000 years ago is tied to the extinction of most of the megafauna (very large animals) which then existed. The famous LaBrea Tar Pits of southern California yielded the remains of twenty-four mammals and twenty-two birds that no longer exist. Among these are the saber-toothed tiger, the giant llama, the twenty-foot ground sloth, and a bison that stood seven feet at the hump and had six-foot-wide horns.

Although many experts believe that human hunting was directly responsible for the destruction of these species, and that a combination of hunting and habitat destruction by humans has led to the extinction of many other species, the link is not always as clear as it might seem at first glance. For example, it is estimated that only about 0.02 percent (1 in 5000) of all species that have ever existed are currently extant. Most of the others (including the dinosaurs) disappeared long before humans ever made an appearance. The simple fact is that all species compete for the limited resources available, and most species have been out-competed, with or without the help of *Homo sapiens*. Just as important is that basic economic principles can help explain why various species are more or less prone to meet their demise at the hands of humans, and what humans might do if they want to delay the extinction of any particular species.[1]

Let's begin with the passenger pigeon, which provides the most famous example of the role of human beings in the extinction of a

---

[1] We say "delay" rather than "prevent" extinction because there is no evidence to date that any species—*Homo sapiens* included—has any claim on immortality.

species. At one time these birds were the most numerous species of birds in North America and perhaps in the world. They nested and migrated together in huge flocks and probably numbered in the billions. When flocks passed overhead, the sky would be dark with pigeons for days at a time. The famous naturalist John James Audubon measured one roost at forty miles long and three miles wide, with birds stacked from treetop down to nearly ground level. Although the Native Americans had long hunted these birds, the demise of the passenger pigeon is usually tied to the arrival of the white man, which increased the demand for pigeons as a source of food and sport. The birds were shot and netted in vast numbers; by the end of the nineteenth century, an animal species that had been looked on as almost indestructible because of its enormous numbers had almost completely disappeared. The last known passenger pigeon died in the Cincinnati Zoo in 1914.

The American bison only narrowly escaped the same fate. The vast herds that roamed the plains were an easy target for hunters; with the advent of the railroad and the need to feed railroad crews as the transcontinental railroads were built, hunters such as Buffalo Bill Cody killed bison by the thousands. As the demand for the fur of the bison increased, it became the target for more hunting. Like the passenger pigeon, the bison had appeared to be indestructible because of its huge numbers, but the species was soon on the way to becoming extinct. Despite the outcries of the Native Americans who found their major food source being decimated, it was not until late in the nineteenth century that any efforts were made to protect the bison.[2]

These two episodes, particularly that of the bison, are generally viewed as classic examples of humankind's inhumanity to our fellow species, as well as to our fellow humans, for many Native American tribes were ultimately devastated by the near demise of the bison. A closer look reveals more than simply wasteful slaughter; it discloses exactly why events progressed as they did and how we can learn from them to improve modern efforts to protect species threatened by human neighbors.

---

[2] For the bison's cousin, the eastern buffalo—which stood seven feet tall at the shoulder, was twelve feet long, and weighed more than a ton—the efforts came too late. The last known members of the species, a cow and her calf, were killed in 1825 in the Allegheny Mountains.

Native Americans had hunted the bison for many years before the arrival of white men and are generally portrayed as both carefully husbanding their prey and generously sharing the meat among tribal members. Yet the braves who rode their horses into the thundering herds marked their arrows so it was clear who had killed the bison. The marked arrows gave the shooter rights to the best parts of the animal. Tribal members who specialized in butchering the kill also received a share as payment for processing the meat. Indeed, the Native American hunting parties were organized remarkably like the parties of the white men who followed: *Once they were killed,* the ownership of the bison was clearly defined, fully enforced, and readily transferable. Moreover, the rewards were distributed in accord with the contribution that each had made to the overall success of the hunt.

Matters were different when it came to the ownership rights to living bison herds. Native Americans, like the whites who came later, had no economically practical way to fence in the herds. The bison could (and did) migrate freely from one tribe's territory into the territory of other tribes. If the members of one tribe economized on their kill, their conservation efforts would chiefly provide more meat for another tribe, who might well be their mortal enemies. This fact induced Native Americans to exploit the bison, so that the herds disappeared from some traditional territories on the Great Plains by 1840—before Buffalo Bill was even born.

Two factors made the efforts of the white man—the railroad hunters—more destructive, hastening the disappearance of the bison herds. First, the white population (and thus the demand for the meat and hides) was much larger than the Native American population. Second, white men used firearms on the bison—a technological revolution that increased the killing capacity of a given hunter by a factor of 20 or more, compared to the bow and arrow. Nevertheless, the fundamental problem was the same for the white man and Native American alike: The property rights to live bison could not be cheaply established and enforced. To own a bison one had to kill it, and so too many bison were killed.

The property rights to a scarce good or resource must be clearly defined, fully enforced, and readily transferable if that resource is to be used efficiently—that is, in the manner that yields the greatest net benefits. This is true whether the resource in question is the

American bison, the water in a stream, or a pepperoni pizza. If these conditions are satisfied, the resource will be used in the manner that best benefits both its owner and society.[3] If they are not satisfied— as they were not for bison on the hoof or passenger pigeons on the wing—the resource generally will not be used in the most efficient manner. In the case of animal species that are competing with human beings, this sometimes means extinction.

In modern times, the government has attempted to limit hunting and fishing seasons and the number of animals that may be taken, by imposing state and federal regulations. The results have been at least partially successful. It is likely, for example, that there are more deer in North America today than there were at the time of the colonists—a fact that is not entirely good news for people whose gardens are sometimes the target of hungry herds. In effect, a rationing system (other than prices) is being used in an attempt to induce hunters and fishermen to act as though the rights to migratory animals were clearly defined, fully enforced, and readily transferable. Yet the threatened extinction of many species of whales illustrates that the problem is far from resolved.

The pattern of harvesting whales has been the subject of international discussion ever since World War II, for migratory whales are like nineteenth-century bison: To own them, one must kill them. It was readily apparent to all concerned that without some form of restraint, many species of whales were in danger of extinction. The result was the founding of the International Whaling Commission (IWC) in 1948, which attempted to regulate international whaling. But the IWC was virtually doomed from the start, for its members had the right to veto any regulation they considered too restrictive, and the commission had no enforcement powers in the event a member nation chose to disregard the rules. Moreover, some whaling nations (such as Chile and Peru) refused to join the IWC, so commission quotas had little effect on them. Some IWC members have used nonmember flagships to circumvent agreed-upon quotas,

---

[3] See Ronald Coase, "The Problem of Social Cost," *Journal of Law & Economics,* October 1960, pp. 1–44. This does not mean that all species will be permanently protected from extinction, for reasons that are suggested in Chapter 3, "Flying the Friendly Skies?" It does mean that extinction will be permitted to occur only if the benefits of doing so exceed the costs.

while others have claimed that they were killing the whales solely for exempt "research" purposes.

The story of the decimation of a species is well told in the events surrounding blue whales, which are believed to migrate thousands of miles each year. This animal, which sometimes weighs almost 100 tons, is difficult to kill even with the most modern equipment; nevertheless, intensive hunting gradually reduced the stock from somewhere between 300,000 and 1 million to, at present, somewhere between 600 and 3000. In the 1930–1931 winter season, almost 30,000 blue whales were taken, a number far in excess of the species' ability to replenish through reproduction. Continued intense harvesting brought the catch down to fewer than 10,000 by 1945–1946, and in the late 1950s the yearly harvest was down to around 1500 per year. By 1964–1965, whalers managed to find and kill only 20 blue whales. Despite a 1965 ban by the IWC, the hunting of blues continued by nonmembers such as Brazil, Chile, and Peru.

Humpback whales have suffered a similar fate. From an original population estimated at 300,000, there remain fewer than 5000 today. Like the blues, humpbacks are now under a hunting ban, but the lack of monitoring and enforcement capacity on the part of the IWC makes it likely that some harvesting is still taking place. IWC conservation attempts designed to protect finbacks, minke whales, and sperm whales have also been circumvented, most notably by the Russians and Japanese, who simply announced their own unilateral quotas.

Whales are not the only seagoing creatures to suffer from an absence of clearly defined, cheaply enforceable, and transferable property rights. Codfish off the New England and eastern Canadian coasts were once so abundant, it was said, that a person could walk across the sea on their backs. The fish grew into six-foot-long, 200-pound giants, and generations of families from coastal communities knew they could count on the fish for a prosperous livelihood. The problem was that, to establish rights to that bounty, the fish first had to be hauled from the sea. The result was overfishing, which led to declining yields and shrinking fish. Over the last thirty years alone, the catch has dropped more than 75 percent, and the typical fish caught these days weighs but twenty pounds. As a result, the Canadians have virtually closed down their cod fishery, and the American fleet is but a ghost of its former self.

The cod is not alone in its demise. In the northeastern Atlantic, haddock, mackerel, and herring are all in serious trouble. Along the West Coast of the United States, lingcod, rockfish, and bocaccio are in trouble as well. Worldwide, 30 percent of fish stocks, including orange roughy, shark, swordfish, and tuna, are declining due to overfishing, and another 40 percent or more of the commercial stocks are on the verge of trouble.

A number of nations have taken legislative action in the hope of stemming the decline. Beginning in 1996, for example, the U.S. National Maritime Fisheries Service was required to begin working with eight regional fishing councils around the country to come up with plans to stem the demise of traditional fish stocks. Yet not all the councils are actually following the plans they have laid out, so the overfishing continues. A more promising approach may be seen in Britain, where under the terms of European Union rules, the catch of all major fish stocks are limited by quotas, which specify the amount of fish that legally may be taken. The British innovation has been to make those quotas transferable—that is, the rights to catch specific numbers of fish can be purchased and sold just like any other good. The quotas assign rights to fish, and their transferability ensures that the lowest-cost, most sensible means of taking those fish will be used. With quotas set at levels consistent with the long-term survival of the fish, and the elimination of the pressure to "catch it or lose it," fish stocks in the affected areas seemed to have begun a turnaround.

The Canadian province of British Columbia has started a similar program covering its halibut fishery, with equally promising results. Since 1923 management of the Pacific halibut fishery has been regulated jointly by the United States and Canada. Yet despite stringent controls, which included limits on the number of vessels that could fish, and reductions in the length of the season, the halibut stock showed signs of collapse by the late 1980s.

Joint efforts by fishers and the Canadian Department of Fisheries and Oceans led to the creation of a system of individual vessel quotas (IVQs) in 1991. Existing license holders now own a percentage of the total allowable catch. In effect, each vessel owner has secure property rights to a specified poundage of fish each year, and the result has been to change their incentives and behavior drastically.

The allocation of individual vessel quotas eliminated the need for a short fishing season, originally created in a futile effort to halt over-fishing. Prior to IVQs, the short season forced the fishers into the same prime areas at the same time, resulting in damaged and lost fishing gear and "ghost fishing," in which lost fishing gear continued to catch fish. From six days in 1990, the season has been lengthened to 245 days, with fishers allowed to choose when they will take the catch that belongs to them. Vessels no longer conflict with one another, preventing substantial losses of gear and fish each season. Moreover, before the individual quotas, vessels had extra crew on board to ensure the most rapid possible harvesting of fish. Under IVQs, the total number of crew members in the fleet quickly dropped by about 20 percent.

Before quotas, vessel owners felt compelled to fish regardless of weather conditions, because the loss of even a day of fishing could make the difference between profit and loss for the season. Now that pressure has been eliminated, greatly enhancing the safety of the fishers. The longer fishing season also has enabled fishers to sell higher quality and fresher fish. Prior to IVQs, only about half the catch could be sold as fresh fish, which are more valuable; now nearly all of it is sold fresh, yielding better product for consumers and higher profits for producers.

The IVQs are transferable (although with some restrictions) and the transferability has added to the benefits of the system. For example, the number of vessels has been reduced, because smaller, less efficient fishers have sold or leased their licenses to more efficient operators. This has decreased capital costs and helped reduce total crew in the fleet. Similarly, average vessel size has risen, increasing the safety of the crews. Transferability also gets the quotas into the hands of the "highliners," the skippers who are best at finding the fish and harvesting them in the lowest-cost manner. And finally, the best news of all is reserved for the halibut themselves. Since the introduction of IVQs, fishers no longer need to harvest the halibut to establish rights to them, so they no longer have an incentive to over-fish. As a result, halibut stocks in the Pacific fishery have begun to grow rapidly—one more illustration that the clear assignment of enforceable, transferable property rights remains the most effective way we know to protect other species from the depredations of *Homo sapiens*.

DISCUSSION QUESTIONS

1.   Has there ever been a problem with the extinction of dogs, cats, or cattle? Why not?

2.   Some argue that the only way to save rare species is to set up private game reserves to which wealthy hunters can travel. How could this help save endangered species?

3.   Is government *ownership* of animals needed to protect species from extinction?

4.   In the United States, most fishing streams are public property, with access available to all. In Britain, most fishing streams are privately owned, with access restricted to those who are willing to pay for the right to fish. Anglers agree that over the past thirty years, the quality of fishing in the United States has declined, while the quality of fishing in Britain has risen. Can you suggest why?

26

Smog Merchants

Pollution is undesirable, almost by definition. Most of us use the term so commonly it suggests we all know, without question, what it means. Yet there is an important sense in which "pollution is what pollution does." Consider, for example, ozone (O_3), an unstable collection of oxygen atoms. At upper levels of the atmosphere it is a naturally occurring substance that plays an essential role in protecting life from the harmful effects of ultraviolet radiation. Without the ozone layer, skin cancer would likely become a leading cause of death, and spending a day at the beach would be as healthy as snuggling up to an open barrel of radioactive waste. At lower levels of the atmosphere, however, ozone occurs as a by-product of a chemical reaction between unburned hydrocarbons (as from petroleum products), nitrogen oxides, and sunlight.[1] In this form it is a major component of smog, and breathing it can cause coughing, asthma attacks, chest pain, and possibly long-term lung-function impairment.

Consider also polychlorinated biphenyls (PCBs), molecules that exist only in human-made form. Because they are chemically quite stable, PCBs are useful in a variety of industrial applications, including insulation in large electrical transformers. Without PCBs, electricity generation would be more expensive, as would the thousands of other goods that depend on electricity for their production and distribution. Yet PCBs are also highly toxic; acute exposure (e.g., from ingestion) can result in rapid death. Chronic (long-term) exposure is suspected to cause some forms of cancer. Illegal dumping of PCBs into streams and lakes has caused massive fish kills

---

[1] Ozone is also produced as a by-product of lightning strikes and other electrical discharges. Wherever and however it occurs, it has a distinctive metallic taste.

and is generally regarded as a threat to drinking-water supplies. And because PCBs are chemically stable (i.e., they decompose very slowly), once they are released into the environment they remain a potential threat for generations to come.

As these examples suggest, the notion of pollution is highly sensitive to context. Even crude oil, so essential as a source of energy, can become pollution when it appears on the shores of Alaska's pristine beaches. Despite this fact, we shall assume in what follows that (1) we all know what pollution is when we see, smell, taste, or even read about it, and (2) holding other things constant, less of it is preferred to more.

There are numerous ways to reduce or avoid pollution. Laws can be passed banning production processes that emit pollutants into the air and water or specifying minimum air- and water-quality levels or the maximum amount of pollution allowable. Firms would then be responsible for developing the technology and for paying the price to satisfy such standards. Or the law could specify the particular type of production technology to be used and the type of pollution-abatement equipment required in order to produce legally. Finally, subsidies could be paid to firms that reduce pollution emission, or taxes could be imposed on firms that engage in pollution emission.

No matter which methods are used to reduce pollution, costs will be incurred and problems will arise. For example, setting physical limits on the amount of pollution permitted discourages firms from developing the technology that will reduce pollution beyond those limits. The alternative of subsidizing firms that reduce pollution levels may seem a strange use of taxpayers' dollars. The latest solution to the air pollution problem—selling or trading the rights to pollute—may seem even stranger. Nevertheless, this approach is now being used around the nation, especially in Los Angeles, the smog capital of the country.

Under the plan that operates in the Los Angeles area, pollution allowances have been established for 390 of the area's largest polluters. Both nitrous oxide and sulphur dioxide, the two main ingredients of southern California's brown haze, are covered. Prior to the plan, which went into effect in 1994, the government told companies such as power plants and oil refineries what techniques they had to use to reduce pollutants. Under the new rules, companies are simply told how much they must reduce emissions each year, and they are then allowed to use whatever means they see fit to meet the standards. Over the initial ten years of the plan, firms had their baseline emissions limits cut by 5 to 8 percent a year. By 2003, emissions of nitrous oxides from these sources should be down by 75 percent and sulphur dioxide by 60 percent.

The key element in the program is that the companies are allowed to buy and sell pollution rights. A firm that is successful in reducing pollutants below the levels to which it is entitled receives emission reduction credits (ERCs) for doing so. The firm can sell those credits to other firms, enabling the latter to exceed their baseline emissions by the amount of credits they purchase.

Presumably, firms that can cut pollutants in the lowest cost manner will do so, selling some of their credits to firms that find it more costly to meet the standards. Because the total level of emissions is determined ahead of time by the area's Air Quality Management District, the trading scheme will meet the requisite air quality standards. Yet because most of the emissions reductions will be made by firms that are the most efficient at doing so, the standards will be met at the lowest cost to society.

A similar market-based plan covering sulphur dioxide has been adopted by the Environmental Protection Agency (EPA) on a nationwide level. This program was kicked off by an auction of 150,000 air pollution allowances granted by the EPA. Each allowance permits a power utility to emit one ton of sulphur dioxide (SO_2) into the air. Based on their past records, utilities have been given rights to emit sulphur dioxide into the air at a declining rate into the future. By the year 2000, for example, utility emissions of sulphur dioxide had to be cut in half. Companies can either use their allowances to comply with the clean air regulations, or they can beat the standards and sell their unused allowances to other utilities.

As it turns out, although the EPA auctions probably helped get the trading process started, the expansion in private trades has been so rapid and extensive that the auctions are now a minor part of the market. Perhaps more importantly, the private market in allowances seems to be quite efficient at doing what it was designed to do—move allowances to their highest-valued locations, permit equalization of control costs across sources, and generate a key source of information about the costs of reducing SO_2 emissions.

Research conducted by Paul Joskow, Richard Schmalensee, and Elizabeth Bailey has found that after an initial twelve- to eighteen-month period in which there were few private trades and relatively high prices for the allowances—some $250 to $300 per ton—the market evolved rapidly. By mid-1994 prices had dropped below $150 per ton and the volume of private trades exceeded the volume offered in the EPA auction. Since then, prices have fallen to about $100 per ton, and private trading of allowances for more than 12 million tons per year now greatly dwarfs the EPA auction.

This research also has uncovered two other quite important facts. First, the transaction costs of trading allowances are quite low—about 2 percent of the prevailing price. In addition, it appears that the prices at which trade takes place at any point in time are all quite close to one another. The spread between average bids and lowest winning bids at EPA auctions is only about 1 to 3 percent, and trading in the private market appears to be similarly concentrated around a single price at any point in time.

Because utilities can freely choose between either abating or emitting each ton of SO_2, they will pay for an allowance only what it will save them in abatement costs. Equivalently, a utility will pay no more for abatement than it would pay for an allowance to emit the SO_2. Thus, the existence of a common price for allowances assures us that the cost per ton of cutting emissions must be at that same level. That is, the costs of abating SO_2 emissions must be running about $100 per ton. According to the U.S. Council of Economic Advisers, the tradable permit plan for SO_2 has not only helped contribute to a 60 percent cut in SO_2 emissions from major sources, it has substantially reduced the costs of achieving this environmental improvement.

There are also EPA trading programs for the emissions produced by heavy-duty on-highway engines (such as found in large trucks) and for nitrogen oxide (NO_x) emissions from power plants. The general consensus seems to be that the heavy-duty engine program has significantly reduced the costs of complying with emissions standards. As yet, the nationwide NO_x program for power plants is still being implemented, so there is no data on its effectiveness, but a better-established NO_x program covering the

Los Angeles area appears to be cutting the costs of achieving emissions reductions there.

Perhaps not surprisingly, the notion of selling the right to pollute has been controversial, particularly among environmental organizations. The activist group Greenpeace, for example, claims that selling pollution allowances "is like giving a pack of cigarettes to a person dying of lung cancer." Nonetheless, other environmental groups have chosen to buy some of the allowances and retire them unused. One such group was the Cleveland-based National Healthy Air License Exchange, whose president said, "It is our intent . . . to have a real effect on this market and on the quality of air."

Some observers have been disappointed that the government has taken so long to approve emissions-trading schemes. There appear to be two key reasons why progress has been so slow. First, many environmentalists are vigorously opposed to the very concept of tradable emissions, arguing that it amounts to putting a price on what traditionally has been considered a "priceless" resource—the environment. Because most of the cost savings that stem from tradable emissions-rights accrue to the polluters and their customers, government agencies have proceeded carefully, to avoid charges that they are somehow selling out to polluters.

Ironically, the second reason for the delay in developing markets for tradable pollution rights has been the reluctance on the part of industry to push harder for them. Similar programs in the past involved emissions credits that could be saved up (banked) by a firm for later use or bartered on a limited basis among firms. Under these earlier programs, environmental regulators would periodically wipe out emissions credits that firms thought they owned, on the ground that doing so provided a convenient means of preventing future environmental damage.

Not surprisingly, some companies believe that any credits purchased under a tradable-rights plan might be subject to the same sort of confiscation. Under such circumstances, firms have been understandably reluctant to support a program that might—or might not—prove to be of real value.[2] Indeed, even under the tradable-emissions plan adopted for Los Angeles, the regulators

---

[2] One can imagine the enthusiasm people would feel toward, say, the market for automobiles if the government announced that because cars were a source of pollution, the property rights to them might be revoked at any time, for any reason.

have explicitly stated that the emissions credits are *not* property rights and that they can be revoked at any time. Sadly, unless obstacles such as these can be removed, achieving environmental improvement at the lowest **social cost** is likely to remain a goal rather than an accomplishment.

DISCUSSION QUESTIONS

1. Does marketing the right to pollute mean that we are allowing too much destruction of our environment?

2. Who implicitly has property rights to the air when the EPA auctions SO_2 permits? Does your answer depend on who gets the revenue raised by the auction?

3. Some environmental groups have opposed tradable pollution-rights on the grounds that this puts a price on the environment, when in fact the environment is a priceless resource. Does this reasoning imply that we should be willing to give up *anything* (and therefore everything) to protect the environment? Does environmental quality have an infinite value? If not, how should we place a value on it?

4. Environmental regulations that prohibit emissions beyond some point implicitly allow firms and individuals to pollute up to that point at no charge. Don't such regulations amount to giving away environmental quality at no charge? Would it be better to charge a price via emissions taxes, for example, for the initial amount of pollutants? Would doing so reduce the amount of pollution?

27

Greenhouse Economics

The sky may not be falling, but it is getting warmer—maybe. The consequences will not be catastrophic, but they will be costly—maybe. We can reverse the process but should not spend very much to do so right now—maybe. Such is the state of the debate over the greenhouse effect—the apparent tendency of carbon dioxide (CO_2) and other gases to accumulate in the atmosphere, acting like a blanket that traps radiated heat, thereby increasing the earth's temperature. Before turning to the economics of the problem, let's take a brief look at the physical processes involved.

Certain gases in the atmosphere, chiefly water vapor and CO_2, trap heat radiating from the earth's surface. If they did not, the earth's average temperature would be roughly $0°F$ instead of just over $59°F$, and everything would be frozen solid. Human activity helps create some so-called greenhouse gases, including CO_2 (mainly from combustion of fossil fuels), methane (from crops and livestock), and chlorofluorocarbons (CFCs—from aerosol sprays, air conditioners, and refrigerators). We have the potential, unmatched in any other species, of profoundly altering our ecosystem.

There seems little doubt that humankind has been producing these gases at a record rate and that they are steadily accumulating in the atmosphere. Airborne concentrations of CO_2, for example, are increasing at the rate of about 0.5 percent per year; over the past 50 years, the amount of CO_2 in the atmosphere has risen a total of about 25 percent. Laboratory analysis of glacial ice dating back at least 160,000 years indicates that global temperatures and CO_2 levels in the atmosphere do, in fact, tend to move together, suggesting that the impact of today's rising CO_2 levels may be higher global temperatures in the future. Indeed, the National Academy of Sciences (NAS) has suggested that by the middle of the twenty-first century, greenhouse gases could be double the levels they were in 1860, and that global temperatures could rise by as much as $2°$ to $9°F$.[1] The possible consequences of such a temperature increase include the following: a rise in the average sea level, inundating coastal areas, including most of Florida; the spread of algal blooms capable of deoxygenating major bodies of water, such as the Chesapeake Bay; and the conversion of much of the midwestern wheat and corn belt into a hot, arid dust bowl.

When an individual drives a car, heats a house, or uses an aerosol hair spray, greenhouse gases are produced. In economic terms, this creates a classic negative externality. Most of the costs (in this case, those arising from global warming) are borne by individuals *other than* the one making the decision about how many miles to drive or how much hair spray to use. Because the driver (or sprayer) enjoys all the benefits of the activity but suffers only a part of the cost, that individual engages in more than the economically efficient amount of the activity. In this sense, the problem of greenhouse gases parallels the problem that occurs when someone smokes a cigarette in an enclosed space or litters the countryside with fast-food wrappers. If we are to get individuals to reduce production of greenhouse gases to the efficient rate, we must somehow induce them to act *as though* they bear all the costs of their actions. The two most widely accepted means of doing this are government regulation and taxation, both of which have been proposed to deal with greenhouse gases.

The 1988 Toronto Conference on the Changing Atmosphere, attended by representatives from 48 nations, favored the regulation route. The Conference recommended a mandatory cut in CO_2 emissions by 2005 to 80 percent of their 1988 level—a move that would require a major reduction in worldwide economic output. The 1997 Kyoto conference on climate change, attended by representatives from 160 nations, made more specific but also more modest proposals. Overall, attendees agreed that by 2012, 38 developed nations

---

[1] This may not sound like much, but it does not take much to alter the world as we know it. The global average temperature at the height of the last ice age 18,000 years ago—when Canada and most of Europe were covered with ice—was 51°F, just 8° or so cooler than today.

should cut greenhouse emissions by 5 percent relative to 1990 levels. Developing nations, including China and India (the two most populous nations in the world), would be exempt from emissions cuts. On the taxation front, one prominent U.S. politician has proposed a tax of $100 per ton on the carbon emitted by fuels. It is estimated that such a tax would raise the price of coal by $70 per ton (about 300 percent) and elevate the price of oil by $8 per barrel, or about 40 percent. These proposals, and others like them, clearly have the potential to reduce the buildup of greenhouse gases but only at substantial costs. It thus makes some sense to ask: What are we likely to get for our money?

Perhaps surprisingly, the answer to this question is not obvious. Consider, for example, the raw facts of the matter. On average over the past century, greenhouse gases have been rising and so has the average global temperature. Yet most of the temperature rise occurred before 1940, whereas most of the increase in greenhouse gases has occurred after 1940. In fact, global average temperatures fell about 0.5°F between 1940 and 1970; this cooling actually led a number of prominent scientists during the 1970s to forecast a coming ice age!

Just as disconcerting is that the facts of global temperature change appear different depending on how and where temperature is measured. For example, if one looks only at ground-based measurements, the decade of the 1990s was clearly the warmest on record. Yet the upward trend in temperature that appears to hold true in these data is directly at odds with the results from other sources. Measurements taken using satellites and balloons, for example, suggest that there is *no* tendency for the average temperature of the atmosphere to rise. Why these discrepancies exist and what they mean for the future are issues still unresolved.

Nevertheless, let us suppose for the moment that, barring a significant reduction in greenhouse gas emissions, global warming is either under way or on the way. What can we expect? According to the most comprehensive study yet of this issue, a report by the prestigious National Academy of Sciences, the answer is a "good news, bad news" story.

The bad news is this: The likely rise in the sea level by one to three feet will inundate significant portions of our existing coastline; the expected decline in precipitation will necessitate more widespread use of irrigation; the higher average temperatures will compel more widespread use of air conditioning, along with the associated higher consumption of energy to power it; and the blazing heat in southern latitudes may make these areas too uncomfortable for all but the most heat-loving souls. The good news is that the technology for coping with changes such as these is well known and the costs of coping surprisingly small—on a scale measured in terms of hundreds of billions of dollars, of course. Moreover, many of the impacts that loom large at the individual level will represent much smaller costs at a societal level. For example, although higher average temperatures could prove disastrous for farmers in southern climes, the extra warmth could be an enormous windfall farther north, where year-round farming might become feasible. Similarly, the loss of shoreline due to rising sea levels would partly just be a migration of coastline inland—current beachfront property owners would suffer, but their inland neighbors would gain.[2]

None of these changes are free, of course, and there remain significant uncertainties about how global warming might affect species other than *Homo sapiens*. It is estimated, for example, that temperate forests can "migrate" only at a rate of about 100 kilometers per century, not fast enough to match the speed at which warming is expected to occur. Similarly, the anticipated rise in the sea level could wipe out between 30 and 70 percent of today's coastal wetlands. Whether new wetlands would develop along our new coastline and what might happen to species that occupy existing wetlands are issues that have not yet been resolved.

Yet the very uncertainties that surround the possible warming of the planet suggest that policy prescriptions of the sort that have been proposed—such as the cut in worldwide CO_2 emissions agreed to at Kyoto—may be too much, too soon. Indeed, the National Academy of Sciences recommended that we learn more before we leap too far. Caution seems particularly wise, because the exclusion of developing nations from any emissions cuts could result in huge costs for developed nations—and little or no reduction in worldwide greenhouse gases. Some sense of the damages that can be wrought by ignoring such counsel and rushing into a politically popular response to a complex environmental issue is well illustrated by another atmospheric problem: smog.

---

[2] There would be a net loss of land area and thus a net economic loss. Nevertheless, the net loss of land would be chiefly in the form of less valuable inshore property.

Although gasoline is a major source of the hydrocarbons in urban air, its contribution to smog is plummeting because new cars are far cleaner than their predecessors. In the 1970s, cars spewed about 9 grams of hydrocarbons per mile; emissions controls brought this down to about 1.5 grams per mile by 1995. The cost of this reduction is estimated to be approximately $1000 for each ton of hydrocarbon emissions prevented—a number that many experts believe to be well below the benefits of the cleaner air that resulted. Despite the improvements in air quality, however, smog is still a significant problem in many major cities. Additional federal regulations aimed primarily at the nine smoggiest urban areas, including New York, Chicago, and Los Angeles, went into effect in 1995. Meeting these standards meant that gasoline had to be reformulated at a cost of about 6 cents per gallon. This brought the cost of removing each additional ton of hydrocarbons to about $10,000—some 10 times the per-ton cost of removing the first 95 percent from urban air.

Just as significantly, EPA rules require that gasoline have a minimum oxygen content to help it burn. But because gasoline does not naturally contain oxygen, these rules effectively require refiners to put additives in their gas. At this point, there are only two additives that meet the EPA requirements: ethanol (refined from corn), and methyl tertiary butyl ether (MTBE). Because adding ethanol would drive the cost of gas up sharply, refiners have felt compelled to add MTBE. Yet MTBE has contaminated water supplies in California, and concern over its possible carcinogenic properties has led that state to ban its use as of 2003. Unless the EPA grants California an exemption from the law, this will leave the state with the choice of switching to the more costly ethanol, or having its citizens walk to work.

The costs of the EPA oxygen standards for gasoline are estimated to add 21 cents per gallon to the price of gas. Moreover, the presence of multiple EPA standards across the country has left supplies of gasoline vulnerable to disruption, because fuel often cannot be transshipped from one area to another to meet temporary shortages. This fact has contributed substantially to large spikes in the price of gasoline in major Midwestern cities, such as Milwaukee and Chicago, every time there has been even a minor supply disruption.

Overall, the costs of EPA-mandated gasoline reformulation are huge, even though the EPA has never shown that the oxygen content requirement is necessary to meet its air quality standards. The potential benefits of reformulated gasoline appear to be trivial compared to the costs, yet we are stuck with this EPA mandate, because few politicians want to be accused of being in favor of smog.

There is no doubt that atmospheric concentrations of greenhouse gases are rising and that human actions are the cause. It is probable that, as a result, the global average temperature is, or soon will be, rising. If temperatures do rise significantly, the costs will be large but the consequences are likely to be manageable. Given the nature of the problem, private action, taken on the individual level, will not yield the optimal outcome for society. Thus the potential gains from government action, in the form of environmental regulations or taxation, are substantial. But the key word here is *potential,* for government action, no matter how well intentioned, does not automatically yield benefits that exceed the costs. As we seek solutions to the potential problems associated with greenhouse gases, we must be sure that the consequences of action are not worse than those of first examining the problem further. If we forget this message, greenhouse economics may turn into bad economics—and worse policy.

DISCUSSION QUESTIONS

1. Why will voluntary actions, undertaken at the individual level, be unlikely to bring about significant reductions in greenhouse gases such as CO_2?

2. Does the fact that the CO_2 produced in one nation results in adverse effects on other nations have any bearing on the likelihood that CO_2 emissions will be reduced to the optimal level? Would the problem be easier to solve if all the costs and benefits were concentrated within a single country? Within a single elevator?

3. The policy approach to greenhouse gases will almost certainly involve limits on emissions, rather than taxes on emissions. Can you suggest why limits rather than taxes are likely to be used?

4. It costs about $80,000 per acre to create wetlands. How reasonable is this number as an estimate of what wetlands are worth?

Part Seven

Global and Macroeconomic Affairs

INTRODUCTION

Many of the key public issues of our day transcend national borders or affect the entirety of our $10 trillion economy. The rapid developments in information processing, communications, and transportation over the past 25 years are gradually knitting the economies of the world closer together. Political developments, most notably the demise of the Iron Curtain and the dissolution of the Soviet Union, have contributed to this growing economic integration, as have reductions in long-standing barriers to international trade. Moreover, the last decade was a period of growing awareness that the economic vitality of individual markets was importantly determined by macroeconomic decisions made in Washington, D.C. The turn of the twenty-first century was also—briefly—the first time in three decades that the federal government managed to spend less than it collected in taxes, a development that surely warrants examination as a public issue.

The passage of the North American Free Trade Agreement (NAFTA) and the creation of the World Trade Organization (WTO) have substantially reduced the barriers to trade between the United States and most of the rest of the world. If we take advantage of these lower trade barriers, we have the opportunity to make ourselves far better off by specializing in those activities in which we have a **comparative advantage** and then trading the fruits of our efforts with other nations. Yet voluntary exchange also often redistributes wealth, in addition to creating it, so there will always be some individuals who oppose free trade. There are many smokescreens behind which the self-interested opposition to free trade is hidden, as we see in Chapter 28, "The Opposition to Free Trade." Nevertheless, although **protectionism**—the creation of trade barriers such as tariffs and quotas—often sounds sensible, it is in fact a surefire way to reduce rather than enhance our wealth. If we ignore the value of free trade, we do so only at our own peril.

To illustrate the tremendous damages that can be wrought when protectionism gains the upper hand, Chapter 29, "The $750,000 Job," examines what happens when tariffs and quotas are imposed in an effort to "save" U.S. jobs from foreign competition. The sad facts are that (1) in the long run, it is almost impossible to effectively protect U.S. workers from foreign competition, and (2) efforts to do so not only reduce Americans' overall living standards, but they also end up costing the jobs of other Americans. The moral of our story is that competition is just as beneficial on the international scene as it is on the domestic front.

For twelve major European nations, New Year's Day 2002 was truly "out with the old, in with the new." That was the day the euro became the common currency for most members of the European Union, replacing some $600 billion worth of francs, marks, lira, and other national currencies with a common currency controlled by the newly-created European Central Bank. As we see in Chapter 30, "The Euro," for individuals living in, traveling to, or doing business with the twelve nations that have adopted the euro, the switch has the potential to make life better. Gone will be the need to keep track of a host of exchange rates, and it will be far easier to compare goods' prices in different countries. But there are risks to the citizens of the euro-nations, risks that some fear could overwhelm the lower transactions costs and greater convenience of having a single money for 300 million people. Broadly speaking, flexibility and independence are the great advantages of having a separate currency with a value that is free to fluctuate against other currencies. With a separate currency a country can respond at lower cost to external shocks, for it can allow its exchange rate to vary, rather than having to wait for domestic prices or factors of production to move. Loss of this flexibility is one of the costs of adopting the euro. Similarly, the twelve nations that have adopted the euro have given up the independence to make their own monetary policies, for they will all be forced to live with the policies of the European Central Bank. Whether advantages of the euro will outweigh its disadvantages is an issue that only experience gained over time will determine.

The issue of money is again our topic in Chapter 31, "Monetary Policy and Interest Rates," where we examine the conduct of **monetary policy** in the United States. The basics of monetary policy are quite simple. An increase in the rate of growth of the **money supply** increases spending on goods and services and thus stimulates the economy, tending to lower unemployment in the short run and raise inflation in the long run. The flip side is that a decrease in the rate of growth of the money supply reduces spending, thereby depressing the economy; the short-run result is higher unemployment, while the longer-run effect is a lower inflation rate. The Fed—short for the **Federal Reserve System**—is America's **central bank** and is charged with the conduct of monetary policy in the U.S. Often the discussion of monetary policy suggests that the Fed somehow controls interest rates throughout the economy. As we see here, although the Fed can cause interest rates to move up or down in the short run via its choice of monetary policy, forces beyond its control determine what interest rates will be in the long run. Ultimately, interest rates are determined just like other market prices—that is, by the choices of millions of individuals and businesses throughout the economy.

Our final issue, covered in Chapter 32, "The Disappearing Surplus," returns us full circle to where we started this book: Our world is one of scarcity. For four brief years between 1998 and 2002, the federal government managed to spend less than it collected in taxes: It ran a budgetary **surplus** after thirty years of budgetary **deficits**. Discussions of the federal budget around this time period routinely suggested to the unwary that the true cost of federal programs was somehow fundamentally altered by whether the government paid for these programs by collecting current taxes, or by borrowing the money. As we show in this chapter, nothing could be farther from the truth. Whenever the government spends more, someone else has to cut spending to release resources to the government: The private sector must give up what the government takes. This is obvious when current taxes are used to pay, but it is equally true when the government borrows. When U.S. government debt is issued, the private sector voluntarily gives up spending in exchange for the bond it receives. Eventually, that debt has to be repaid through higher taxes in the future—added taxes that must cover both the interest and the principal. Thus, the real issue is not the surplus or the deficit. The real issue is how much of our total annual income the government spends, and therefore how much is left over for you and everybody else to spend. Higher government spending means fewer resources are available for the private sector—and that means fewer resources for you, whether the higher taxes happen to be now or in the future. In a world of scarcity, no choices are without cost.

28

The Opposition to Free Trade

Much of the last decade has been a time of great change on the international trade front. The North American Free Trade Agreement (NAFTA), for example, substantially reduced the barriers to trade among citizens of Canada, the United States, and Mexico. On a global scale, the Uruguay round of the General Agreement on Tariffs and Trade (GATT) was ratified by 117 nations including the United States. Under the terms of this agreement, GATT was replaced by the World Trade Organization (WTO), whose membership now numbers more than 140, and **tariffs** were cut worldwide. Agricultural **subsidies** were reduced, patent protections extended, and the WTO is establishing a set of arbitration boards to settle international disputes over trade issues.

Many economists believe that both NAFTA and the agreements reached during the Uruguay round were victories not only for free trade, but also for the citizens of the participating nations. Nevertheless, many non-economists, particularly politicians, opposed these agreements, so it is important we understand what is beneficial about NAFTA, the Uruguay round, and free trade in general.

Voluntary trade creates new wealth. In voluntary trade, both parties in an exchange gain. They give up something of lesser value in return for something of greater value. In this sense, exchanges are always unequal. But it is this unequal nature of exchange that is the source of the increased productivity and higher wealth that occurs whenever trade takes place. When we engage in exchange, what we give up is worth less than what we get—for if this were not true, we would not have traded. And what is true for us is also true for our trading partner, meaning that partner is better off too.

Free trade encourages individuals to employ their talents and abilities in the most productive manner possible, and to exchange the fruits of their efforts. The **gains from trade** lie in one of the most fundamental ideas in economics—a nation gains from doing what it can do best *relative* to other nations, that is, by specializing in those endeavors in which it has a **comparative advantage**. Trade encourages individuals and nations to discover ways to specialize so that they can become more productive and enjoy higher incomes. Increased productivity and the subsequent increase in the rate of economic growth are exactly what the signatories of the Uruguay round and NAFTA sought—and are obtaining—by reducing trade barriers.

Despite these gains from exchange, free trade is routinely opposed by some (and sometimes many) people, particularly in the case of international trade. There are many excuses offered for this opposition, but they all basically come down to one issue. When our borders are open to trade with other nations, some individuals and businesses within our nation face more competition. As we saw in Chapter 18, most firms and workers hate competition, and who can blame them? After all, if a firm can keep the competition out, profits are sure to rise. And if workers can prevent competition from other sources, they can enjoy higher wages and greater selection among jobs. So the real source of most opposition to international trade is that the opponents to trade dislike the competition that comes with it. There is nothing immoral or unethical about this—but there is nothing altruistic or noble about this, either. It is self-interest, pure and simple.

Opposition to free trade is, of course, nothing new on the American landscape. One of the most famous examples of such opposition resulted in the Smoot-Hawley Tariff of 1930. This major federal government statute was a classic example of protectionism—an effort to protect a subset of American producers at the expense of consumers and other producers. It included tariff schedules for over 20,000 products, raising taxes on affected imports by an average of 52 percent.

The Smoot-Hawley Tariff encouraged beggar-thy-neighbor policies by the rest of the world. Such policies represent an attempt to improve (a portion of) one's domestic economy at the expense of foreign countries' economies. In this case, tariffs were imposed to discourage imports, in order that domestic import-competing industries would benefit. The beggar-thy-neighbor policy at the heart of the Smoot-Hawley Tariff Act of 1930 was soon adopted by the United Kingdom, France, the Netherlands, and Switzerland. The result was a massive reduction in international trade. According to many economists, this caused a worsening of the ongoing worldwide depression of the period.

Opponents of free trade sometimes claim that beggar-thy-neighbor policies benefit the United States by protecting import-competing industries. In general, this claim is not correct. It is true that some Americans benefit from such policies, but two large groups of Americans lose. First, there are the purchasers of imports and import-competing goods. They suffer from higher prices and reduced selection of goods and suppliers caused by tariffs and import **quotas**. Second, the decline in imports caused by protectionism also causes a decline in exports, thereby harming firms and employees in these industries. This follows directly from one of the most fundamental propositions in international trade: *In the long run, imports are paid for by exports.* This proposition simply states that when one country buys goods and services from the rest of the world (imports), the rest of the world eventually wants goods from that country (exports) in exchange. Given this fundamental proposition, a corollary becomes obvious: *Any restriction on imports leads to a reduction in exports.* Thus any business for import-competing industries gained as a result of tariffs or quotas means at least as much business *lost* for exporting industries.

Opponents to free trade often raise a variety of objections in their efforts to restrict it. For example, it is sometimes claimed that foreign companies engage in dumping, that is, selling their goods in America below cost. The first question to ask when such charges are made is this: Below *whose* cost? Clearly, if the foreign firm is selling in America, it must be offering the good for sale at a price that is at or below the costs of American firms, or else it could not induce Americans to buy it. But the ability of individuals or firms to get goods at lower cost is one of the *benefits* of free trade, not one of its damaging features.

What about claims that import sales are taking place at prices below the *foreign* company's costs? This amounts to arguing that the owners of the foreign company are voluntarily giving some of their wealth to us, namely, the difference between their costs and the (lower) price they charge us. It is possible, though unlikely, they might wish to do this, perhaps because this could be the cheapest way of getting us to try a product that we would not otherwise purchase. But even supposing it is true, why would we want to refuse this gift? As a nation, we are richer if we accept it. Moreover, it is a gift that will be offered only in the short run: There is no point in selling at below cost unless one hopes to soon raise price profitably above cost!

Another argument sometimes raised against international trade is that the goods are produced abroad using unfair labor practices (such as the use of child labor) or using production processes that do not meet American environmental standards. It is surely the case that such charges are sometimes correctly levied. But we must remember two things here. First, although we may find the use of child labor (or perhaps sixty-hour weeks with no overtime pay) objectionable, such practices were at one time commonplace in the United States. They used to be engaged in here for the same reason they are currently practiced abroad: The people involved were (or are) too poor to do otherwise. Some families in developing nations literally cannot survive unless all members of their family contribute. As unfortunate as this is, if we insist on imposing our tastes—shaped in part by our extraordinarily great wealth—on peoples whose wealth is far smaller than ours, we run the risk of making them worse off even as we think we are helping them.

Similar considerations apply to environmental standards.[1] It is well established that individuals' and nations' willingness to pay for environmental quality is very much shaped by their wealth: Environmental quality is a luxury good; that is, people who are rich (such as Americans) want to consume much more of it per capita than do people who are poor. Insisting that other nations meet environmental standards that we find acceptable is much like insisting that they wear the clothes we wear, use the modes of transportation we prefer, and consume the foods we like. The few people who manage to afford it will indeed be living in the style to which we are accustomed, but most people will not be able to afford much of anything.

Our point is not that foreign labor or environmental standards are, or should be, irrelevant to Americans. Our point instead is that

[1] There is one important exception to this argument. In the case of foreign air or water pollution generated near enough to our borders (for example with Mexico or Canada) to cause harm to Americans, good public policy presumably dictates that we seek to treat such pollution as though it were being generated inside our borders.

achieving high standards of either is costly, and trade restrictions are unlikely to be the most efficient or effective way to achieve them. Just as importantly, labor standards and environmental standards are all too often raised as smokescreens to hide the real motive: keeping the competition out.

If it is true that free trade is beneficial and that restrictions on trade generally are harmful, we must surely raise the question: How does legislation like the Smoot-Hawley Tariff (or any other trade restriction) ever get passed? As Mark Twain noted many years ago, the reason the free traders win the arguments and the protectionists win the votes is this: Foreign competition often clearly affects a narrow and specific import-competing industry such as textiles, shoes, or automobiles, and thus trade restrictions benefit a narrow, well-defined group of economic agents. For example, restrictions on imports of Japanese automobiles in the 1980s chiefly benefited the Big Three automakers in this country: General Motors, Ford, and Chrysler. Similarly, long-standing quotas on the imports of sugar benefit a handful of large American sugar producers. Because of the concentrated benefits that accrue when Congress votes in favor of trade restrictions, sufficient monies can be raised in those industries to convince members of Congress to impose those restrictions.

The eventual reduction in exports that must follow is normally spread in small doses throughout all export industries. Thus no specific group of workers, managers, or shareholders in export industries will feel that it should contribute money to convince Congress to reduce international trade restrictions. Additionally, although consumers of imports and import-competing goods lose due to trade restrictions, they too are typically a diffuse group of individuals, none of whom individually will be affected a great deal because of any single import restriction. It is the simultaneous existence of concentrated benefits and diffuse costs that led to Mark Twain's conclusion that the protectionists would often win the votes.

Of course the protectionists don't win all the votes—after all, about one-eighth of the American economy is based on international trade. Despite the opposition to free trade that comes from many quarters, its benefits to the economy as a whole are so great it is unthinkable that we might do away with international trade altogether. Thus, when we think about developments such as the North American Free Trade Agreement (NAFTA) and the World Trade Organization (WTO), it is clear that both economic theory and empirical evidence indicate that, on balance, Americans will be better off after—and because of—the move to freer trade.

DISCUSSION QUESTIONS

1. During the late 1980s and early 1990s, American automobile manufacturers greatly increased the quality of the cars they produced, relative to the quality of the cars produced in other nations. What effect do you think this had on (1) American imports of Japanese cars, (2) Japanese imports of American cars, and (3) American exports of goods and services other than automobiles?

2. Over the last twenty years, some Japanese automakers have opened plants in the United States so that they could produce (and sell) "Japanese" cars in the United States. What effect do you think this had on (1) American imports of Japanese cars, (2) Japanese imports of American cars, and (3) American exports of goods and services other than automobiles?

3. For a number of years, Japanese carmakers voluntarily limited the number of cars they exported to the United States. What effect do you think this had on (1) Japanese imports of American cars, and (2) American exports of goods and services other than automobiles?

4. Until recently, American cars exported to Japan had driver controls on the left side of the car (as in America) even though the Japanese drive on the left side of the road, and thus Japanese cars sold in Japan have driver controls on the right side. Suppose the Japanese tried to sell their cars in America with the driver controls on the right side. What impact would this likely have on their sales in this country? Do you think the unwillingness of American carmakers to put the driver controls on the correct side for exports to Japan had any effect on their sales of cars in that country?

29

The $750,000 Job

In even-numbered years, particularly years evenly divisible by four, politicians of all persuasions are apt to give long-winded speeches about the need to protect U.S. jobs from the evils of foreign competition. To accomplish this goal, we are encouraged to buy American. If further encouragement is needed, we are told that if we do not voluntarily reduce the amount of imported goods we purchase, the government will impose (or make more onerous) either tariffs (taxes) on imported goods or quotas (quantity restrictions) that physically limit imports. The objective of this exercise is to save U.S. jobs.

Unlike black rhinos or blue whales, U.S. jobs are in no danger of becoming extinct. There are an infinite number of potential jobs in the American economy, and there always will be. Some of these jobs are not very pleasant, and many others do not pay very well, but there will always be employment of some sort as long as there is scarcity. Thus when a steelworker making $72,000 per year says that imports of foreign steel should be reduced to save his job, what he really means is this: He wants to be protected from competition so he can continue his present employment at the same or higher salary, rather than move to a different employment that has less desirable working conditions or pays a lower salary. There is nothing wrong with the steelworker's goal (better working conditions and higher pay), but it has nothing to do with saving jobs. (Despite this, we may even use the term in the discussion that follows, because it is such convenient shorthand.)

In any discussion of the consequences of restrictions on international trade, it is essential to remember two facts. First, *we pay for imports with exports.* It is true that, in the short run, we can sell off assets or borrow from abroad if we happen to import more goods and services than we export. But we have only a finite amount of assets to sell, and foreigners do not want to wait forever before we pay our bills. Ultimately, our accounts can be settled only if we provide (export) goods and services to the trading partners from whom we purchase (import) goods and services. Trade, after all, involves *quid pro quo* (literally, something for something). The second point to remember is that *voluntary trade is mutually beneficial to the trading partners.* If we restrict international trade, we reduce those benefits, both for our trading partners and for ourselves. One way these reduced benefits are manifested is in the form of curtailed employment opportunities for workers. In a nutshell, even though tariffs and quotas enhance job opportunities in import-competing industries, they also cost us jobs in export industries; the net effect seems to be reduced employment overall.

What is true for the United States is true for other countries as well: They will buy our goods only if they can market theirs, since they too have to export goods to pay for their imports. Thus any U.S. restrictions on imports to this country—via tariffs, quotas, or other means—ultimately cause a reduction in our exports, because other countries will be unable to pay for our goods. This implies that import restrictions inevitably must decrease the size of our export sector. So imposing trade restrictions to save jobs in import-competing industries has the effect of costing jobs in export industries.

Just as important, import restrictions impose costs on U.S. consumers as a whole. By reducing competition from abroad, quotas, tariffs, and other trade restraints push up the prices of foreign goods and enable U.S. producers to hike their own prices. Perhaps the best documented example of this is found in the automobile industry, where voluntary restrictions on Japanese imports were put in place.

Due in part to the enhanced quality of imported cars, sales of domestically produced automobiles fell from 9 million units in 1978 to an average of 6 million units per year between 1980 and 1982. Profits of U.S. automobile manufacturers plummeted as well, turning into substantial losses for some of them. United States automobile manufacturers and autoworkers' unions demanded protection from import competition. They were joined in their cries by politicians from automobile-producing states. The result was a voluntary agreement entered into by Japanese car companies (the most important competitors of U.S. firms), which restricted U.S. sales of Japanese cars to 1.68 million units per year. This agreement—which amounted to a quota even though it never officially bore that name—began in April 1981 and continued into the 1990s in various forms.

Robert W. Crandall, an economist with the Brookings Institute, has estimated how much this voluntary trade restriction has cost U.S. consumers in terms of higher car prices. According to his estimates, the reduced supply of Japanese cars pushed their prices up by $1500 apiece, measured in 2002 dollars. The higher price of Japanese imports in turn enabled domestic producers to hike their prices an average of $600 per car. The total tab in the first full year of the program was $6.5 billion. Crandall also estimated the number of jobs in automobile-related industries that were saved by the voluntary import restrictions; the total was about 26,000. Dividing $6.5 billion by 26,000 jobs yields a cost to consumers of better than $250,000 *per year* for every job saved in the automobile industry. United States consumers could have saved nearly $2 billion on their car purchases each year if, instead of implicitly agreeing to import restrictions, they had simply given $75,000 to every autoworker whose job was preserved by the voluntary import restraints.

The same types of calculations have been made for other industries. Tariffs in the apparel industry were increased between 1977 and 1981, saving the jobs of about 116,000 U.S. apparel workers at a cost of $45,000 per job each year. At about the same time, the producers of citizens band (CB) radios also managed to get tariffs raised. Approximately 600 workers in the industry kept their jobs as a result but at an annual cost to consumers of over $85,000 per job. The cost of protectionism has been even higher in other industries. Jobs preserved in the glassware industry due to trade restrictions cost $200,000 apiece each year. In the maritime industry, the yearly cost of trade protection is $270,000 per job. In the steel industry, the cost of preserving a job has been estimated at an astounding $750,000 per year. If free trade were permitted, each worker losing a job could be given a cash payment of half that amount each year, and the consumer would still save a lot of money.

Even so, this is not the full story. None of these studies estimating the cost to consumers of saving jobs in import-competing industries have attempted to estimate the ultimate impact of import restrictions on the flow of exports, the number of jobs lost in the export sector, and thus the total number of jobs gained or lost.

When imports to the United States are restricted, our trading partners can afford to buy less of what we produce. The resulting decline in export sales means fewer jobs in exporting industries. And the total reduction in trade leads to fewer jobs for workers such as stevedores (who unload ships) and truck drivers (who carry goods to and from ports). On both counts—the overall cut in trade and the accompanying decline in exports—protectionism leads to job losses that might not be obvious immediately.

Several years ago, Congress tried to pass a domestic content bill for automobiles. In effect, the legislation would have required that cars sold in the United States have a minimum percentage of their components manufactured and assembled in this country. Proponents of the legislation argued that it would have protected 300,000 jobs in the U.S. automobile manufacturing and auto parts supply industries. Yet the legislation's supporters failed to recognize the negative impact of the bill on trade in general and its ultimate impact on U.S. export industries. A U.S. Department of Labor study did recognize these impacts, estimating that the domestic content legislation would actually cost more jobs in trade-related and export industries than it protected in import-competing businesses. Congress ultimately decided not to impose a domestic content requirement for cars sold in the United States.

In principle, trade restrictions are imposed to provide economic help to specific industries and to increase employment in those industries. Ironically, the long-term effects may be just the opposite. Researchers at the World Trade Organization (WTO) examined employment in three industries that have been heavily protected throughout the world—textiles, clothing, and iron and steel. Despite stringent trade protection for these industries, employment actually declined during the period of protection, in some cases dramatically. In textiles employment fell 22 percent in the United States and 46 percent in the European Union. The clothing industry had employment losses ranging from 18 percent in the United States to 56 percent in Sweden. Declines in employment in the iron and steel industry ranged anywhere from 10 percent in Canada to 54 percent in the United States. In short, WTO researchers found that restrictions on free trade were no guarantee against job losses—even in the industries supposedly being protected.

The evidence seems clear: The cost of protecting jobs in the short run is enormous. And in the long run, it appears that jobs cannot be protected, especially if one considers all aspects of protectionism. Free trade is a tough platform on which to run for office. But it looks as if it is the one that will yield the most general benefits if implemented. Of course, this does not mean that politicians will embrace it, and so we end up "saving" jobs at a cost of $750,000 each.

DISCUSSION QUESTIONS

1. Who gains and who loses from import restrictions?

2. What motivates politicians to impose tariffs, quotas, and other trade restrictions?

3. If it would be cheaper to give each steelworker $375,000 per year in cash than impose restrictions on imports of steel, why do we have the import restrictions rather than the cash payments?

4. Most U.S. imports and exports travel through our seaports at some point. How do you predict that members of Congress from coastal states would vote on proposals to restrict international trade? What other information would you want to know in making such a prediction?

30

The Euro

For twelve major European nations, New Year's Day 2002 was truly "out with the old, in with the new." That was the day the euro became the common currency for most members of the European Union, replacing some $600 billion worth of francs, marks, lira, and other national currencies with a common currency controlled by the newly-created European Central Bank. For Americans traveling to Europe, the switch to the euro will make life better, eliminating the need to keep track of a host of exchange rates, and making it far easier to compare goods' prices in different countries. Citizens of the twelve nations that have adopted the euro will enjoy those same benefits, but they are subject to more of the risks associated with the new currency—risks that some fear could overwhelm the lower transactions costs and greater convenience of having a single money for 300 million people.[1]

The notion of a single monetary system for Europe dates back at least as far as 1940, when Adolf Hitler proposed a "Bank of Europe." Not until 1969, however, was there actually a decision by European nations to seriously investigate the feasibility of a common currency. In 1991, the Maastricht treaty was signed, marking a formal agreement to have a common currency. Many nations wanted to name the new (but as yet hypothetical) currency the ECU, which stood for European Currency Unit. The Germans objected, however, one of their complaints being that this would sound too much like "Eku," a German beer. It was not until 1995

---

[1] For the record, the twelve nations adopting the euro are: Austria, Belgium, Finland, France, Germany, Greece, Ireland, Italy, Luxembourg, Netherlands, Portugal, and Spain. The three members of the European Union that chose to keep their own national currencies rather than adopt the euro are Denmark, Sweden, and the United Kingdom.

that the name "euro" was approved. Finally, on January 1, 2002 ten billion bank notes and thousands of tons of coins made their way into circulation across Europe, beginning a two-month process in which the euro gradually displaced the national currencies of the twelve nations adopting it.

The push to create the euro was importantly driven by the substantial costs and inconveniences of having many different currencies in a place as economically integrated as Europe. Every time individuals or businesses wanted to transact with someone in another country, they had to make price comparisons involving multiple currencies; convert payments or receipts between a foreign currency and their own; and insure themselves against the risks of holding foreign currencies subject to fluctuations in value. Although the situation was perhaps not quite so extreme, you can get a flavor for the problem by imagining a different currency in every state across America. Interstate travel and trade would be a costly nuisance, fraught with risk and inconvenience. Just as Americans benefit from having the dollar as our single currency, the twelve nations adopting the euro hope to benefit from that currency. Overall, experts think, the European adopters of the new monetary unit will save perhaps 0.5 percent of national income each year—roughly $120 per year for each person.

Yet there are risks and thus potential costs associated with the adoption of a single currency. Broadly speaking, flexibility and independence are the great advantages of having a separate currency with a value that is free to fluctuate against other currencies. Let's consider flexibility first, by contrasting the United Kingdom, a nation that chose not to adopt the euro, with France, which opted to give up the franc in return for the euro. If the U.K. suffers a decline in the demand for the goods it makes, this also implicitly represents a decline in the demand for its currency (the pound), because if foreigners are not buying British goods, there is no reason for them to acquire pounds. One simple way for Britain to adjust to the drop in demand is to allow the value of the pound to fall relative to other currencies. This will make British goods cheaper in other countries, and thus help counteract the lower demand for British products.

Let's contrast this with France, which is using the euro. Because France is only a small part of the sum of the economies using the euro, if there is a decline in the demand for French goods, the value of the euro will decline little if at all. Hence the French are forced to respond to the shock in one of two other (and more costly) ways. France must either endure a deflation—a fall in the prices of goods and services throughout France relative to elsewhere—or wait until factors of production, such as labor, leave the country to find employment elsewhere. Both of these processes are likely to be more painful and protracted than the simple expedient of allowing the exchange rate to decline, as the British are able to do. Our conclusion, then, is that with a separate currency a country has much more flexibility in responding to external shocks, for it can allow its exchange rate to vary, rather than having to wait for domestic prices or factors of production to move. Loss of this flexibility is one of the costs of adopting the euro.

There is also the matter of independence. Consider, for example, the contrast between Germany and Greece. For whatever reason, for the past half century, the Bundesbank—the central bank of Germany—has chosen a relatively slow rate of monetary growth, which has led to a very low inflation rate in Germany. In contrast, the central bank of Greece has opted for a relatively high rate of growth in that nation's money supply, and thus a relatively high inflation rate in Greece—five times higher than Germany's rate during the 1990s alone. Under the European Central Bank, both Germany and Greece (as well as the other ten member nations) are stuck with a common monetary policy. We cannot know now what that policy will be, but given the historical differences between the policies of the countries involved, some nations are likely to be looking at a monetary policy that is very different than that to which they are accustomed—and one that is thus likely to be quite painful for their citizens. For better or worse, by not adopting the euro, the British have retained the independence to make their own monetary policy, and thus avoided one of the costs of having a common currency.

The trade-offs involved in adopting the euro are central to the issue of defining an **optimal currency area**. The larger the economic area covered by a common currency, the greater are the potential benefits (due to the facilitation of trade), but the greater too are the potential costs (due to the reduced flexibility and inde-

pendence). The real question concerns where the marginal benefits equal the marginal costs. The United States, for example, basically has been a single currency area since its inception. Yet according to Professor Hugh Rockoff of Rutgers, until about seventy
years ago, the benefits of having a common currency were probably outweighed by the costs. Different areas of the country, such as
the agrarian South and West versus the industrial North and East,
were simply far too different from each other; moreover, there
were no mechanisms in place that permitted the differences in desired monetary policies to be reconciled. Some experts believe
that the twelve-nation euro currency area is likewise too big, with
a set of member nations that are simply too different, to permit
the euro to work. Indeed, the desire to avoid the political and economic frictions that are sure to arise is likely an important reason
why Britain, Sweden, and Denmark opted to stay out—at least for
the moment.

Apart from facilitating trade among member nations, there is
actually quite another incentive for European nations to agree to
a common currency. As things stand today, the American dollar is
the premier "trading currency" of the world. That is, many businesses and people around the world use the dollar in conducting
international trade, even though they stick with their own national
currencies at home. To do this, of course, these economic agents
must hold balances of dollars—either cash or bank accounts—
which effectively act as interest-free loans to the United States.
Thus America is able to enjoy a higher level of income simply because our currency is held in such high regard around the world.
There is little doubt that the nations adopting the euro hope it will
some day rival or surpass the dollar as an international trading
currency, enabling them to reap some of the benefits America has
enjoyed.

This brings us to the other reason that may have helped per-
suade Britain to eschew the euro. Until World War II, the British
pound was a major trading currency around the world, especially
in Britain's former colonies. If the euro fails because of internal di-
visions among the countries using it, the British pound will likely
be the only European currency left standing to challenge the dollar as a trading currency. And quite apart from national pride,
there is little doubt that the citizens of the United Kingdom would

like nothing better than the added income that would mean—especially if it came at the expense of some of their rivals across the English Channel.

DISCUSSION QUESTIONS

1. What economic factors would you want to examine to make a prediction about whether Denmark, Sweden, or the United Kingdom is likely to adopt the euro sometime in the future?

2. Many European nations have government restrictions that impede the mobility of labor across national borders. How does this fact affect the desirability of having a common currency area in those countries?

3. Until about 30 years ago, many nations chose to have **fixed exchange rates**, in which the value of their domestic currency was fixed at a specified number of U.S. dollars. How did America benefit from this system? To what sort of risks were other countries subjected because they had fixed exchange rates with the dollar?

4. Until about 1930, most of the major nations of the world were on the gold standard: Although each had a national currency, such as the dollar or the pound, the exchange rate between each currency and gold was fixed, which meant that the exchange rate between each national currency was fixed. How is a gold standard like the euro? How do you think it might differ? (Hint: What controls the amount of gold in the world? Is this different than what controls the amount of euros in existence?)

31

Monetary Policy and Interest Rates

"The Fed lowers interest rates by one-half point." That is one of numerous headlines seen in the financial press during the early part of the 2000s. The Fed—short for the **Federal Reserve System**—is America's **central bank**. Interest rates can be affected by the Fed; when they are, that is part of **monetary policy**, defined as the use of changes in the amount of money in circulation so as to affect interest rates, credit markets, inflation, and unemployment.

The theory behind monetary policy is relatively simple. An increase in the rate of growth of the money supply by the Fed increases spending on goods and services and thus stimulates the economy, tending to lower unemployment in the short run and raise inflation in the long run. (One important version of the **money supply** is comprised of checking-type account balances and currency in the hands of the public.) The flip side is that a decrease in the rate of growth of the money supply reduces spending, thereby depressing the economy; the short-run result is higher unemployment, while the longer-run effect is a lower inflation rate.

Congress established the Federal Reserve System in 1913. A Board of Governors consisting of seven members, including the very powerful chairperson, governs it. All of the governors, including the chair, are nominated by the president and approved by the Senate. Their appointments are for fourteen years (although the chair serves in that role for only four years at a time).

Through the Fed, and its Federal Open Market Committee (FOMC), decisions about monetary policy are made eight times a year. The Federal Reserve System is independent; the Board even has its own budget, financed with interest earnings on the portfolio of bonds it owns. The president can attempt to convince the Board, and Congress can threaten to merge the Fed with the Treasury or otherwise restrict its behavior. But unless the Congress took the radical step of passing legislation to the contrary, the Fed's chair and governors can do what they please. Hence, talking about "the president's monetary policy" or "Congress's monetary policy" is inaccurate. To be sure, the Fed has, on occasion, yielded to presidential pressure to pursue a particular policy, and it's true that the Fed's chair follows a congressional resolution directing him to report on what the Fed is doing on the policy front. But now, more than ever before, the Fed remains the single most important and truly independent source of economic power in the federal government. Monetary policy is Fed policy and no one else's.

Federal Reserve monetary policy, in principle, is supposed to be counter-cyclical. That is, it is supposed to counteract other forces that might be making the economy contract or expand too rapidly. The economy goes through so-called **business cycles**, made up of recessions (and sometimes depressions) when unemployment is high, and boom times when unemployment is low and businesses are straining their productive capacity. For the Fed to stabilize the economy, it must create policies that go counter to other forces affecting business activity. Although Fed policy can be put into place much faster than most federal policies, it still does not operate instantaneously. Indeed, researchers have estimated that it takes almost fourteen months for a change in monetary policy to become effective. Thus, by the time monetary policy goes into effect, a different policy might be appropriate.

Researchers who have examined the evidence over the period from 1913 until the 1990s have concluded that, on average, the Fed's policy has turned out to be pro-cyclical, rather than counter-cyclical. That is, by the time the Fed started pumping money into the economy, it was time to do the opposite; by the time the Fed started reducing the rate of growth of the money supply, it was time for it to start increasing it. Perhaps the Fed's biggest pro-cyclical blunder occurred during the Great Depression. Many economists believe that what would have been a severe recession turned into the Great Depression in the 1930s because the Fed's action resulted in almost a one-third decrease in the amount of money in circulation, drastically reducing aggregate spending. It has also been argued that the rapid inflation experienced in the 1970s was importantly the result of excessive monetary expansion by the Fed.

In the 1990s, few commentators were able to complain about monetary policy. Inflation almost disappeared by the end of the decade, which also saw the unemployment rate drop to its lowest level in nearly forty years. Why the Fed was successful in the 1990s remains unclear. It could have been due to the uniquely superior insights of its chair, Alan Greenspan. Or it might be that the Fed has learned from its lessons of the past. Or, it might simply have been a run of good luck. But whatever the reason, it is clear that the Fed remains far from perfect. Late in the decade it tightened monetary policy sharply, reducing monetary growth and thereby contributing to the recession that began in 2001. Moreover, some economists are worried that the Fed may have increased the rate of growth of the money supply too much in 2001 and 2002 to counter that recession. If they are correct, this means that the Fed will have set the stage for renewed inflation later.

Most newspaper discussions of Fed policy focus on its decisions to raise or lower interest rates. Before we can make any sense out of such discussions, we need to first understand the relationship between **nominal interest rates**, that is, the rates that you see in the newspaper and pay for loans, and the **expected rate of inflation**.

Let's start in a hypothetical world in which there is no inflation and so expected (or anticipated) inflation is zero. In that world, you might be able to borrow—obtain a mortgage to buy a home, for example—at a *nominal* rate of interest of, say, 6 percent. If you borrow the funds and your anticipation of zero inflation turns out to be accurate, neither you nor the lender will have been fooled. The dollars you pay back in the years to come will be just as valuable in terms of purchasing power as the dollars that you borrowed. In this situation, we would say that the **real rate of interest** (defined to be the nominal rate of interest minus the anticipated rate of inflation) was exactly equal to the nominal interest rate.

Contrast this to a situation in which the expected inflation rate is, say, 5 percent. Although you would be delighted to borrow at a 6 percent interest, lenders would be reluctant to oblige you, and based on exactly the same reasoning you would be using: the dollars with which you would be repaying the debt would be declining in purchasing power every year of the debt. Lenders would likely insist upon (and you would agree to) an *inflationary premium* of 5 percent, to make up for the expected inflation. Hence, the nominal interest rate would rise to about 11 percent, keeping the real rate at its previous level of 6 percent.

There is strong evidence that inflation rates and nominal interest rates move in parallel: During periods of rapid inflation, people come to anticipate that inflation fairly promptly, and thus higher nominal interest rates are the result. In the early 1970s, when the inflation rate was between 4 and 5 percent, nominal interest rates on mortgages were around 8 to 10 percent. At the beginning of the 1980s, when the inflation rate was near 9 percent, nominal interest rates on mortgages had risen to between 12 and 14 percent. By the middle of the 1990s, when the inflation rate was 2 to 3 percent, nominal interest rates had fallen to between 6 and 8 percent.

Now let's go back to Fed policy and the headlines. When the chair of the Fed states that the Fed is lowering "the" interest rate from, say, 5.75 percent to 5.25 percent, he really means something else. In the first place, the interest rate referred to is the **federal funds rate**, or the rate at which banks can borrow excess reserves from other banks. Any effects of Fed policy here will show up in other rates only indirectly. More importantly, even when the Fed decides to try to alter the federal funds rate, it can do so only by actively entering the market for federal government securities (usually Treasury bills). So if the Fed wants to lower "the" interest rate, it essentially must buy Treasury bills from banks and other private holders of them. This action bids up the prices of these bills, and simultaneously lowers the interest rates on them. This in turn lowers the interest rates at which banks are willing to lend to each other and to the public. (In terms of our earlier discussion, this policy also has the effect of increasing the money supply, and so increases spending throughout the economy.) Conversely, when the Fed wants to increase "the" rate of interest, it *sells* Treasury bills, driving their prices down and pushing interest rates up. The result is a reduction in the money supply and a reduction in spending throughout the economy. The pre-announcement of the policy change, which comes in the form of a Fed declaration that interest rates are going to change, simply serves to alert people that a new policy is on the way.

The other key point to note is that the changes in interest rates we have been talking about here are very much short-term changes—and are occurring over a period of time short enough that the expected inflation rate is constant. Once the effects of the Fed's new policy begin to kick in, however, the expected inflation rate will tend to respond, which can create a whole new set of problems. For example, suppose the Fed decides to "lower interest rates," i.e., increase the money supply by buying Treasury bills. In the early weeks and months, this will indeed lower interest rates and stimulate spending. But for a given level of productive capacity in the economy, this added spending will eventually get translated into a higher inflation rate. This will soon enough cause nominal interest rates to *rise*, as inflationary expectations get added onto the real interest rate.

The fact of the matter is that although the Fed can cause interest rates to move up or down in the short run via its choice of monetary policy, forces beyond its control determine what interest rates will be in the long run. The real rate is determined by the underlying productivity of the economy and the consumption preferences of individuals, and the expected inflation rate is determined by people's beliefs about future policy. Thus, when you read that the chair of the Fed has lowered "the" interest rate, you know that the money supply has been increased. But you also now know that whether the Fed likes it or not, if this policy persists long enough, the eventual result will be more inflation in the future, and thus higher, not lower, interest rates.

DISCUSSION QUESTIONS

1. Why do you suppose the Fed likes to signal its intentions about monetary policy ahead of time?

2. Some economists have argued that the Fed should stick to a simple "monetary rule," which might consist of a stable rate of growth of the money supply, regardless of what is going on in

the economy. Given the Fed's performance history, can you suggest why we might benefit from the introduction of such a rule?

3. In light of your answer to the previous question, why do you think the Fed has steadfastly refused to implement such a rule?

4. In the long run, the Fed can determine only what the inflation rate will be, not what the unemployment rate or real growth of the economy will be. If you were chair of the Fed, what inflation rate would you pick? Why?

32

The Disappearing Surplus

When George H. W. Bush left the White House in January 1993, the federal government was awash in red ink—year after year it was running budget **deficits**. Indeed, it had been spending more than its revenues for decades. Yet when his son George W. Bush, took office in January 2001, federal tax receipts exceeded federal spending: The government was running a **surplus**, and both government officials and private economists predicted that the federal government would continue to run surpluses for many years to come. Indeed, some government statisticians confidently proclaimed that over the following decade, the federal government would show a cumulative $10 trillion surplus. Less than a year after the younger Bush took office, though, the surplus had disappeared.

Before we go into the events behind this vanishing surplus, let's first examine how it is even possible for the federal government to run budget deficits. When the government spends more than it receives, by definition its spending exceeds its tax revenues. The government has to finance this shortfall somehow. Typically, the U.S. Treasury sells IOUs on behalf of the U.S. government, in the form of securities that are normally called **bills** (short-term debt) or **bonds** (long-term debt). In effect, the federal government asks Americans and others to lend it money to cover its deficit. For example, if the U.S. government spends $100 billion more than it receives in revenues, the Treasury will raise that amount by selling $100 billion of new Treasury bonds. The people who buy the bonds are lending money to the U.S. government and will receive interest payments over the life of the bond, plus the return of their original loan amount at the end of the bond's life. In return, the Treasury receives immediate purchasing power.

When the government creates a budget deficit or surplus, that deficit or surplus is a flow, that is, a magnitude with a time dimension: It is something that happens over a time period, in this case one year. Each year the government runs a deficit, it adds to its accumulation of debt, called the public debt, which is a stock—that is, a magnitude without a time dimension. At any point in time, the public debt is simply some number, such as $4 trillion. Hence, if at the beginning of a year the public debt is $4 trillion and during the year the federal government has a deficit of $200 billion, then at the beginning of the next year the public debt will be $4.2 trillion.

All federal public debt, taken together, is called the **gross public debt**. When we subtract from the gross public debt the portion that is held by government agencies (what the federal government owes to itself), we arrive at the **net public debt**. Because of deficits year after year, the net public debt grew continuously for many years until 1998. From then until 2002, the federal government ran surpluses, and so the net public debt actually shrank during those years. Expressed as a percentage of our nation's total national income, the net public debt reached its peak after World War II when it exceeded 115 percent of annual income. This ratio fell from then until the early 1970s before it started to rise again, reaching over 50 percent in the early 1990s. Today, the ratio of net public debt to total income is somewhat over 30 percent.

Now let's tackle the question of why there was a disappearing surplus. During the later part of the 1990s and into early 2001, the economy was booming. The federal government was collecting large amounts of revenues, and for the first time in decades, it was spending less than it was receiving, thereby running annual surpluses. Then two things happened. First, early in 2001, the economy started into an economic recession. This reduced the federal government's tax receipts (because taxpayers' incomes were lower) and increased the government's outlays, on programs like unemployment benefits, for example. The September 11 terrorist attacks on the World Trade Center and the Pentagon also forced up federal spending and cut tax receipts. The combined effect of recession and the attacks was that federal government spending came to exceed the amount it was receiving in tax revenues, and hence the surplus became a deficit.

We know that when the government runs a deficit, it typically finances such a deficit by selling U.S. government bonds. Is this a problem? Alternatively, is there any difference between the government raising current taxes to meet spending or allowing deficits to mount? Consider the following analysis.

When bonds are sold by the United States government (the Treasury), the government incurs a liability of future payments of interest on that debt and, eventually, repayment of the principal. Ignoring for the moment the repayment of the principal, any increase in the net public debt means an increase in *future* interest payments. This means that when George W. Bush sent Congress a suggested budget for 2003 that was approximately $100 billion in deficit, the net public debt was going to increase $100 billion. Interest payments on that $100 billion would have to be paid out of future tax revenues. All other things held constant, that meant that taxpayers of the future would have to pay more taxes to meet these increased interest payments. There is a popular saying in economics that there is no such thing as a free lunch, and this saying applies to government spending also, regardless of what the spending is on.

Whenever the government spends more, someone else has to reduce spending to release resources to the government: At any given time, the economic pie that is to be divided among alternative uses is only so large. The private sector must give up what the government takes. Thus, to find out how much the government takes out of the private sector, we do not look at explicit *taxes* collected in any one year. Rather, we look at the total amount of government *spending,* because that spending must be paid for one way or another. When U.S. government debt is issued to pay for it, some parts of the private sector voluntarily give up spending in exchange for the bond they receive—which is the government's promise to pay interest on a U.S. Treasury bond, and eventually repay the principal. In later years, other sectors of the economy—that is taxpayers in general—not so voluntarily give up some of their spending capacity in the form of higher taxes to pay the interest on government bonds already issued. In any event, net public debt domestically purchased is a debt that we owe ourselves. And eventually, that debt has to be repaid.

In this sense, there is little difference between taxation and debt financing of government spending. So, George W. Bush could have proposed a 2003 budget with higher taxes and no government deficit, but the fact would have remained that government spending was going to rise. In the extreme case, there is *no* difference at all between higher taxes and deficit spending. If taxpayers are not fooled by the accounting numbers, they know that when the government runs a deficit and issues more debt, they will be forced to cough up more tax dollars in the future to pay for the interest payments on that increased debt. When taxpayers have complete foresight, they alter their behavior accordingly by saving more than they would otherwise when there are large increases in the government deficit. This increased saving by taxpayers yields them interest with which to pay higher future taxes levied to pay interest on higher government debt, and means they'll ultimately have the savings needed to eventually repay the principal.

Thus, whatever the reason for the disappearing federal government surplus today—increased homeland security spending, increased military spending, or simply higher unemployment benefits—the real issue is not the surplus or the deficit. The real issue to you as an American is how much of total annual income the government spends, and therefore how much is left over for you and everybody else to spend. Higher government spending means fewer resources are available for the private sector—and that means fewer resources for you, whether the higher taxes happen to be now or in the future.

DISCUSSION QUESTIONS

1. In 1751 the government of Britain began to consolidate all of its debt by issuing "consols." These were bonds that promised to pay a fixed rate of interest, or annuity, each year, but they had no maturity date—that is, the government was never actually obligated to repay the initial amount of the loan. Why would anyone lend money to the government under such circumstances?

2. Referring back to the previous question, some people claim that, as a practical matter, the U.S. government will never really repay the debt it issues—instead, it will simply issue more

debt. Suppose the government in fact does this. Does it in any way affect the analysis of this chapter that debt issue acts just like higher taxes?

3. During wartime, there is a temporary increase in the demand for currently available resources, that is, resources that can be used to fight the war. What impact should this temporary increase in demand for current resources have on interest rates? Does the expected impact differ whether the extra spending is paid for with higher current taxes or issuance of debt?

4. In addition to borrowing from ourselves, by selling bonds to Americans, we could (and do) borrow from foreigners to help us finance the debt. Does the fact that the foreigners make the loans affect the analysis?

Glossary

Bills: Short-term debt; as applied to the federal government, it has a maturity of less than one year.

Bonds: Long-term debt; as applied to the federal government, it has a maturity in excess of five years.

Business cycles: Fluctuations in the overall level of business activity in the economy, including recessions (and sometimes depressions) when unemployment is high, and boom times when unemployment is low and businesses are straining their productive capacity.

Cartel: A group of independent businesses, often on an international scale, that agree to restrict trade, to their mutual benefit.

Central bank: A banker's bank; usually an official institution that also serves as a country's treasury's bank and often the regulator of commercial banks.

Comparative advantage: The ability to produce goods at a lower cost.

Competition: Rivalry among buyers or sellers of outputs, or among buyers or sellers of inputs.

Cost: Highest-valued (best) foregone alternative; the most valuable option that is sacrificed when a choice is made.

Deficits: As applied to the government, an excess of spending over tax receipts.

Demand curve: A graphic representation of the demand schedule; a negatively sloped line showing the inverse relationship between the price and the quantity demanded.

Demand schedule: A set of number pairs showing various possible prices and the quantities demanded at each price. This schedule shows the rate of planned purchases per time period at different prices of the good.

E-commerce: Commercial transactions executed over the Internet.

Economic good: Any good or service that is scarce.

Economies of scale: A cost structure for the firm that has the characteristic that the average costs of production decline as the level of output increases. See also *increasing returns*.

Elastic demand: A characteristic of a demand curve in which a given percentage change in price will result in a larger inverse percentage change in quantity demanded. Total revenues and price are inversely related in the elastic portion of the demand curve.

Elasticity: A measure of the responsiveness of one variable to changes in the value of another variable; it equals percentage change in the dependent variable, divided by the percentage change in the independent variable.

Elasticity of demand: The responsiveness of the quantity of a commodity demanded to a change in its price per unit. See also *Price elasticity of demand.*

Elasticity of supply: The responsiveness of the quantity of a commodity supplied to a change in its price per unit. See also *Price elasticity of supply.*

Equilibrium price: The price that clears the market when there is no excess quantity demanded or supplied; the price at which the demand curve intersects the supply curve. Also called *Market-clearing price.*

Expected rate of inflation: The rate at which the average level of the prices of goods and services is expected to rise.

Externalities: Benefits or costs of an economic activity that spill over to a third party. Pollution is a negative spillover, or externality.

Federal funds rate: The *nominal interest rate* at which banks can borrow excess reserves from other banks.

Federal Reserve System: America's *central bank*, it consists of a seven-member Board of Governors with headquarters in Washington, D.C., and twelve Reserve Banks located in major cities throughout the United States.

Fixed exchange rates: A system of legally fixed prices (rates) at which two or more national currencies trade (exchange) for one another.

Free good: Any good or service available in larger quantities than desired at a zero price.

Gains from trade: The extent to which individuals, firms, or nations benefit by engaging in exchange.

Gross public debt: The total indebtedness of the federal government, including debt it owes to itself; the sum of all past deficits and surpluses.

Human capital: The accumulated training, education, and knowledge of workers.

Increasing returns: A cost structure for the firm that has the characteristic that the average costs of production decline as the level of output increases. See also *economies of scale.*

Inelastic demand: A characteristic of a demand curve in which a given change in price will result in a less-than-proportionate inverse change in the quantity demanded. Total revenue and price are directly related in the inelastic region of the demand curve.

Inflation: A sustained rise in the weighted average of all prices over time.

Intellectual property: Creative ideas, including inventions that are patented, trademarks, industrial designs, copyrights, and the like.

Law of demand: A law stating that quantity demanded and price are inversely related—more is bought at a lower price, less at a higher price (other things being equal).

Law of supply: A law that states that a direct relationship exists between price and quantity supplied (other things being equal).

Marginal analysis: The analysis of what happens when small changes take place relative to the status quo.

Marginal benefits: The additional (marginal) benefits associated with one more unit of a good or action; the change in total benefits due to the addition of one more unit of production.

Marginal costs: The change in total costs due to a change in one unit of production.

Market clearing price: See **Equilibrium price.**

Market share: The proportion of total sales in an industry accounted for by the sales of a specific firm or group of firms in that industry.

Market supply: Total quantities of a good offered for sale by suppliers at various prices.

Median age: The age that exactly separates the younger half of the population from the older half.

Merger: The joining together into common ownership of two or more formerly independent companies.

Minimum wage: The lowest hourly wage firms may legally pay their workers.

Models, or theories: Simplified representations of the real world used to make predictions or to better understand the real world.

Monetary policy: The use of changes in the amount of money in circulation so as to affect interest rates, credit markets, inflation, and unemployment.

Money supply: The sum of checking-type account balances and currency in the hands of the public.

Monopolist, or **Monopoly:** Literally, a single supplier. More generally, it is a firm that faces a downward-sloping demand curve for its output and therefore can choose the price at which it will sell the good; an example of a *price searcher.*

Monopsonist, or **Monopsony:** Literally, a single buyer. More generally, it is a firm that faces an upward-sloping supply curve for its input and therefore can choose the price at which it will buy the good; an example of a *price searcher.*

Natural monopoly: A monopoly that arises when there are large *economies of scale* relative to the industry's demand.

Negative externality: A cost, associated with an economic activity, which is paid by third parties. Pollution is a negative externality because, for example, someone other than the driver of an automobile bears part of the cost of the car's exhaust emissions.

Net public debt: *Gross public debt,* minus the debt the federal government owes to itself.

Network effect: A change in the benefit that an agent derives from a good when the number of other agents consuming (or using) the same kind of good changes.

Nominal interest rate: The premium, in percent per year, that people are willing to pay to have dollars sooner rather than later.

Oligopoly: A firm that is one of very few sellers (or buyers) in a market; in such a case, each firm reacts to changes in the prices and quantities of its rivals.

Opportunity cost: The highest valued alternative that must be sacrificed to attain something or to satisfy a want.

Optimal currency area: A geographical or political area in which the net benefits of having a single monetary currency are at their greatest.

Per capita income: Total income divided by population.

Perfectly elastic: An infinite value for the ratio of the percentage change in quantity over the percentage change in price, measured along a demand or supply curve; visually, a perfectly elastic curve appears horizontal.

Positive-sum game: A process or setting in which more than one participant gains. Voluntary exchange is said to be a positive-sum game because both parties are simultaneously made better off.

Price discrimination: Selling at prices that do not reflect differences in marginal costs; different prices with the same marginal costs, for example, or the same prices with different marginal costs.

Price elasticity of demand: The percentage change in quantity demanded divided by the percentage change in price. See also *Elasticity of demand.*

Price elasticity of supply: The percentage change in quantity supplied divided by the percentage change in price. See also *Elasticity of supply.*

Price searcher: Literally, a firm that must search for the profit-maximizing price, because it faces a downward-sloping demand curve (if it is a seller) or an upward-sloping supply curve (if it is a buyer); often used as a synonym for *monopoly* or *monopsony.*

Price taker: Any economic agent that takes the market price as given; often used as a synonym for a firm operating in a market characterized by *pure competition.*

Profit: The income generated by selling something for a higher price than was paid for it. In production, the income generated is the difference between total revenues received from consumers who purchase the goods and the total cost of producing those goods.

Product differentiation: The distinguishing of products by brand name, color, and other minor attributes.

Property rights: The set of rules specifying how a good may be used and exchanged.

Protectionism: A set of rules designed to protect certain individuals or firms from competition, usually competition from imported goods.

Public debt: The dollar amount owed by the federal government to the owners of the bills, notes, and bonds it has issued.

Public goods: Goods with these two characteristics: consumption by one person does not diminish the amount available for others to consume, and it is extremely costly to prevent nonpaying customers from consuming them.

Purchasing power: The capacity of money to buy goods; the amount of goods that can be purchased with a given amount of money.

Pure competition: A market structure in which participants individually have no influence over market prices; all act as *price takers.*

Quotas: Limits on the amount of a good or activity; often used in international trade to limit the amount of some foreign good that legally may be imported into a country.

Rate of return: The net benefit, in percentage terms, of engaging in an activity. For example, if the investment of $1.00 yields a gross return of $1.20, the net benefit is $0.20 and the rate of return is equal to ($0.20/$1.00) = 20 percent.

Real interest rate: The premium, in percent per year, that people are willing to pay to have goods sooner rather than later.

Regulated monopoly: A *price searcher* whose key business decisions, such as the price at which it sells its output, are regulated by a government agency.

Rent control: A system in which the government tells building owners how much they can charge for rent.

Resource: An input used in the production of desired goods and services.

Scarce good: Any good that commands a positive price.

Scarcity: A state of nature in which resources are limited even though wants are unlimited. Scarcity means that nature does not freely provide as much of everything as people want.

Shortage: A situation in which an excess quantity is demanded or an insufficient quantity is supplied; the difference between the quantity demanded and the quantity supplied at a specific price below the market clearing price.

Social cost: The full cost that society bears when a resource-using action occurs. For example, the social cost of driving a car is equal to all private costs plus any additional cost that other members of society bear (e.g., air pollution and traffic congestion).

Stock: The quantity of something at a point in time. An inventory of goods is a stock. A bank account at a point in time is a stock. Stocks are defined independent of time, although they are assessed at a point in time.

Subsidies: Government payments for the production of specific goods, generally designed to raise the profits of the firms receiving the subsidies and often intended to increase the output of the subsidized goods.

Supply curve: The graphic representation of the supply schedule, which slopes upward (has a positive slope).

Supply schedule: A set of prices and the quantity supplied at each price; a schedule showing the rate of planned production at each relative price for a specified time period.

Surplus: An excess quantity supplied or an insufficient quantity demanded; the difference between the quantity supplied and the quantity demanded at a price above the market clearing price. As applied to the government budget, an excess of tax receipts over expenditures.

Tariffs: Taxes levied on imports.

Trade barriers: Any rules having the effect of reducing the amount of international exchange. *Tariffs* and *quotas* are trade barriers.

Trade-off: A term relating to opportunity cost. In order to get a desired economic good, it is necessary to trade off (give up) some other desired economic good in a situation of scarcity. A trade-off involves making a sacrifice in order to obtain something.

Type I error: An error of commission, such as might arise when an unsafe drug is errantly permitted to be sold.

Type II error: An error of omission, such as might arise if a beneficial drug is errantly prevented from reaching the market.

Index

Abortion(s), 30–31, 52–58
  illegal
    cost of, 53, 54, 55–56
    deaths due to, 54, 56
    information regarding, 54–55
  legal
    cost of, 53–54, 57–58
    deaths due to, 54, 57
    under English common law, 52–53
    information regarding, 57
    restrictions on, 57–58
    Supreme Court on, 52, 53, 54, 57–58
Acquired immune deficiency syndrome. *See*
    AIDS
AIDS (acquired immune deficiency
    syndrome)
  drugs for treating, 14, 15
  prostitution and, 30, 36
Air pollution
  air pollution allowances and, 173–176
  gasoline and, 181–182
  generated near borders with free trade
    partner and, 190n
  ozone and, 171
  property rights to increase, 154, 172–176
Air pollution allowances, 173–176
Air travel. *See also* Airline industry
  price discrimination and, 93, 108–109,
    110
  safety of, 3, 17–22
    marginal analysis of, 3, 17–18
Airbags, 1–2, 4–8
Airline industry
  price discrimination in fares and, 93,
    108–109, 110
  regulation of, 108
  safety in, 3, 17–22
    marginal analysis of, 3, 17–18
Alaska, North Slope oil and, 101

Alcohol
  during Prohibition, 30, 32, 34, 35, 37
  quality of, variations in, 36–37
Algeria, OPEC and, 102
Amazon.com
  first profit of, 95
  price discrimination and, 106
American bison, 153, 164–165
Animal species. *See also individual species*
  destruction of, by humans, 153–154,
    163–169
  extinction of, 153–154, 163–164
  global warming and, 180
  property rights and, 153, 165–166, 168–169
Apparel industry, effect of trade restrictions
    on, 195, 196
Armstrong, Neil, 114
AT&T, 118
Audubon, John James, 164
Australia
  diamond discovery in, 103
  immigration laws in, 145
Austria, adopted euro as currency of, 198n
Automobile(s)
  airbags and, 1–2, 4–8
  domestic content requirements and, 196
  domestically produced, sales of, 194
  fuel economy of, regulations regarding,
    123–124, 126–130
  imported from Japan, restrictions on, 191,
    194–195
  safety and, 1–2, 4–8, 22, 124, 127, 128, 129,
    130
  seat belts and, 4, 5, 7, 8
Azidothymidine (AZT), 14, 15
AZT (azidothymidine), 14, 15

Baby boomers, retirement of, 124–125, 141,
    143. *See also* Senior citizens